The Crazy Ape

DAVID MACSWEENEY

The Crazy Ape

Sanity, Madness, Your Brain and You

PETER OWEN · LONDON

ISBN 0 7206 0565 2

PETER OWEN LIMITED
73 Kenway Road London SW5 0RE

First published 1982

Printed in Great Britain by
Daedalus Press Somers Road Wisbech Cambs

To my wife Dale and my children
Alana, Eve and Shane

Man, though successful biologically, is in many ways an unsatisfactory species; but, whatever he is, we have to live with him.

ANTHONY STORR, *Human Aggression*

Contents

III

Acknowledgements

I wish to thank my publisher, Peter Owen, for his consistent enthusiasm, encouragement and support throughout the difficult gestation of this book, and my editor, Dan Franklin, for his tolerance and flexibility and the definitive care he lavished on the final draft. I am also much indebted to the late Michael Dempsey for help and advice so generously and freely given.

I must also thank Sir Denis Hill, F.R.C.P., who very kindly read an early draft of Chapter 12, 'Of Masks and Motivation'. His critical comments stung exquisitely in all the hyperalgesic places and occasioned much pain and revision but little repentance.

I am grateful to Dale Pring-MacSweeney for drawing the diagrams and most especially for the innumerable hours she spent patiently correcting and advising me on early and subsequent drafts of the manuscript. My thanks are also due to Beatrice Musgrave for her cheerful *advocatus diaboli* and her perceptive criticisms during the early phase of editing.

David MacSweeney, M.A., M.B., B.S., M.R.C.S., M.R.C.Psych.
February 1982

PART ONE

I

Superape

Pindar (522-442 BC), the Greek poet, believed that 'Men and gods are of the same family; we owe the breath of life to the same mother' – that is, the Earth-mother Gaea, whose son and husband was Uranus, the starlit sky. In this he was at odds with Greek tradition, which maintained that Prometheus created mankind; using earth and water – some said his own tears – he fashioned and kneaded the body of the first man, into which Athene breathed soul and life.

Superape man, a somewhat muddled-together, psycho-biophysical conglomerate, literally personifies all that has happened in the physical and non-physical universe since time or change began. Indeed, since, with hindsight, he must have ever been in the mind's eye of evolution or the 'destiny' which shapes our ends, he may be said to have antedated time. Not only does he play host to the spiritual and the bestial, he even harbours and carries about, in the self-maintaining, self-replenishing hamper that is his body, a naturally-occurring, measurable quantity of radioactivity in the inorganic element potassium – an element that forms an essential part of his body's survival kit. Philosophers and scientists can be as negative or evasive about what happened during the 'coming-into-being' of this self-aware ape as they are about what happens at his 'ceasing-to-be', when physiological disintegration occurs and he seems, overtly at least, to become inorganic yet once more; they seem reluctant to speculate on what happens to him at death, when the viability of the brain ebbs away beyond recall and mind, ego or self has permanently lost its medium or instrument of liaison.

Man is, as we shall see, a sort of Minotaur, part god, part beast, part frog – one might add to the mix an elemental pinch of salt or clay, a mythological tear or a little radioactive stardust. Two outstanding contemporary neurobiologists sum up, at least in part, what I am attempting to sketch in. John Eccles says in his book *Facing Reality*: 'Because of the mystery of our being, as unique self-conscious existence, we can therefore have hope, as we set our own soft, sensitive and fleeting personal experiences against the terror and immensity of illimitable space and time. Are we not participants in the meaning where there is else no meaning? Do we not experience a delight in fellowship, joy, harmony, truth, love and beauty – where there is else only the mindless universe?' Commenting more cautiously, and on an evolutionary continuum of brain development that is less speculative and more phylogenetically biased than Eccles' postulation, M. S. Gazzaniga says: 'The structure of our thought processes, with our ability to grasp relationships, causality and all the rest, emerges from our deep-core information-processing capacity that is probably in a continual state of evolution, and is present in some form in the chimpanzee (ape), monkey, and dog, as it is in us.'

It is when this 'deep-core information-processing capacity', which is modulated neurochemically, becomes deranged in man, that crazy behaviour may result.

What a machine – what a piece of work is man. When looked at anatomically and behaviourally, in comparison to other animals he is a sort of Hydra-brained, huge-headed freak, going about his sophisticated, self-seeking rascalities on his two hind legs, the most surly, intelligent and interesting beast chance and evolution have yet cast up from the leavening mudpies of the primordial swamp.

He is unique among mammals and most lower animals in that he kills members of his own species – indeed he has devised skilful methods to kill his unborn offspring; he has also been known to kill his young, or his neighbour's young, after they have already been born and without their permission. He is the only animal who murders himself. He sometimes murders his wife or mate; he murders strangers. He is probably mass-murdering now, and has in the recent and distant past banded together with other men and set out to exterminate whole races. He officially threatens, tortures and kills members of his own species using primitive, traditional or more ingenious devices – the woeful reality or threat of atomic bombs and nuclear weapons; the gas chamber, the electric chair, the electrode, the shotgun, hanging or suspension, the club, the axe, the guillotine. Visitors from outer space could not help but be impressed by the consistency and ingenuity with which *Homo sapiens* satisfies the ill-construed sado-masochistic hankerings of his conscious and unconscious mind.

Modern man kills with bad grace. Why? One can only speculate. Unlike other animals he no longer has to grow, wield or necessarily wear on his own person the weapons he uses for killing or maiming. Thus he is able, by the use of sophisticated machines of his own invention, to destroy his enemy at a distance, thereby avoiding the discipline, chivalry or embarrassment of making eye-to-eye contact, or of having to utter a verbal greeting, even a war whoop. Our fighting etiquette has deteriorated since the days of Homer.

In spite of these barbarities man is still the only animal who seems to laugh (at himself and others) and who is capable of deliberately performing heroic altruistic acts, literally self-sacrifice, in the interests of members of his co-species and their survival.

The male of the species is (currently at least) more intelligent, more murderous and more rancorous than the female. Physically too he is more preposterous; while he possesses a uterus, in the middle of his prostate gland, which is vestigial and useless as an organ of reproduction (the uterus masculinus), he grows two breasts, which though also vestigial, can nevertheless be made to yield milk, and sometimes do so spontaneously. He has testes in which, if one of the primitive pluripotent cells in the tissue of this gland fertilizes another primitive cell, he occasionally begets monstrous 'clones', or teratomas, and thus a new organism is conceived. This may then develop into a bizarre motley collection of hair, teeth and other tissue, which is sometimes found on surgical exploration of a lump. These organisms can also occur in other organs of his body. None of these man-made monsters has ever been known to live independently of the host, though they themselves in turn may likewise go on to reproduce in themselves other little monsters or 'miniclones'. Somewhat similar events occur even more frequently in the organs of the female, including the brain and ovary; a girl of thirteen is on record as having no less than five (human) embryos removed from her brain. 'Clones', 'miniclones', teratomas, 'parthenogenesis' (virgin conception), human hermaphrodites (each complete with an ovary and a testis), girls who become normal men at puberty, people with tails long enough to pull or wag or with vestigial fish-gills on the sides of their necks – it would seem that where nature and man are concerned, there is nothing really new under the sun, moon or electron microscope.

Man carries about inside the exoskeleton that is his skull (partly formed from fused vertebrae) the soft, jellied, dull-pink pot-pourri of at least half a dozen superimposed evolutionary brains, all 'wired up' into what may be regarded for the sake of simplicity and clarity as two anatomically discrete, but interconnected and interacting compound brains : the cerebrum and the cerebellum (see Figure 1). Their job is to function in unison to keep man in touch with his external and internal environments. As a result, man's head, compared with those of other animals, is huge in relation to his body. It is probable that if the Lernaean Hydra existed today and was suddenly confronted for the first time with a close-up of modern man, its eighteen eyes would all go pop in total astonishment. Indeed, on first beholding man, most animals do take to their heels or wings, to the water or to the safety of the earth. To their bucolic eyes, the huge size of man's head in ratio to the rest of his body must appear grotesque and very frightening.

But why man as the evolutionary supremo? And how come his unique invention of the symbolic shorthand of language, his development of a non-material, essentially useless culture, his brilliant discovery of himself, his invention or discovery of the gods, his awareness of life and death and the possibilities even of a life beyond the grave? The complexity and size of man's brain compared with those of other primates, lower mammals and amphibians give us some sort of clue as to his superiority.

Man's brain, as we shall see in more detail later, relegates even the most sophisticated modern computer to a lower, almost reptilian league. The number of neurons or nerve cells that make up the three to three-and-a-half pounds of the human brain is in the order of a hundred thousand million. If synapses rather than neurons are estimated and considered as the elements of the nervous system, then we are talking in the order of a hundred trillion or 100,000,000,000,000.

The synapse is the specialized structure whereby nerve cells communicate or pass on positive or negative messages to one another, usually by releasing a specific chemical transmitter from the ter-

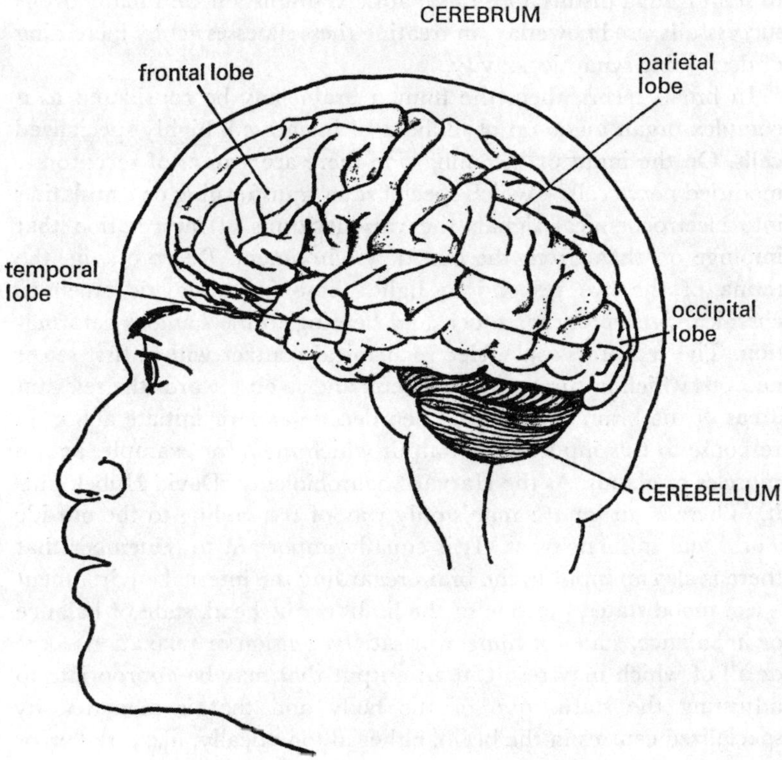

Figure 1: THE HUMAN CEREBRUM AND CEREBELLUM

minals of one neuron that are close to the cell membrane of the adjacent neuron. The synapse is probably the focal and crucial area for mediating memory, skills and mood itself, and for establishing, altering, maintaining or eliminating other behavioural happenings – and all this probably in terms of synaptic circuits. Already over twenty transmitter substances have been identified. Our recent, immensely improved understanding of synapse chemistry has made a major impact on brain physiology in general and psychiatry in particular; for example, disorders of brain function like Parkinson's disease, psychotic (suicidal) depression, mania and schizophrenia appear to stem from a disturbance of synaptic transmission, and many drugs successfully used nowadays in treating these illnesses act by increasing or decreasing synaptic activity.

In broad terms, then, the human brain may be considered as a complex organ made up of millions of integrated, highly specialized cells. On the input or incoming side there are groups of receptors – modified nerve cells – which specialize in transforming or translating into electrochemical signals the various forms of information that impinge on them from the outside environment. Receptors in the retina of the eye respond to light, those for taste and smell to chemicals, receptors for touch and hearing to mechanical deformation. The receptors make electrochemical contact with a first set of neurons which in turn contact others; and so on towards the relevant areas of the brain which may then decode and/or initiate action in response to this input by an output which may, for example, act on muscles or glands. As the Harvard neurobiologist, David Hubel, puts it, 'There is an input : man's only way of responding to the outside world and influencing it.' It is equally important to remember that there is also an input to the brain regarding the internal environment – e.g. mood states, position of the limbs or the head, state of balance or imbalance, states of hunger or satiety, tension or relaxation, some or all of which may result in an output that may be appropriate to adjusting the status quo of the body and that is mediated by specialized centres in the brain, either automatically, like a reflex, or consciously, as in voluntary movement.

The purpose of this book is to attempt to survey and to understand the human animal's exalted biological status in terms of the past and the present, and to look hopefully into, and guess at, his future. This entails observing his behaviour dispassionately, especially his irrational or crazy behaviour, in an attempt to understand what makes him act in certain ways under certain prevailing external or internal environmental circumstances. This in turn entails some elementary knowledge of the human brain, the organ which not only mediates our subjectivity and internal behaviour, our overt and observable behavioural patterns and sleep behaviour, but also subserves consciousness and self-awareness itself.

It is intended that the reader, whether a lay person without any scientific background, a physician (with the usual occult smattering of science) or a specialist in any job or profession, scientific or otherwise, will gain additional and more sympathetic insight into his own, as well as into his fellow man's, eccentricities and foibles. This book is also intended to help the reader towards a sympathetic understanding of those among us who are behaving in an obviously mad or deluded manner. We are all more or less mad at certain times and potentially mad at any time.

Finally, I hope to try to put even the craziest of man's social, sexual and other aberrations into a readily understood and normative socio-biological context.

REFERENCES

John C. Eccles, *Facing Reality: Philosophical Adventures by a Brain Scientist*, Springer, New York, 1970.

M. S. Gazzaniga, 'Consistency and Diversity in Brain Organization', *Annals of the New York Academy of Sciences*, Vol. 299, 1977, pp. 415-23.

David Hubel, 'The Visual Cortex of the Brain', *Scientific American*, 1967; reprinted in *From Cell to Organism*, Freeman, San Francisco, 1967.

2

Man's Central Nervous System:
A Brief Outline of How It Works

The human brain weighs only 1.5 kilograms, less than 3½ pounds. When first seen in the operating theatre it is as unimpressive as butter, and in the pathology museum even less so. Yet, as Eccles says, it is 'without any qualification the most highly organized and most complexly organized matter in the universe'.

Man's nervous system has developed and evolved over millions of years from fish, some of whom came ashore about 350 million years ago to become amphibians. From amphibians, reptiles, dinosaurs and primitive mammals, who first appeared about 200 million years ago, evolved the more sophisticated mammals, including primates.

From these zooish, haphazard, humble origins, we arrive at what was probably the first hominid, *Ramapithecus punjabicus*, who appeared five to fifteen milion years ago. His descendants were *Australopithecus robustus,* who petered out, and *Australopithecus africanus,* who didn't, and who derives his name from fossil remains found at a number of sites in Africa, including Olduvai in Kenya.

Side by side with these fossils were found stone implements of the pebble-tool type and the bashed-in skulls of baboons probably killed by the well-aimed missiles of our ancestral hunter. He very probably also pelted manually-sharpened stones at any neighbour or stranger who tried to seduce or abduct his wife.

Homo erectus, who may have descended from *Australopithecus africanus* via the tool-making *Homo habilis,* appeared about 700000 BC. There is archaeological evidence that he was culturally almost as advanced as some of the less civilized black or white races of today

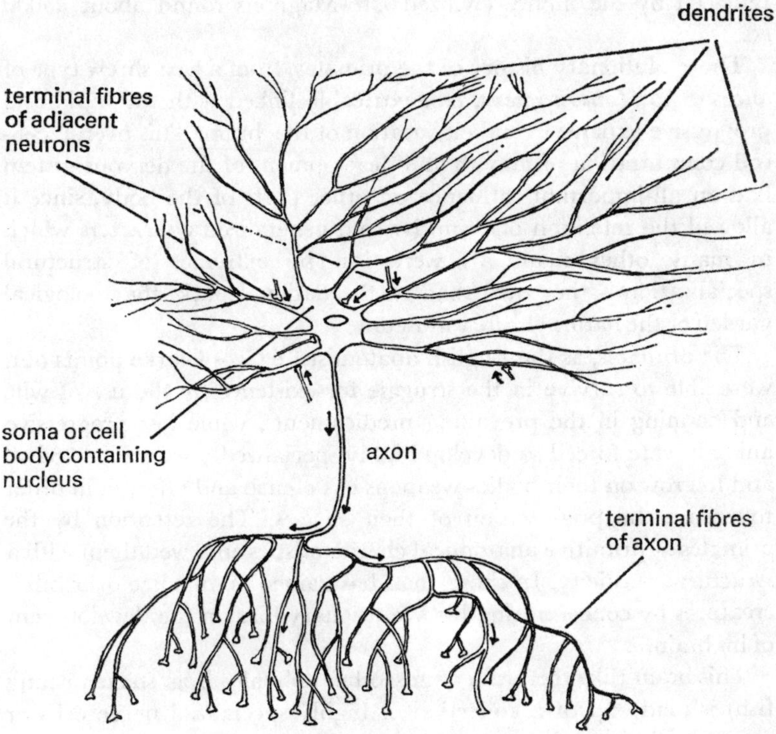

Figure 2: THE NEURON (the arrows indicate the direction of the electrochemical 'message')

and that he had discovered the domestic use of fire. Next, about 100,000 to 200,000 years ago, appeared *Homo sapiens*, and later, about 1000000 to 35000 BC, a 'generalized' Neanderthal type. Archaeological evidence suggests that a Neanderthal group split off into a more specialized type whose skull capacity, and therefore brain size, was even larger than that of modern man. This more specialized group became extinct and modern man (*c.* 40000 BC – AD ?3000) resembles much more closely in his skull configuration and brain size his more generalized, probably less sophisticated, Neanderthal forebears. The surviving group of Neanderthals evolved into or were replaced by the highly civilized Cro-Magnons round about 35000 BC.

The evolutionary history of the primates, from a tree-shrew type of ancestor to *Homo sapiens*, is inextricably linked with the rapid and progressive expansion and elaboration of the brain. This overall central concentration of growth and development of the nervous system had an all-important influence on other parts of the body, since it allowed the retention of primitive and generalized characters which in many other mammals were lost by extremes of structural specialization – the royal road to the national park, the zoological garden or the natural history museum.

The primates, as the English anatomist Le Gros Clarke points out, were able to survive in the struggle for existence by the use of wile and cunning in the prevailing predicaments, while less progressive animals were forced to develop highly specialized organs for survival and to grow on their bodies weapons of defence and offence, in order to ensure the preservation of their species. The retention by the primates of primitive anatomical characteristics endowed them with a structural plasticity. In short, man has gained dominance over other creatures by concentrating his evolutionary bias on the development of his brain.

This brain (like the brain of any other animal – frog, snake or lung fish) is made up of a collection of highly specialized nerve cells or neurons, whose job is to pass on messages or impulses from one part of the body to another. The human cerebrum comprises about 10,000 million neurons, the cerebellum about 80 million.

Each neuron is a living cell with a nucleus and the other components common to all cells. Its three main parts are the cell body (or soma) containing the nucleus; the dendrites, which branch out from the cell and receive impulses (information); and the axon, the principal nerve fibre along which these impulses may travel on to the next neuron (see Figure 2). A nerve itself is no more or no less than an elongated bundle of hundreds of neurons. Nerve impulses usually move from the dendrites, through the cell body and then along the axon to the dendrites or cell body of the next neuron, or to a gland or a muscle. Interwoven among the neurons are glial cells which serve supportive, nutritive and other functions not as yet understood. So specialized is the neuron that, unlike most other cells in the body, it can never divide again into two more cells. It has reached its ultimate developmental end-point; it has nothing up its biological sleeve and

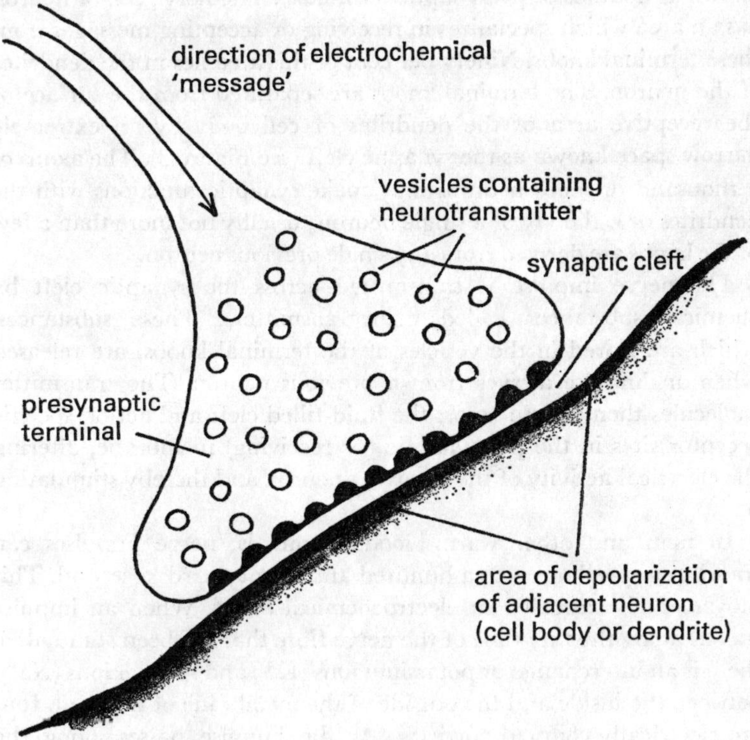

Figure 3: THE SYNAPSE

cannot even digress into producing cancer cells. (Brain tumours made up of neurons are almost unknown, though tumours of the supporting glial cells are relatively common.)

The central nervous system is unique in the complexity of the actions it can perform. It constantly receives thousands of bits of information (in the currency of electrochemical impulses) from the sensory organs and integrates all this information to determine the response to be made by the body as a whole. More than 99 per cent of this information is discarded by the brain as irrelevant. The nerve impulse travels along the axon, which finally breaks up into a large number of branching fibrils, at the end of which are tiny knobs (also known as boutons or presynaptic terminals). The nerve cell or neuron has an area which specializes in receiving or accepting messages from these terminal knobs. Ninety per cent of this area lies in the dendrites of the neuron. The terminal knobs are separated from the surface of the receptive area of the dendrites or cell body by an extremely narrow space known as the synaptic cleft (see Figure 3). The axons of a thousand or more neurons may make synaptic junctions with the dendrites or cell body of a single neuron; usually not more than a few of the knobs are derived from any single previous neuron.

The nerve impulse is transmitted across the synaptic cleft by chemical substances called neurotransmitters. These substances, which are stored in the vesicles of the terminal knobs, are released when an impulse arrives from a previous neuron. The transmitter molecules then diffuse across the fluid-filled cleft and act on specific receptor sites in the postsynaptic (or receiving) membrane, altering the electrical activity of the receiving neuron and thereby stimulating it.

In man and other warm-blooded animals, nerve impulses can travel at a speed of up to a hundred and twenty yards a second. This movement is basically an electrochemical event. When an impulse travels along the tiny tube of the nerve fibre that has been stimulated, there is an interchange of potassium ions (K^+) and sodium ions (Na^+) between the inside and the outside of the membrane of that cell. Ions are electrically charged particles. As the impulse passes along the neuron, the inside of the cell becomes positively charged with respect to the outside; this is the opposite to what is happening when the neuron is in the resting phase, which is usually at about minus seventy millivolts.

The presynaptic knobs may contain an excitatory or an inhibitory transmitter. An excitatory transmitter, when released into the synaptic cleft, excites or 'switches on' the receiving neuron; an inhibitory transmitter inhibits or 'switches off' the neuron. Switch-on/switch-off mechanisms are of equal importance. If only excitatory transmitters existed, the neurons could go on firing inappropriately and for too long.

The importance of the neurotransmitters, which include noradrenaline, adrenaline, serotonin (also known as 5-Hydroxytryptamine), dopamine and acetylcholine, cannot be too highly stressed. These substances are the 'vital spirits' that fuel the brain. By turning receptor areas or centres off and on appropriately they mediate adaptive behaviour to the internal or external environment. Derangement of neurotransmission within the brain can lead to a host of subjective and behavioural aberrations, as we shall see later.

To remain usefully viable the neuron must not only maintain itself and keep itself alive, but must also manufacture adequate supplies of transmitter. To do this it requires oxygen, vitamins, amino acids, sodium, potassium and other electrolytes and raw materials.

In summary then, the nervous system is made up of cells highly specialized in the direction of sensitivity and conductivity. It is designed primarily for the reception of incoming sensory stimuli (from the external or internal environments) and for the transmission of this information to effector organs, whether muscular or glandular structures. By passing on electrical impulses in the manner outlined above, the brain not only controls the muscles of locomotion, the release of hormones from glands, the speed of the heart-rate, the flow of blood through the arteries, but also acts as the substrate for mediating self-awareness and the act of reasoning and thinking itself. The neural complexity of the system provides the anatomical basis for the modification of behavioural reactions to the requirements of any given situation. Clearly the more elaborate the central nervous system, the greater is the repertoire of adjustments which the animal can effect in relation to its total environment, and the more readily it is able to determine its immediate and long-term behavioural plans in accordance with the results of past experience and the stored memory of this experience.

The nervous system has much in common with the more complex electronic computer, in which the output, or the answer or appropriate behavioural response, is determined not only by the input or received information, but also by the way in which these signals have gone through the input circuits, and have had access to information already stored in the computer. We will see in the next chapter how memories of past events seem to be stored in the temporal lobes of the brain. The output or behavioural response is mediated in the animal 'computer' by the signals sent out to the effector organs, which can be the muscles of the legs (resulting in fleeing from danger) and/or the adrenal gland (resulting in the secretion of hormones which prepare the body for fight or flight), to give just two examples.

REFERENCE

John C. Eccles, *The Understanding of the Brain*, McGraw-Hill, New York, 1977.

3

Ancestral Voices:

Multi-Brained Man and His Built-in Ancestral Brain Souvenirs

Trammelled up in the human brain are evolutionary vestiges of three of our basic ancestors. This 'triune brain', as it was referred to by the American neurobiologist Paul D. MacLean, is made up of three evolutionary relics : the reptilian brain , which includes important arousal mechanisms both in the reptile and in man ; the paleomammalian brain (or limbic system), inherited from primitive mammals and intimately concerned with the mediation of emotionality; and the neomammalian brain, or most recently developed brain component, which reaches its highest developmental status in man and in whom it subserves the modalities of thinking, speech, vision and willed or voluntary movement. Each one of these brains, inherited from the past, seems to try, with varying degrees of success, to venge an outlet for its repertoire of archaic, ancestral 'memories', responses and predispositions.

Each of these basic brains might in engineering terms be regarded as a biological computer, programming or influencing man's behavioural reaction to his internal and external environment. For example, MacLean has suggested that the reptilian brain in man (a legacy from dinosaur, snake, crocodile, turtle, tortoise) programmes us for repetitive, stereotyped behaviour according to instructions based on ancestral memories – searching for food, mating, chewing, eating and migratory behaviour, hunting, homing, forming social hierarchies. There is some experimental evidence for this. If you damage – i.e. put a lesion in – the reptilian part of the rat's brain in an area called the substantia nigra, the lesioned animal ceases to drink or eat and exploratory and food-seeking behaviour is reduced. In man, over-stimulation of this part of the brain by large doses of the drug amphetamine can lead to the development of repetitive, neurotic, 'obsessive-compulsive', stereotyped behaviour – chewing and gnawing movements, repeating or writing the same word over and over again.

Reptiles behave as though they are slaves to precedent, as though they are 'obsessional'. For example, the sea turtle returns year after year to the same place to lay its eggs and never forgets to cover them over. These obsessional, repetitive traits are also found in higher animals, including man. MacLean hypothesizes that it would be interesting to know how much the reptilian counterpart of man's brain contributes to his superstitions, his obeisance to precedent in organized rituals and to his vulnerability to religious and political indoctrination.

How does the shrew-brain, rat-brain, horse-brain, donkey-brain counterpart in man help to regulate our emotional behaviour? The paleomammalian brain, more often known now as the limbic lobe or limbic system, is concerned with emotional and sexual behaviour and subconscious drives and instincts. It is the neural fulcrum from which we experience the intrinsic feelings of pain and pleasure. Part of this limbic system, especially the hypothalamus and related structures, controls many of the internal functions of the body, including the biological clocks – the menstrual cycle, temperature, blood pressure, the body fluids, appetite and therefore body weight. Many of these functions and the areas of brain tissue involved can be 'sampled' or demonstrated in conscious man and in lower animals by electrical stimulation or by ablation experiments in which certain parts of the brain are removed or destroyed.

The limbic system is an interconnected complex of brain elements in the midst of which is the hypothalamus. It is this central part of the brain which is fundamentally bamboozled each month in women who take the contraceptive pill. The hypothalamus is also intimately tied up with emotional behaviour. Other elements in the limbic system include the amygdala, associated with mediating the emotions, including rage; the hippocampus, which helps to mediate memory; and the septal nuclei, which are tied up with motivation and pleasure.

In addition to its role in olfaction or smell, stimulation and ablation

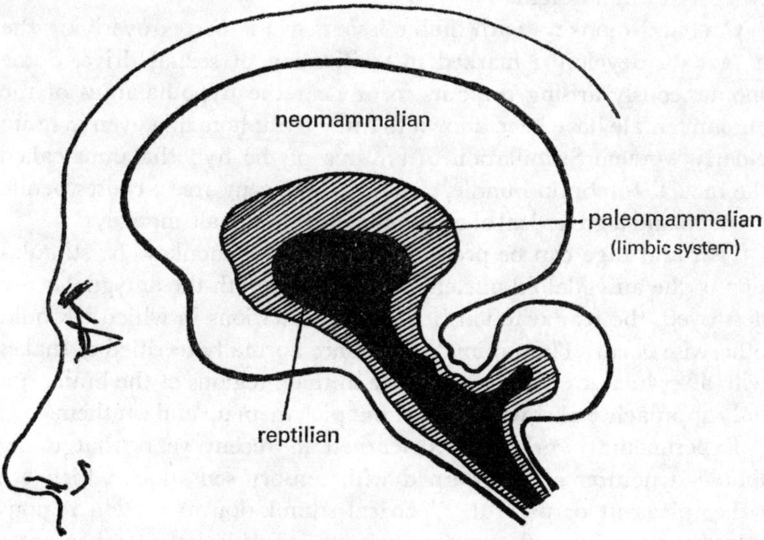

Figure 4: THE TRIUNE BRAIN

experiments indicate that the limbic system is also concerned with feeding behaviour, in which the hypothalamus also plays a central role. The hypothalamus also regulates sexual behaviour, the emotions of rage and fear and, very important for man and lower animals, the physiology of reward or motivation. Only a few experiments will be referred to here because subsequent chapters will discuss in some detail the physiology of sex and mating, the brain's pleasure (reward) and pain centres and their relation to human behaviour, normal and psychotic.

The hypothalamic regulation of appetite for food depends on the interaction of a 'feeding centre' and a 'satiety centre'. Electrical stimulation of the feeding centre in conscious animals evokes feeding behaviour; its destruction causes severe fatal anorexia in otherwise healthy animals. Stimulation of the satiety centre when the animal is feeding causes it to stop eating. Destruction of this region will lead to hyperphagia : a rat in which this region of the brain is destroyed will continue to eat when food is present even after it has become over twice its normal weight.

Cats and monkeys with limbic lesions in the cortex overlying the amygdala develop a marked intensification of sexual drive. Some spontaneously arising tumours in or near the hypothalamus of the human female have been known to cause nymphomania even in quite elderly women. Stimulation of an area of the hypothalamus called the medial forebrain bundle, and of its adjacent areas, causes penile erection and a great deal of emotional display in male monkeys.

Fear and rage can be produced in conscious monkeys by stimulation of the amygdaloid nuclei. Conversely, if both the amygdalae are destroyed, the fear reaction is absent in situations in which it would otherwise occur. Thus animals which are normally terrified of snakes will, after bilateral lesions are made in these regions of the brain, not only approach snakes without fear but pick them up and eat them.

Experimental workers have learned in recent years that many limbic structures are concerned with sensory sensations which are either pleasant or painful. Electrical stimulation of certain regions 'pleases' or satisfies the animal, whereas stimulation of other areas seems to cause pain, fear and defence or escape reactions. Clearly these two oppositely responding systems greatly influence the animal's behaviour in its natural habitat. If the animal is trained to press a lever and thus to switch on an electrode which stimulates a reward centre, he may proceed to press the lever many thousands of times an hour; rats press the bar or lever five to twelve thousand times per hour, while monkeys have been clocked at seventeen thousand presses per hour. When offered the choice between their favourite food and self-stimulation, these animals often choose to press the lever. Normally, starved rats will cross an electrified grid to obtain food only when the current is below seventy microamperes, but when self-stimulation is the 'bait' they will cross currents of three hundred microamperes or more.

The major reward centres are located in the septum and in certain nuclei of the hypothalamus. Punishment centres are also located in the hypothalamus and in adjacent areas of the limbic system. Stimulation of the pain or punishment centres, while the reward or pleasure centres are already being stimulated, can frequently inhibit these latter centres completely, suggesting that the mediation of pain can take precedence over pleasure and reward. Since almost everything we do depends on reward and punishment (carrots and sticks), the importance of centres which mediate motivation in lower animals and humans need hardly be stressed.

A number of lever-pressing experiments have been carried out with humans who have had electrodes implanted permanently in their brains. (Most were schizophrenics or epileptics, others suffered from inoperable cancer which caused severe intractable pain.) Like animals, humans pressed the levers repeatedly to turn on the reward centres. They usually reported a general sensation of well-being, experiencing pleasurable sensations expressed in phrases like 'quiet relaxed feeling' or 'relief of tension'. However, they rarely reported happiness, ecstasy or joy. Some subjects who had the highest self-stimulation rates were unable to explain why they continued to press the lever.

When electrodes were placed in areas in the brain which human subjects learned to avoid 'turning on', the subjects reported sensations ranging from vague fear and anxiety to absolute terror. Should central neural structures mediating anxiety or terror in appropriate situations (as for example when a man is confronted suddenly with the prospect of being shot dead) be turned on inappropriately by disease or some biochemical imbalance, then the unfortunate person will experience subjectively severe, persistent anxiety, or severe terror or panic attacks, without the appropriate external environmental situation. This is known as 'free-floating' anxiety or 'free-floating' panic attacks. Many of these people may be branded by psychiatrists and others as hysterics.

The 'new' or neomammalian brain, the most highly developed of the three ancestral brains, reaches its evolutionary heights in the ape, the dolphin and, pre eminently, in man himself, in whom it has become the instrument subserving the higher mental functions : speech, writing, reasoned choice, logic, mathematics, the creative arts, and the calculation of space and time.

The human cerebral cortex, a thin layer of grey matter, about one-tenth of an inch thick but up to four hundred square inches in area, forms the outer shell of the 'new' brain. It may contain up to 14,000 million nerve cells. It is literally man's thinking cap. In the last five hundred thousand years, this cortex has involuted, extended and evolved spectacularly, partly by chance, partly because of the unremitting and, for man, ever-changing challenges of the environment (which 'unmasked' his indwelling genetic 'acorns' of adaptive and readaptive biological potential), and also because, *pari passu* with the evolution of the cerebral cortex, man has developed an increasingly complex cerebellum.

The cerebellum, which is situated behind and below the cerebrum (see Figure 1), is intimately involved in the mediation of emotionality or mood. More important, however, is the role it plays in the regulation of muscular movement in the limbs. In man it is especially important in the control of the subtle muscular movements of the larynx.

Without this cerebellum, the elegantly precise muscular movements required for speech could not have evolved. (No cerebellum, no Maria Callas.) As he evolved, it became possible for man to develop vocalizations or grunts, cries of pain or fear, gasps for help, cries of joy, anger, frustration or recognition, into a systematic language which could be used in day-to-day living and subsequently recorded graphically and symbolically, thus permitting acquired knowledge or know-how to be passed on to future generations.

The higher intellectual functions of *Homo sapiens* – abstract and symbolic thought, concept formation – are correlated in no uncertain way with the activity of the cerebral cortex of the 'new' brain. Without the abstractions of language, man would have remained a mere 'stimulus-response', concrete, almost off-the-cuff thinker and problem-solver. Consciousness itself, however, the pale tip of a black, ill-construed iceberg, depends on a primitive subcortical arousal or alerting mechanism anatomically ill-defined and neurophysiologically as ill-understood as an act of human creativity itself. This area is called the reticular activating system of the brain-stem, part of the 'reptilian' brain. Man, having extended communication beyond the limited repertoire of pragmatic grunts and the usage of his muscles of facial expression, to the refinements of a language which became more and more abstract, thereby endowed with ever-evoking, ever-increasing, central, cerebral 'augmentation-value' the tangible environmental objects about him, and so could increasingly assume more control over the primitive, humdrum, season-ruled social milieu in which he had both to survive and plan his continuing survival.

It is best to think of the environment and the brain as a 'two-way-arrow' system, each acting and reacting on the other. For example, if you constrict the rat's environment simply by immobilizing him, you can alter his brain levels of 5-Hydroxytryptamine. Similarly, newly born rats taken away from their mother for short periods during the weeks after birth will develop larger brains than their litter mates.

By understanding, and more precisely defining, his external environment, using intelligence, insight and language, man thereby accelerated the evolution of central mechanisms, especially the cerebral cortex of the 'new' brain. In turn, he could now ever more precisely define the phenomena of his environment, thereby further extending the repertoire of his responses. Thus may have arisen the possibility of culling from his scavenging ranks an Aristotle or a Da Vinci.

As with certain areas of the limbic system and in the reptilian brain, so too experimentation on conscious humans has demonstrated areas of localization of function in the cerebral cortex and other centres. Electrical stimulation of the motor cortex in man, a narrow strip which lies immediately in front of a central fissure called the fissure of Rolando, gives rise to discrete movements of the various parts of the body. Crude visual impressions can be induced by stimulating points on the occipital or posterior end of the cerebral cortex. If this area is damaged in man, eyesight is impaired or may be lost forever. Broca's speech area is situated in a defined area of the cortex, usually on the left side of the brain. Stimulation produces vocalization; one conscious patient reported (on being stimulated) that his voice was being 'pulled out of him'. Disease in this area, as one would expect, produces defects of speech.

Patients with temporal lobe disease suffer from memory impairment. Stimulation of the temporal lobe may evoke detailed memories of events that occurred in the remote past, often beyond the power of voluntary recall. The memories produced by temporal lobe stimulation are 'flash-backs'. The subject experiences them as replays of previous real-life experiences. The temporal lobe may therefore be a 'key' area to unlock memory-traces neurochemically recorded in other areas of the brain. We have all experienced the *déjà vu* phenomenon, an inappropriate feeling of familiarity with new events or in new surroundings. This often resembles the sort of warning or 'aura' experienced by patients with temporal lobe epilepsy before having a fit.

It is not surprising that patients with temporal lobe epilepsy whose fits are caused, as they are in other forms of this disease, by the spontaneous, inappropriate firing-off of groups of cells, frequently report auditory and other hallucinations immediately before or during a fit. For example, a woman reported hearing a lullaby her mother had sung long ago. In another case, a girl of fourteen with scars in this area of her brain had fits during which she felt terrified, and in every fit witnessed a scene in which she identified herself as a child of seven being attacked in a field by a man; throughout the attack she had an horrific fear lest she be struck or smothered from behind. Her mother confirmed that this episode had occurred in real life when the girl was aged seven. The resemblances between certain types of temporal lobe epilepsy and schizophrenia, and between schizophrenia and drug-induced psychotic states, as can occur with LSD abuse and chronic amphetamine intoxication, have been well documented.

While man is probably the most complex and the most interesting, he is, paradoxically, apart from his intelligence, the least specialized vertebrate that has ever crawled out of the teeming sea on four seal-like fins. The dolphin's brain is larger both absolutely and relative to its total body weight, but during its evolution this mammal has probably 'digressed' and enlarged its brain into literally mere 'hearsay' or a specialized 'listen-whistle mediating device', rather analogous to the pig whose entire tactile or touch-receiving area of the brain appears to be devoted to the snout. The supreme non-specialized handy man himself, if he can be said to have specialized at all, has done so slowly, almost negatively, by his reluctance to over-react or over-specialize in response to an ever-changing terrestial environment, and in his ability to 'forget' or to discard those minor adaptations or novel skills which at a point in time had enabled him to survive temporarily prevailing hazards. Later on, when the climate of survival changed yet again, he was able to discard, 'ungrow' or readapt these skills and somatic augmentations. The biological survival-value of forgetting or despecializing (or being able to 'ungrow') – in other words, of maintaining adaptive plasticity – tends to be forgotten by some biologists, some anthropologists and many psychiatrists. Failure to 'despecialize' has probably led to the demise of a species as often as has failure to adapt to new environmental conditions. Indeed, the natural history museums of the world are cluttered with the skeletons and fossils of species whose complex and ingenious adaptive specializations left them literally high and dry when the climate of survival changed – alas poor *Megalosaurus*, alas poor *Australopithecus*.

It should be evident that, in spite of its boggling complexity, the human brain is nevertheless, like every other organ in the body, a mere collection of cells, though very highly specialized cells; that it still retains, recorded in some neurochemical way, ancestral memories and predispositions inherited from our more humble vertebrate ancestors: from long-lost species that resembled the gill-breathing fish, lung-fish, amphibians and reptiles of today, and so on through primitive and more highly developed mammals, and on again via a common early primate stem, consisting of the rat-sized insect-eaters of seventy million years ago, that deviated and evolved over time into 'species', some of which later became extinct, but also into our primate-stem 'cousins', still alive today – tree shrews, lemurs, lorises, tarsiers, monkeys, orang-outangs, gibbons, gorillas and chimpanzees.

But why man as the cognitive and creative evolutionary maestro? At present it is only possible to speculate. It seems likely that central to *Homo sapiens*' spectacular ascent over the last three and a half million years or so were the following features: the emergence and the refinement of a spoken language, the dawning of self-awareness, and the birth and development of a culture which would ultimately permit man to impose his will on both the environment and himself, depending on the social mores he chose to construct and follow. Almost certainly language came first and played the key role.

Only those two well-known eastern passerines, the parrot and the mina bird, can simulate human speech. 'Why is it,' ask Richard Leakey and Roger Lewin in *People of the Lake*, their study of the origins of man, 'that during the evolutionary journey from a speechless ape-like ancestor we learned the trick of stringing together complex sounds in a meaningful and articulate way?' How, in the twentieth century AD, do we look for the signs of emerging language in our remote past? There are a number of possibilities. Firstly, we could examine the changes in the size and shape of those ancestral hominid skulls that are still available to represent developments over the past three million years, hoping to find clues regarding whatever expansion and reorganizing of the brain may have occurred in order to make language possible – a daunting task; second, and more realistically, we could look at the stone tools and ritualistic objects which may tell us as much about what was in the minds of the individuals who made them as they do about the manipulative skills of their hands. Another approach is to study the evolution of language development in the modern child during the early months and years of life; we might also perhaps seek for clues in the communication systems of those apes who have been taught American Sign Language (Ameslan for short), devised especially for and used by hundreds of thousands of deaf Americans and pioneered in 1966 as a means of communication for, and to, chimpanzees by the American psychologists Allen and Beatrice Gardner, at a research centre in the Nevada Rockies. It might also be of interest to examine data that has recently become available in comparative neurobiology and comparative neuropsychology.

At some point between three million and a hundred thousand years ago man's brain almost doubled in size, from the modest gorilla-resembling 600 cubic millimetres of *Australopithecus* to an impressive 1,500 cubic millimetres, the size it still remains today. Recent reports in the scientific literature have demonstrated that during this period of expansion not only did one hemisphere of the brain (in about 98 per cent of persons the left side) become the dominant or speech hemisphere, but that it is also somewhat larger and asymmetrical when compared with the right hemisphere.

It has been known for over a hundred years that the left cerebral hemisphere is intimately tied up with the comprehension of language and the modality of speech. In the 1860s a French investigator, Paul Broca, pointed out that damage to a particular region of the cerebral cortex gave rise to an aphasia or speech disorder. This area is on the side of the frontal lobes and is now called the language area, or simply Broca's area. Broca then went on to make another major discovery. He demonstrated that whereas damage to this area on the left side of the brain caused aphasia, similar damage to the identical area on the right side left speech intact.

Another type of aphasia was identified in 1874 by the German investigator, Carl Wernicke, and was associated with an area of damage in the cortex of the temporal lobe, also on the left side. Damage to Wernicke's area results in a sort of word salad, a form of speech that includes nonsensical syllables and nonsensical or inappropriate words. Wernicke's area not only plays an important role in speaking, it also has a major role in the comprehension of the spoken word and in the other typically human activities of reading and writing.

Until recently, there was no anatomically recognizable structure to match this brain unilaterality of speech and language. In the early 1970s, however, the American workers, Geschwind and Levitsky, examined a hundred post-mortem brains and found that the part called the planum temporale, which forms part of Wernicke's area, is generally larger on the left side and, moreover, that this disparity could easily been seen with the naked eye. More recently Wada, of the University of British Columbia, demonstrated that asymmetry and enlargement of the planum temporale is present at birth in human infants, indeed it can be detected in the seven-month-old foetus. It seems clear from Wada's fascinating discovery that the enlargement on the left planum cannot be in response to the development of linguistic competence in childhood. On the contrary, the linguistic talent of the left hemisphere very probably results from an anatomical bias that is genetically determined. Did this chance genetic-anatomical bias towards communication mediated via language enhance our more recent ancestors' survival value and thereby 'drive', as Leakey and Lewin suggest, the internal reorganization, expansion and growth of our hominid ancestors' brains? For example, *Ramapithecus* survived longer than the australopithecines, who probably lived easy-going lives that put few pressures of natural selection on their brains to get bigger, and who may therefore have remained more dim-witted.

The Harvard scientist Le May has recently reported finding asymmetries in cranial endocasts made from the fossil skulls of Neanderthal man and other hominids. The pattern of asymmetry was similar to that observed in modern man, suggesting that hemispheric dominance had already emerged at least 30,000 years ago. She has also demonstrated that similar asymmetries exist in the great apes, but not in monkeys. Since apes are our phylogenetic next-of-kin, this should not come as a great surprise. All this reminds us again of Gazzaniga's formulation that man's developmental superiority, even uniqueness, may derive from his 'deep-core information-processing capacity', and that this capacity probably remains in a continual state of evolution even now, and is present, Gazzaniga stresses, in some form in the ape and in more humble mammals. In other words, man may not be as qualitatively unique as Eccles' eulogy would have us believe.

Since the endocasts of our protohuman and more recent ancestors merely provide us with vague, tantalizing clues regarding the origins of human language, we will consider briefly what can be learned from man's tools and other artifacts, and from his early culture, about how he came to be what and where he is today. Dispassionate observation – that is, observation unbiased and uncluttered by teleological argument of either a quasi-scientific or a religiose nature – forces us to accept that in his cerebral-intellectual, ethical, rational, aesthetic and technological achievements and activities, man has outstripped and outgrown his animal ancestry to an impressive and seemingly unprecedented degree. Nevertheless, as Darwin, Lorenz and others have stressed, he betrays in his emotional and social behaviour, as vividly as he does in the nails at the extremities of his limbs, his humble, lower-animal origins.

Sir Karl Popper, John Eccles and David Leakey have emphasized in their various ways how a developing language, with its descriptive, argumentative and conceptualizing functions, would give considerable selective advantages to our primitive ancestors, not only in coming together and forming themselves into tribes, but also in communal grouping for hunting, gathering, defence and attack.

Leakey and Lewin draw attention to the socio-technological factors and possibilities in man's progression towards a more sophisticated language and culture. The earliest stone artifacts come from the Hadar site in Ethiopia, 'crude flakes and choppers . . . the purposive products of hominid minds and hands of more than three million years ago'. The tools left behind on the shores of Lake Turkana a million years or so later are only moderately more impressive – bigger and somewhat better razor-sharp blades manufactured by banging rocks together, as at Hadar. Leakey and Lewin believe that it was not until about one and a half million years ago that a better, newer dimension of technology arrived in the symmetrical and beautiful hand-axes of the Acheulian culture, which lasted till about 100,000 years ago. It was not, however, until about 50000 BC and onwards that strictly non-utilitarian artifacts in the shape of paintings and carvings become evident, presumably when the time-ruling, time-consuming exigencies of mere survival no longer dominated ancestral thinking.

Eccles suggests that the more recent artistic-cultural products of Paleolithic man – as seen, for example, on the walls of the Lascaux cave – postulate 'a kind of early art school operating by linguistic description and criticism', since, he argues, a highly developed form of communication would be necessary to visualize, remember and pictorially represent the shape and movements of the animals so vividly and beautifully painted. Leakey and Lewin, like Eccles, emphasize that the evolving structure of language and the process of making tools and other artifacts, overlap, since both are made up of individual elements – i.e. words in language, and types of strokes in tool-making – and both are ordered according to a basic form – grammar in language, and the necessary sequence of strokes in manufacturing the particular tool that is already a predetermined or a conceptualized implement in the mind of the artisan. And so we progress to the earliest example of 'figurative art', a two-inch-long statue of a horse, carved out of mammoth ivory over 32,000 years ago, found in a cave in Vogelherd in Germany and probably carried about as a 'fetish' or 'good luck' charm. (Is superstition the precursor of organized religion – the creator of gods?)

Leakey and Lewin conclude their joint thesis by suggesting that while it is just about conceivable to imagine complex stone-tool cultures being produced by non-verbal hominids, it is impossible that the abstract symbolism produced and elaborated during the past thirty thousand years or more could have arisen in a speechless animal. 'Without words with which to name them, a statuette of a horse, a rock painting, or a nation's flag, could never exist: they would be meaningless.' In other words, 'social behavioural factors', which of necessity include language, were of outstanding importance.

What of the sign language, as distinct from speech, acquired by young apes in a human-type learning situation in Reno and in other centres in the United States? The first chimp to be taught Ameslan by the Gardners at Reno was called Washoe. She had been captured in the wild in Africa, and was about eleven months old when the Gardners began to teach her. Washoe proved to be a keen student who did not require carrots or raisins as a bribe to learn items in the sign language. She was soon demonstrating that she understood basic concepts. For example the Ameslan sign for a (human) 'baby' is to display one's cradled arms. Washoe could generalize this sign and apply it to pictures of pups and kittens, as well as to human infants; at the same time she could still make the sign for dog when shown a picture of a grown dog, even if the picture was smaller than those of the puppies. By the time she was three she had a vocabulary of eighty-five words, and was regularly able to use three sign words in combination. Indeed earlier, at the age of about 18-24 months, she was using two words in combination, rather like the human infant does at the same stage of its development.

In 1974 the Gardners produced a study comparing early language development in child and chimpanzee. They demonstrated that, in answering questions or merely communicating in two-word combinations, the proportion of nouns, adjectives, verbs and the word order used by the chimpanzee is very close to those found in the more recent and careful studies of children. For example, both young children, before they have picked up syntax properly, and the chimpanzee, telescope sentences into a word or two, missing out the definite article and the possessive pronoun.

Washoe loved to look at pictures in magazines, often signing to handlers 'What is that?' Chimps can be toilet-trained easily in early life and can also be taught to do the washing and wiping-up after meals. Even more impressively, Duane Rumbaugh, a psychologist at the Yerkes Regional Primate Centre in Atlanta, Georgia, has taught chimps to communicate with one another using special large typewriters, the keys of which are stamped with arbitrary abstract symbols, each one representing a word – noun or verb. A gorilla (a more lowly primate than the chimp) has mastered a vocabulary of 100 signs in Ameslan in a primate centre in San Francisco.

Will the day come when an ape will be able to tell us in Ameslan, or in any other symbolic language, what it's like to be an ape? Or alternatively, will man some day be asked, by an intelligent, sympathetic and inquisitive ape, what it's like to be human? At the present state of knowledge in this exciting and expanding field of investigation, one can only guess. Perhaps man's future space-time explorations should be more in the direction of trying to communicate with our only available living ancestry, the chimps (what stories we might swop!), rather than in advancing our necessarily one-way cosmo-physical and astronomical dialogue with the available contemporaneous relics of the big-bang creation of the universe. We certainly seem more likely, at the present time, to manage to have a chat with brother Ape than we are with some intelligent, self-maintaining, self-replicating, planetary mushroom on Mars or from outer space.

There seems little doubt that man's central nervous system, or more accurately, both his 'hemisphere' brains, will continue to evolve and complexify, if only because the ever-increasing ingenuity of his technology and creativity will evoke and consubstantiate in his brain an ever-increasing, neurochemobiologically-mediated repertoire of responses to internal and external enviromental events, past, passing and to come. He will continue actively being, that is, becoming his more potential self – '*dasein*' – the way the acorn continues actively to be and to 'struggle' to realize the leaf-fledged oak even in its transitory and seeming demise in the autumn clay.

Our knowledge and understanding of how the brain is 'compartmentalized', how it has evolved and continues to evolve, has been much increased by post-operative studies of two dozen or so American patients who suffered from severe chronic epileptic seizures, and had to have the corpus callosum of the brain surgically divided in order to control their prolonged and frequently-occurring fits. The corpus callosum is the great tract, made up of about two hundred million fibres, which links together almost all areas of the left and right hemispheres and keeps one hemisphere informed about what's happening in the other.

The dominant, or major hemisphere, which contains the speech centres, is nearly always on the left. Because there is a partial discussation, or crossing-over, of the nerve fibres from the retinas at the optic chiasma, the right visual field for both eyes projects to the visual cortex in the left or major hemisphere. Similarly, the left visual field projects to the right visual cortex. Sperry and his associates in the United States have demonstrated, in a series of elegant and humane experiments on those patients with 'split' brains, that the 'goings-on' in the minor hemisphere are unknown to the subject, i.e. that he is only in liaison with the 'goings-on' in the major hemisphere. The major hemisphere alone can communicate by the use of language – it is the talking hemisphere. If, for example, we position the subject in a special apparatus and flash-display HAT BAND so that HAT goes to the right hemisphere and BAND to the left (speaking) hemisphere and then ask what word the subject saw, he will say 'BAND'. The speaking hemisphere had no idea that the right hemisphere had received the word 'HAT' at the same time; indeed there is never even a trace of cross-transfer from the right to the left, that is, to the conscious experience of the subject.

But despite its inability to speak, the minor hemisphere has some independent ideational existence of its own, and in some ways it is quite clever. It can, for example, write the names of words flashed or displayed to it alone. If what it writes is hidden from the total field of vision, the major hemisphere knows only that something has been written (because it feels the writing movement coming through the body) but has no idea what the word is. Though the minor hemisphere gives a good performance in naming (writing or manually identifying) common objects, simple verbs are rarely, if ever, comprehended by it. It can, however, recognize descriptive phrases as signals to retrieve particular objects from a collection of other objects : 'for lighting fire' results in the retrieval of a match, 'measuring instrument', a ruler, and so on. Its delayed responses are impressive; for example, if a signal of an object is flashed to it, and there is an enforced delay of five minutes, it can correctly retrieve the object from a bag containing twenty or so other items – no non-human primate can match this. In brief, it is a highly intelligent brain, except that it cannot speak or express itself adequately in language, or really disclose any experience of consciousness that can be recognized. Sperry postulates, however, that another consciousness does exist in the minor hemisphere, but that its existence is obscured by its lack of expressive language.

By contrast, the major hemisphere has a normal linguistic ability. To it, therefore, we must accord the prior existence of the self, or the ego, with full access to all the memories of the past before the commissural section was performed by the surgeon. As Levy and Sperry have also demonstrated recently, this major hemisphere is also the specialized organ 'in respect to fine imaginative details in all descriptions and reactions, i.e. it is analytical and sequential.' It can also add, subtract and multiply and perform other computer-like operations. Its dominance derives from its verbal and ideational-conceptional abilities and its liaison with consciousness itself. It may not be the old-fashioned 'seat of the soul', but it certainly seems to be the physical substrate through which the mind, or the ego, mediates in its dialogue with the outside and inside worlds.

In normal brains the two hemispheres have complementary functions. The evolutionary advantage of this is clear, since it helps to reduce or avoid the redundancy of neuronal duplication and leaves more space available for further specialization, while at the same time allowing the normal individual the advantage of presiding over the whole of his cerebral performance in a cumulative and integrated manner. Gazzaniga has recently suggested that the major hemisphere, because of the early, embryological (ontogenetic) emergence of the 'language' brain (e.g. the left planum temporale that is present even in the foetus's brain), 'becomes filled up, synaptically speaking, and therefore has little remaining neural space available for those executing skills involved in manipulating items in external space which mature later. In other words, language matures in the left, leaving the right to acquire manipulative spatial skills later on in life.' There are still considerable areas of the brain that remain 'silent' or comparatively 'unused'. Therein lie our cerebral potentialities, man's as yet unexploited, encephalized, neuronal riches.

Yet it is salutary to be reminded that not only can animals as lowly as the rat employ two bits of previously learned behaviour to solve a new problem – that is, they show intelligent behaviour – but that even more humble non-intelligent organisms, the song-birds studied by Nottebohm of Rockefeller University, display a neural laterality of the brain for singing. Similarly, J. H. Dewson, now at Stanford University, has shown that the left hemisphere is dominant in the recognition of cries (confined to their own species) in Japanese macaque monkeys, who, like their local human counterparts, display an exotic and unusual variety of such signals.

It is the spectacular development of the human cortex and cerebellum that accounts for man's current evolutionary supremacy, for his intelligence, self-awareness and inventiveness. Ironically, however, man's very inventiveness may continue to exacerbate his ancient habit of killing members of his own species and could lead ultimately to the total destruction of all life on this planet.

We should, whether we subscribe to a religious belief or not, acknowledge honestly both our humble origins and the vulnerability of our present exalted phylogenetic status. The dolphin's brain is larger than ours, both absolutely and relative to its total body weight. Thus, if this seemingly happy philanthropist, who has few natural enemies, should decide to leave the easy-going sea and submit to the dangerous but cerebrally-enhancing challenges of terrestial living, man might end up as his house-boy or in his zoological garden.

Before concluding our brief discussion of the specialized centres of the brain which modulate behaviour, it is important to stress that none of these organizational areas functions independently from the rest of the brain. Each specialist structure is integrated with the rest of the brain, physiologically, anatomically or neurochemically. It must not be assumed that there is a direct one-to-one relationship between a specific neurochemical event and a behavioural happening.

Reductionist or deterministic attempts to interpret or understand the psyche in terms of brain chemistry, conditioning, reinforcement or computerization, are not only inadequate, but make a poor *philosophe's* joke of consciousness, self-analysis and self-awareness, and reduce reason, logic and imaginative speculation and creativity to drab, repetitive cybernetics. I think of the mind/body liaison metaphorically as a two-way prism through which psyche and soma endlessly altercate.

Finally, on a more romantic level, perhaps man's endless, insatiable hankering after what is beautiful, magical or divine – illustrated in the cave paintings of Cro-Magnon man so expertly etched and dappled thirty thousand years ago, and in the abstract sculpture and paintings of present-day artists – intimate, if ever so faintly, at a future for the human ape somewhat more Olympian than the psychotic nuclear brinks of prevailing national and international madness. Man's hankering after what is beautiful may even hint at the long-truanting sabbatical of some benign but absent-minded divinity who in a not too obtrusive way shapes our stars, rough-hews our teleological instincts while permitting us, nevertheless, some sort of small, pitiful free choice.

REFERENCES

John C. Eccles, *The Understanding of the Brain*, op. cit.

M. S. Gazzaniga, 'Consistency and Diversity in Brain Organization', op cit.

Richard Leakey and Roger Lewin, *People of the Lake; Man: His Origins, Nature and Future*, Collins, London, 1979.

J. C. T. Levy and R. W. Sperry, 'Perception of Bilateral Chimeric Figures Following Hemispheric Deconnexion', *Brain*, Vol. 95, 1972, pp. 61-78.

4
Psychosurgery Old and New

The human brain is the ultimate paradox. It is still constantly, almost tautologically, trying to catch up on, explore and decipher its own near-limitless complexities and resources – literally brain-picking itself, and necessarily having to use (despite advances made in computers, in neurophysiology and in related sciences) its own pathetically limited knowledge of its very own self to pick with. The historical vicissitudes of psychosurgery provide an excellent ongoing example of this exploration. By psychosurgery I mean brain surgery which specifically attempts to understand and alter behaviour and mental life, rather than surgery to relieve some physical malformation – for instance, a brain tumour in a frontal lobe, requiring a lobectomy or partial lobectomy (i.e. removal of all or a portion of that lobe) – or to treat an injury to the brain itself, as may occur in a traffic accident or at birth.

The history of psychosurgery goes back more than ten thousand years to the New Stone Age which began about 9000 BC in the Near East and endured in north-west Europe until about 2000 BC, when it was succeeded by the Bronze Age. Archaeologists have abundant evidence that the operation of trephination was carried out in prehistoric times. This entailed cutting an opening through the skull into the brain, an operation which was performed in those distant days on men, women and quite young children. These openings varied from a tiny hole to an opening about two inches in diameter. Not infrequently, skulls are found which show that these burr holes were trephined on more than one occasion on the skull of the same individual. Evidence suggests that the New Stone Age specialist used a flint knife or scraper to perform the 'operation'; in the days of classical Greece a metal drill, actually called a trephine (*trupanos*), was used to cut the hole. Few prehistoric trephined skulls show any sign of fracture, so the operation must have been carried out for some other reason. It is possible that in those distant times certain nervous or mental conditions may have been attributed to a demon which had possessed the patient, a belief still common not only in primitive races, but which has lingered on in the ritual floggings and in other more sophisticated punishments meted out to the unfortunate lunatic right up to the present time. The ancient brain surgeon probably made a hole in the skull to let the demon escape. The round plate of bone cut from the skull was often highly prized and hung round the neck of the patient as an amulet. Here we have not only the treatment of mental disease itself, but also prevention – an attempt to ward off recurrence – a sort of prehistoric lithium.

The first 'breakthrough' (literally) in more modern times occurred at 4.30 pm on 13 September, 1848, when Phineas P. Gage, a man of twenty-five noted for his temperate habits and employed as a foreman on the Rutland and Burlington Rail Road in Vermont, was preparing a hole with powder, preparatory to blasting. While he was in the act of tamping the power, it exploded and blew the tamping iron up through the left cheek and eye and through the left lobe of the brain, making its exit through the median line of the frontal area of the skull. The tamping iron was 3 feet 7 inches long, $1\frac{1}{4}$ inches in diameter and weighed $13\frac{1}{4}$ pounds. Gage was thrown on his back, but after a few twitches spoke within minutes of his misadventure. His friends sat him up in an ox-cart and drove him three-quarters of a mile to a local hotel where he was later seen by a physician, John M. Harlow.

Gage recovered, but after his accident there was a dramatic and permanent change in his personality and behaviour. In the words of Dr Harlow, who later reported the event in the *Boston Medical and Surgical Journal*, Gage changed from a hard-working, temperate miner into a 'fitful, irreverent' man, 'indulging at times in the grossest profanity . . . manifesting but little deference for his fellows . . . at times pertinaciously obstinate, yet capricious and vacillating, devising many plans of future operation, which are no sooner arranged than they are abandoned in turn for others appearing more feasible. . . . His mind was radically changed, so decidedly that his friends and acquaintances said he was "no longer Gage".'

There was, of course, no rationale behind Gage's unfortunate accident, and if the enthusiasts of the ensuing seventy years had familiarized themselves with Dr Harlow's account of the personality disruption which followed Gage's informal lobectomy, as well as previous accounts in the literature, they might have been less scalpel or ice-pick happy with the brains of the mentally deranged patients handed over to their ministrations by psychiatrists.

Gottlieb Burckhardt is an example. In 1891 Burckhardt published the first account in the literature of the brain operations which he himself carried out at an 'insane asylum' in Préfargier, Switzerland, of which institute he was director. His rationale for surgical interference was stated with Hitlerian élan. It was also totally fallacious. He believed that the agitation, excitement and impulsivity of his more disturbed and uncontrollable patients were due to abnormal impulses arising from the cerebral cortex. 'If,' he argued, 'we could remove these exciting impulses from the brain mechanism, the patient might be transformed from a disturbed to a quiet dement. . . .' And so he undertook to bring about the desired pacification by destroying what he believed were the offending regions.

He experimented with six of his patients. One died as a consequence of surgery. Burckhardt's account of the other operations suggests that some of the patients were transformed into manageable, self-locomoting vegetables, but that others remained psychotic. He concluded that his efforts had met with only limited success, but nevertheless justified his (undoubtedly well-intentioned) efforts in a way that chills the spine today : 'I believe one has the right to excise such parts of the cortex that one can consider as starting points and centres of psychological malfunctions and, furthermore, to interrupt connections whose existence is an important part of pathological processes.' Burckhardt's rationale for psychosurgery was that our 'psychological existence is composed of single elements, which are localized in separate areas of the brain'.

Almost half a century was to pass before any psychosurgeon claimed better results than Burckhardt. Puusepp's experiments on his Russian patients, carried out around 1920, were at least no worse.

Our story now continues at the International Neurological Congress in London in 1935, when, tragically for many patients subsequently, monkeys and chimpanzees briefly steal the limelight, in particular an adult female chimp called Becky. Before her brain operations and laboratory adventures, Becky was described by the American experimenters, Jacobsen, Fulton and colleagues, as 'extremely eager to work and apparently well motivated'. She was happy and friendly and conscientious too, 'highly emotional and profoundly upset whenever she made an error'. She was to have portions of her two frontal lobes removed (lobectomy) during separate operations, and the behavioural changes resulting from these manoeuvres would be recorded.

In the introduction to their published report, Jacobsen, Fulton and colleagues point out with exquisite euphemism that 'the extirpation of the frontal association area in monkeys and chimpanzees causes behavioural disturbances strikingly similar to those described in man after this lesion, namely, a marked reduction in complexity of behaviour.' They then add : 'Utilization of this essential equivalence of frontal lobe symptoms in man and chimpanzee enables one to pursue an experimental analysis of frontal lobe function necessarily precluded in man.'

Becky was given two types of tests. One was designed to measure her spatial intelligence. For example, she was given sticks, graded in length, with which to scoop in longer sticks and finally food, which was placed outside her cage at the radius of the longest single stick. The second series was designed to test her recent memory. In one typical test, food was hidden under two similar cups and the animal was distracted for varying lengths of time; she was then tested to see if she remembered the cup under which the food was hidden. By continued exposure to this second sort of problem-solving, too difficult for her to master, Becky had two nervous breakdowns or 'experimental neuroses' similar to those provoked by Pavlov in dogs who had to make increasingly fine visual discriminations between a circle and an ellipse, which ultimately so resembled each other that it was beyond their ability.

Becky's neuroses took the form of 'violent temper tantrums' after she had made a mistake; she often rolled on the floor, defecated and urinated at the experimenters – bad manners, but what a fair criticism of her masters! Later she refused to co-operate and 'it was necessary to drag the animal' into the experimental cage. She was then given a break from work and 'gradually reaccustomed to the experimental set-up by generous feeding and play sessions in the experimental apparatus'.

The same tests were repeated after Becky had had 17 grams of brain removed from the left frontal lobe and had recovered from her operation. Again she broke down under experimental testing. Four months later, 14 grams of brain were removed from her right frontal area. 'When this animal was rendered a bilateral preparation, a profound change occurred.' The chimp was no longer surly, 'offered its usual friendly greeting', resumed the 'cups and bait' experiment having gone to the experimental cage 'with its customary eagerness and alacrity', and didn't seem to give a damn how often she made a mistake: 'it was quite impossible to evoke even a suggestion of an experimental neurosis. It was as if the animal had joined the "happiness cult of the Elder Micheaux" and had placed its burdens on the Lord.' It should be stated that throughout all this time, that is, before and after both her operations, Becky was doing as well as ever in her 'spatial intelligence' tests. In short, bilateral lobectomy left her intelligence intact but disrupted her recent memory. It also cured her of her neurosis and converted her to an emotionally stable, 'normal' chimp.

Among those attending the International Congress in London was a Portuguese neurologist, Egas Moniz. When Jacobsen, who read the joint paper, had finished, Moniz, enraptured, compared and equated in his own mind 'the querulous, the deluded, the agitated and obsessed' with Becky and the other experimental apes and monkeys of Fulton and Jacobsen. He later sought Fulton out and asked him about the possibility of applying such an operation to human sufferers. This was too much for Fulton; he later allowed that he was quite shocked by Moniz's suggestion. Jacobsen's reply is not on record. Undaunted, Moniz returned home convinced that a scientific basis now existed to justify the use of brain surgery to modify behaviour and thereby to improve 'the mental life of some lunatics . . . and, in particular of obsessed and melancholic patients'. Moniz's rationale was a somewhat more subtle version of Burckhardt's. 'Normal psychic life', he reasoned, 'depends on the good functioning of brain synapses, and mental disorders appear as a result of synaptic derangement.' He considered it was necessary only to alter surgically the synaptic adjustments of the prefrontal lobes in his disturbed patients in order 'to modify the corresponding ideas and force thought [*sic*] into different channels'. (This last statement puts one in mind of ancient Chinese acupuncture and its quite non-existent meridians or channels through which Ch'i, the vital force, 'circulates'.)

Moniz was not himself a neurosurgeon, but his purpose was 'to annihilate a great number of associations . . . to attack en masse the cell-connecting fibres of the anterior portion of both frontal lobes'.

An attack was mounted as soon as Moniz had persuaded a neurosurgeon, Almeida Lima, to join forces with him. As Moniz later recalled, 'all fears were swept aside by the hope of obtaining favourable results' – note the cavalier bravery of the man. Stephan Chorover, of the Massachusetts Institute of Technology, comments: 'What Moniz lacked in originality he made up for by sheer immodesty and total lack of self-critical judgement.'

At first Lima used injections of alcohol to destroy the white nerve-fibre tracts that connect the frontal lobes with the rest of the brain, including the limbic system. Later a special blunt instrument called a 'leucotome' was developed. It was blunt in order to avoid severing arteries and veins as it was pushed into the brain and moved up and down. Blunt knives were also used to make the desired lesions. The operation of cutting the nerve tracts between the frontal lobes and the rest of the brain became known as 'leucotomy' or (in the United States) 'lobotomy'.

In 1936 Moniz described the first twenty cases of pre-frontal leucotomy with swashbuckling enthusiasm, providing a minimum of clinical detail and maximum promotional gusto. Not only was his style of presentation aped in the publications of other psychosurgeons of the day, but pre-frontal psychosurgery spread rapidly throughout the world as a consequence of Moniz's glowing report. He commented later, true to form, that 'we obtained cures and improvements but no failures to make us draw back'; he claimed that seven patients had been cured, and another eight especially violent patients made calm and tractable. Most of these patients were probably schizophrenic. (It would be interesting to know whether Moniz himself was, in fact, a true manic-depressive, one of whose elated, over-confident phases coincided with his visit to London and subsequently recurred at intervals.)

By the end of 1936 the neurosurgeon Walter Freeman and his colleague James Watts had introduced pre-frontal leucotomy into the United States. Freeman, by the time of his retirement in 1970, had performed or supervised more than 3,500 operations. It has been estimated that about 50,000 pre-frontal leucotomies of various kinds were performed in the USA between 1936 and 1955. In 1947 standard leucotomy carried a 6 per cent mortality rate.

In fairness, Moniz himself referred no more than one hundred patients for brain surgery before, in 1944, he was assaulted by a leucotomized patient who put a bullet in his spine, leaving one side of his body paralysed. The final crazy irony occurred in 1949, when this well-intentioned but over-enthusiastic physician was awarded the Nobel Prize in medicine for his discovery of 'the therapeutic value of pre-frontal leucotomy in certain psychoses'. This was an operation which, at best, to quote Freeman himself, left the patients 'direct, practical and uninspired', but at worst, we might add, dead or only half alive – epileptic, apathetic or irresponsible and asocial, often with blunted memory and sensibilities and a severely blunted intellect.

It cannot be denied, however, that for a proportion of patients life became more bearable and some did recover. Moniz shared his Nobel Prize with Walter Hess, the Swiss brain physiologist. Hess received his award for studies on the effects of stimulating deep portions of the brain in cats, using implanted electrodes. There is no record of Moniz offering to share his half of the prize money with poor old Becky or with Jacobsen and Fulton.

By the end of the 1950s the early advocates of leucotomy in the USA, UK and elsewhere had lost, for good and obvious reasons, much of their enthusiasm. Their younger, newer, somewhat better-informed and more sophisticated psychosurgical and psychiatric colleagues have been openly critical of those early surgeons whose excessive enthusiasm for surgical attack on the mind brought psychosurgical methods of treatment into disrepute.

Many of the patients in the early days were schizophrenic, and at that time there were virtually no effective treatments for this condition. In 1971 the *British Journal of Psychiatry* published a paper by Freeman in which he reported on a long-term follow-up of 415 schizophrenic cases on whom he had performed the standard, old-fashioned pre-frontal leucotomy. His findings were unimpressive, and his suggestion that the operation was more successful in illnesses of relatively short duration than in the chronic form was then quite irrelevant, since no British psychiatrist in his proper senses would then or now advocate leucotomy for early-onset schizophrenia. This operation has long been abandoned in the UK and elsewhere because of its disappointing results, morbidity and mortality rates, and also because the introduction of the phenothiazine drugs like largactil in the early

1950s revolutionized the treatment of schizophrenic illness. The experienced neurosurgeon, Geoffrey Knight, clearly stated in 1973 that even the less traumatic stereotactic operation should rarely if ever be used on schizophrenics, and then only to alleviate severe concomitant depression. In short, with the advent of drug therapy, prefrontal leucotomy became essentially redundant as a treatment for schizophrenia.

This was not, however, the end of psychosurgery. Nowadays, more sophisticated and accurate manoeuvres are employed, mostly in the treatment of severe depressions and to alleviate severe anxiety and obsessional neuroses which have failed to respond to other, more conventional methods of treatment such as psychotherapy, anti-depressant drugs or electro-convulsive therapy (ECT). Operations are usually carried out at specialized centres and with the patient's full consent.

The most sophisticated and successful psychosurgical operation currently in use is stereotactic subcaudate tractotomy, which was conceived and pioneered by Geoffrey Knight.

'Stereotactic' means three-dimensional. In 1908 Victor Horsley, a British neurosurgeon, and an associate, Robert Clarke, invented a stereotactic instrument which gave a three-dimensional picture of the brain and could direct with considerable accuracy a needle, electrode or probe to any desired point in the brain. A number of variations of the Horsley-Clarke instrument (which was first used experimentally on monkeys) have since been developed to enable depth probes to be inserted into the brains of many species of animal, including man.

It was not until the late 1960s and the 1970s that the Leksell stereotactic frame and a variation of this, McCaul's device, were specifically designed for psychosurgery. Before that, a variety of modified, 'free-hand' operations were used – indeed some of these 'free-hand' operations are still performed today. The advantage of the stereotactic technique, however, is that, by using X-rays to outline the skull and the ventricles of the brain, and a probe guidance system, it is possible to locate a target in three-dimensional space by making discrete, orderly measurements. After the calculations have been made, a stimulating electrode and then a lesion-making probe can be introduced to any position within the brain to an accuracy of one millimetre.

Stereotactic subcaudate tractotomy, the operation devised by Geoffrey Knight in the late 1960s, entails making discrete lesions in the inner corners of the frontal lobes in the white matter anterior to the head of what is called the caudate nucleus. The lesions are produced by using an array of small ceramic rods containing the radioactive element yttrium; each rod is only 7 mm long and 1 mm in diameter. They are very accurately placed, by means of stereotaxis, into the target sites. Yttrium causes localized damage, for about two and a half days only, a few millimetres distant around each rod. The radioactivity then disappears completely. The operation takes only one and a half hours and the patient is up on the third post-operative day.

To date, approximately 1,000 operations have been performed in Knight's unit. Nearly two-thirds of patients with severe and intractable depressive illnesses, some present for over ten years, had a complete cure or virtually so. Sixty per cent of cases with severe anxiety and fifty per cent of patients with obsessional neurosis also recovered. All these patients had failed repeatedly to respond to conventional therapies. There were no serious personality changes or other unwanted side-effects.

Patients with obsessional neuroses may find a slightly different operation of more benefit. Stereotactic limbic leucotomy involves making small lesions in the lower medial quadrant of the frontal lobes, and also in the adjacent cingulum, by means of radiofrequency coagulation. The (unconscious) patient is first stimulated electrically and the physiological responses – e.g. rise in blood pressure and heart-rate – indicate that the correct target areas have been found. Patients with severe anxiety states also benefit from limbic leucotomy.

Stereotactic operations designed to make bilateral lesions in the amygdala and in the hypothalamus are also sometimes carried out. These two structures are intimately related to behaviour and especially to emotional expression (including rage reactions and aggressive display) and these operations, amygdalotomy and posterior hypothalamotomy, are thus the cause of some controversy. They will be considered in more detail in the next chapter.

In their article 'Psychosurgery : Yesterday and Today', P. K. Bridges and J. R. Bartlett, the psychiatrist and neurosurgeon who are now in charge of Knight's unit at Brook General Hospital in London, point to amygdalotomy and posterior hypothalamotomy as a possible origin of 'the erroneously alleged intention of psychosurgery in general to modify behaviour'. They decry the fact that controversy over amygdalotomy 'has tended to embrace the whole of psychosurgery indiscriminately' and advocate that 'the available evidence for and against the different operations should be considered separately and dispassionately'.

Their plea, made in 1977, seems to have fallen on deaf ears. Recently psychosurgery has been the object of renewed criticism, and the target has been not amygdalotomy but Bridges' and Bartlett's speciality, stereotactic subcaudate tractotomy. Within the profession, not all psychiatrists are convinced by the statistical evidence of the operation's benefits; outside it, pressure groups have turned their attention to the problem of obtaining legal consent from patients who are severely disturbed. MIND, the mental health pressure group in the UK, has recently suggested that each proposed psychosurgical operation should be reviewed by an independent panel, which would have the right to stop the operation taking place if there was doubt about its suitability or about the patient's ability to consent. Other critics go further still, and are proposing a complete ban on psychosurgical operations in the United Kingdom.

A major cause of disquiet seems to be that no one can explain why operations of this sort work. But if one accepts that, in many cases, they *do* work, is it right to withhold them? Depression of any type carries a 15 per cent risk of suicide; severe neuroses carry a mortality rate three times the expected frequency. In the USA the suicide risk in neurotic patients was found to be twenty-five times higher than the national average. In Niskanen's 1974 study of hospitalized neurotic patients in Finland, 'in almost two-thirds of cases the illness either followed a chronic course, developed into a psychosis, or led to suicide'. Clearly it is not always possible or indeed wise to put severely ill patients suffering from suicidal depression, suicidal anxiety or temporal lobe epilepsy associated with potentially homicidal aggressivity into 'cold storage' until such time as a wonder drug appears or until neuroscientists have worked out definitively the biological minutiae of normal and abnormal brain function and behaviour. One has to balance diagnosis, degree of risk and the patient's misery against what is currently available in pharmacotherapy, ECT, psychosurgery or any other useful form of therapy.

As Bridges and Bartlett pointed out, one area of psychosurgery that has been the subject of constant concern and controversy is its potential use for pacification or behaviour control. Can psychosurgery actually be usefully deployed to pacify violent patients or violent criminals? Has it been used, or is it currently being used for this purpose? If so, is this use of psychosurgery ever justified? In the next chapter I shall attempt to answer these questions.

REFERENCES

P. K. Bridges and J. R. Bartlett, 'Psychosurgery: Yesterday and Today', *British Journal of Psychiatry*, Vol. 131, 1977, pp. 249-60.

Gottlieb Burckhardt, 'Ueber Rindenexcisionen, als Bertrag zur operativen Therapie der Psychosen', 1891; quoted, in translation, in E. Valenstein, *Brain Control*, John Wiley, New York, 1973.

Stephan L. Chorover, 'The Pacification of the Brain: From Phrenology to Psychosurgery', in T. P. Morley (ed.), *Current Controversies in Neurosurgery*, W. B. Saunders, Philadelphia, 1976, pp. 730-67.

C. F. Jacobsen, J. B. Wolfe and T. A. Jackson, 'An Experimental Analysis of the Functions of the Frontal Association Areas in Primates', *Journal of Nervous and Mental Disorders*, Vol. 82, 1935, pp. 1-14.

5

Psychosurgery as a Means of Pacification

Ever since the early 1940s, when Freeman and Watts were pioneering pre-frontal leucotomy in the United States, the possible use of psychosurgery for pacification or social control seems to have had a curious appeal for a number of American psychosurgeons. Freeman himself openly maintained that psychosurgery made otherwise intractable offenders against society easier to manage. 'As a matter of fact,' he said, 'lobotomised patients seldom come in conflict with the law precisely because they lack the imagination to think up new devilries and the energy to perpetrate them – maybe it was the abnormal development of these intellectual-emotional defects that got the patient into trouble originally.'

'Pacification', that rather sinister-sounding euphemism, has been advocated for two broad categories of people, patients and non-patients. In both cases the common factor that singles them out as potential subjects for treatment is a tendency towards violent or aggressive behaviour.

In the patient group we find three sub-groups : individuals subject to periodic outbursts of rage or violence who do not have demonstrable brain disease (and who may or may not have come to the notice of the psychiatrist); patients with organic disease in the limbic system who are deemed to act violently at certain times as a consequence of this disease; and patients with organic disease of the temporal lobes who suffer from epilepsy and who also have outbursts of violent behaviour attributable to their disease. It may not be possible to use drugs successfully to treat patients of these three types.

Some of them may be found in prisons, maximum security hospitals or psychiatric hospitals.

The non-patient group is much broader and more difficult to define, but it includes individuals who may sometimes band together and resort to violent or aggressive behaviour in protest against what they regard as political or social injustice. This group may include idealists, liberals and well-intentioned activists, as well as others with less lofty motives. The group in general does not find favour with the establishment – police, politicians, government administrators, the armed forces, etc.

Before we consider the means of pacification advocated for this second group and actually practised on the first group, it is important to look at aggressive behaviour itself. Recent psychobiological studies of aggressive intraspecies behaviour, carried out in Africa, America and elsewhere, have helped to elucidate the origins and development of this type of behaviour in primates, including man.

A number of studies suggest that the male of the species is more aggressive than the female, and that this in turn may be related to the influence of the male sex hormones. Goodall has filmed a ten-month-old male chimpanzee making threatening gestures typical of the adult and noted that these early aggressive patterns are much more characteristic of males than females, suggesting a gender-hormonal influence. It has also been observed that even brief treatment of new-born female rats with the male hormone testosterone causes a lifelong abolition of female sexual behaviour as well as patterns of aggressive behaviour as adults. Pregnant rhesus macaque monkeys, carrying females, which were given testosterone during the second quarter of gestation, produced offspring with aggressive behavioural characteristics of the male type; these female offspring were also much more aggressive than normal females. At Johns Hopkins University, John Money has followed up twenty-two girls whose mothers were exposed to androgens while pregnant. As teenagers, these girls were 'tomboys', enjoying rough play and showing little interest in clothes or other female preoccupations when compared to a normal group of girls of similar age.

Other studies suggest that aggression-submission behaviour is innate or inherited. In one experiment monkeys were raised in total isolation for the first nine months of life. Between 2½ and 4 months the animals were exposed to coloured slides showing adult monkeys displaying a species-typical aggressive or threat expression. These slides elicited a much more dramatic degree of behavioural arousal in these young isolates than did neutral slides. This suggests that at least a predisposition to recognizing aggressive behaviour may be inherited in some animals.

What is even more fascinating and particularly relevant to our present discussion is the observational learning that takes place socially in many species. The following sequence has been described in primates by a number of field-workers : close observation of one animal by another; imitation by the observing animal of the behaviour of the observed animal; practice of the observed behaviour, often for hours after its occurrence, especially in the play group of young animals. This sequence of observation, imitation and practice has been reported in relation to several adaptive ambiences, for example, food gathering, tool using and making, nest building, infant care, copulation and aggressive interactions. Essentially, the young have access to virtually the full gamut of adult behaviour to learn patterns of adaptation both aggressive and non-aggressive. Moreover, the motivation for such observational learning seems to be very well-established in the young primate.

Young humans also demonstrate the same susceptibility to learn aggressive behaviour patterns by observing models which act aggressively. The elegant studies of Bandura showed this clearly. For example, pre-school children were exposed to an aggressive model attacking a target object for ten minutes in a laboratory, while another (control) group experienced the same situation without an aggressive model. When the children were tested six months later, the first group was much more aggressive to the target object than the control group.

To sum up, the studies reported above suggest that where primates (including man) are concerned, although there may be an inherited predisposition in the young animal towards recognizing and performing certain types of aggression-submission behaviour, and that while aggressivity itself is more often found in the male of the species and is therefore probably related to the influence of testosterone, it would seem, nevertheless, that aggression is for the most part a pattern of behaviour which the young primate learns from others in an ongoing social or environmental setting.

With this model in mind, it would seem absurd to suppose that psychosurgery could play any part in alleviating aggressive behaviour in individuals who do not have demonstrable brain disease. Yet in the United States there do seem to be physicians who make this supposition. On 9 July, 1972, the *National Enquirer* reported that the Californian psychosurgeon, M. Hunter Brown, had claimed that 'brain surgery could transform the most violent murderer into a normal citizen'.

In many countries, aggression, violence and social turmoil continue to preoccupy public officials; in America, however, these social manifestations also seem to have an especial interest for certain physicians and neuroscientists. Both camps seem to perceive the causes of this turmoil as lying in the direction of individual derangement. Accordingly, both camps seem to think that a mutual interest is served by making research on brain function and behaviour relevant to the solution of problems that are essentially social, political or environmental.

In the autumn of 1967, after the political protests of the 'long, hot summer', a group of American doctors and neuroscientists wrote a joint letter to the *Journal of the American Medical Association* concerning 'the role of brain disease in riots and urban violence'. Having dutifully referred to the 'urgent needs of the underprivileged' slum-dwellers, they suggested the possibility of brain dysfunction in those among the rioters who engaged in arson, sniping or physical assault. The writers concluded that 'the real lesson of the urban rioting is that . . . we need intensive research and clinical studies of the individuals committing the violence.' They were frank about the purpose of these studies : 'to pinpoint, diagnose, and treat those people with low violence thresholds before they contribute to further tragedies'.

This suggestion seems to me about as logical and realistic as attempting to resolve the food shortage and consequent hunger and misery in the Third World by getting brain surgeons to remove the offending hypothalamic 'feeding centres' from the brains of the near-starving millions, thus eliminating their ability to feel hunger pangs.

This excessive obeisance towards officialdom is sadly reminiscent of the excessive zeal and unquestioning fervour with which many German doctors and scientists avidly seized the opportunity to perform what were for the most part badly-designed experiments on Jews during the Hitler régime, once this type of experimentation had been given the respectability of official sanctioning. Such a hankering, jingoistic segment of the general public exists today – now – in every country under the sun : a segment on heat to serve the régime currently in power. (It would be outside the scope of this discussion to suggest how mental health professionals should deal with high public figures who order the violent decimation of an entire sub-continent, though there might well be a place for the experienced psychosurgeon here.)

The likelihood, now or in the future, of political activists or aggressive prisoners being subjected to psychosurgical pacification is far from being a bee in an alarmist's bonnet. In May 1973 M. Hunter Brown presented a paper entitled 'Multiple Limbic Targets for Schizophrenia and Aggression' at a meeting of the American Psychiatric Association. He claimed good results in over 200 cases with 'hard core schizophrenia and [in] a variety of cases showing violent-aggressive states including explosive personality'. Brown believes the cingulum (part of the limbic system) to be the locus of disturbed brain function in a wide array of socially deviant individuals. It is consequently his favourite target site. Like some of the 'old masters' before him, he describes his patients' or prisoners' case histories with scant detail and an excess of jargonized, self-congratulatory stultiloquence, which is intended to convey that 'modern psychiatric surgery has moved a long way from the bitter backwash of lobe-cutting twenty-five years ago'.

But Brown has gone even further than this. At least from 1972 onwards, he maintained that 'a majority of the captive patients in our mental institutions and prisons have major neuropsychiatric illness such as paranoid schizophrenia, psychomotor epilepsy, or impulse dyscontrol with explosive personality'. He reckoned that only 6,000 dollars would be needed to transform a 'violent young criminal' into a responsible, well-adjusted citizen', in contrast to the 100,000 dollars required to pay for twenty years' incarceration. I have been unable to discover any reports on which Brown might have based his therapeutic zeal, or indeed his seemingly off-the-cuff 'epidemiological' statistics for prisons and mental institutions in the USA. There are of course patients and prisoners with the illnesses he describes in such institutions, but surely only a minority.

Even before Brown's pronouncements, it had been proposed in 1971 to screen prisoners at the California Medical Facility at Vacaville for psychosurgical evaluation and treatment in a 'maximum psychiatric diagnostic unit' (MPDU). Plans for the MPDU at Vacaville were actually sent to Governor Ronald Reagan, but had to be abandoned when they fell into the hands of ex-prisoners. It is possible, however, that pacification projects are being carried out at other MPDUs. As Chorover has rightly warned us, for some American psychosurgeons the distance seems short 'from brain disease to social disorder and from brain surgery to behaviour control'.

One illustration should suffice. On 15 November, 1970, the brain researcher, José Delgado, was reported to have asked, 'What sort of humans would we like, ideally, to construct?' Delgado conducts laboratory experiments on animals, including the human variety. One of the experiments involves implanting in the brain electrodes which are connected to a transmitter/receiver or computer carried on the patient's body. It is then possible unobtrusively to monitor and indeed manipulate behaviour and brain activity. Delgado reportedly looks forward to the day when 'assaultative or anti-social activity could be recognized by the computer before they ever reach consciousness, in order to trigger pacification of the subject.'

Delgado's question is a good one, and he appears not unaware of the moral and other implications of his work. He prefaced his enquiry by pointing out that 'the human race is at an evolutionary turning point. We're very close to having the power to construct our own mental functions . . . through a knowledge of the cerebral mechanisms which underlie our behaviour.' Nevertheless, one cannot help wondering whether a better, more pertinent, question is not, 'Is Delgado a person?' If so, is he a person fit to construct another person? Or, to put it another way, are the humans he may currently be constructing people or just law-abiding robots? Who has the right to speak *ex cathedra* on how human animals should behave?

To sum up, since aggressive behaviour may be learned, triggered off by environmental signals from the past, related to current endocrine status or indeed endocrine influences that prevailed *in utero*, or due simply to sheer institutional monotony and boredom, the possibilities for neurosurgical misdiagnosis, interpretation and abuse are only too obvious, especially among a captive population (who seem to be the prime target of the neuroscientists' misguided zeal). Economic and social deprivation, parental neglect, class barriers and prejudice are more likely to contribute to aggressive, reparative or psychopathic behaviour than an unsymphonied amygdala, an explosive temporal lobe or a leaky hypothalamus. If we are determined to intervene in this area, a more contractual relearning/behaviouristic approach – even one as draconian as that adopted by Stürup in Denmark, who offers good old-fashioned castration to violent, habitual sexual offenders, with post-operative parole – might prove not only more humane but more 'politically' and socially effective.

If pacification is unsuitable, indeed unethical, in the case of individuals who may exhibit aggression but have no demonstrable brain disease, should it be used in the case of individuals who do have such disease? I believe that there can be no reasonable objection to offering surgical treatment to patients suffering from temporal lobe epilepsy (whether or not this is associated with aggressive outbursts), which is not responding to drug therapy, or to patients with organic limbic brain disease.

In 1973 the British surgeon Murray Falconer reviewed the effects of his own unilateral temporal lobe and other resections on the behaviour abnormalities of 250 temporal lobe epileptics. Pathological findings in the resected specimens, which included the hippocampus and the amygdala, showed mesial temporal sclerosis, or brain hardening, in about 50 per cent, hamartomas (tumours) in 20 per cent and miscellaneous lesions, such as scars, in 10 per cent. The remainder had non-specific lesions. Falconer's patients were also followed up and assessed, six to twenty years after their operations, by psychiatrists who had not been involved with the neurosurgical team. In one series of 100 patients, twenty-seven, who had also suffered from hyperaggressiveness, had this symptom relieved by unilateral temporal lobectomy. This included seven of thirteen with mesial sclerosis of the temporal lobe.

In 1974 the Americans, Mark and Sweet, offered evidence linking organic limbic brain disease to abnormal aggressiveness. They concluded that a relationship existed between limbic brain tumours, infection, injury or epilepsy and some abnormal aggressive states exibited by patients suffering from these forms of brain disease. To deny these patients brain surgery would in my opinion be quite irresponsible and unethical.

Subjecting patients without demonstrable brain pathology to limbic leucotomy is more debatable. However, Dr Desmond Kelly, who until recently worked at the Atkinson Morley Hospital in London, has reported in favourable terms on the outcome of this operation in 66 of 100 patients who did not have evidence of organic brain damage. In Kelly's study, the least favourable of the ratings by independent psychiatrists was used for statistical purposes. Eighty-seven per cent of patients with obsessional neuroses (27) had a good clinical outcome, with 89 per cent improvement (after a mean interval of sixteen months). Of those with anxiety states (15), 66 per cent had improved, and of patients suffering from depression (9), 78 per cent had improved. Of the seven schizophrenics, six were rated as improved; in some of these very carefully selected patients, the quality of their lives was dramatically changed for the better by the operation. Nevertheless, Kelly, like Knight, advises that 'for limbic leucotomy to be considered in schizophrenia, symptoms of severe anxiety, depression or obsessional rituals or ruminations need to be present'. The overall improvement in a group of eight miscellaneous patients suffering from anorexia nervosa (2), personality disorder with depression and anxiety (3), depersonalization with depression (1), post-encephalitic Parkinsonism (1) and dementia with depression (1), was 76 per cent.

Operations for bilateral stereotactic amygdalotomy and bilateral hypothalamotomy are rarely performed and, as we have noted, their usefulness and ethical justification are somewhat in debate.

The historical background to the operation of amygdalotomy is somewhat reminiscent of the bad old days of Becky and Burckhardt. In 1938 Klüver and Bucy reported in America on the drastic effects and devastating changes in social and emotional behaviour which developed in monkeys following bilateral destruction of portions of the limbic system together with the overlying temporal lobes of the cortex of the brain. These disruptions included a compulsive orality in which food and non-food, including in one case the lighted end of a cigarette, were repeatedly placed in the mouth. An odd form of psychic blindness, in which the animals were unable to recognize objects by sight, was also noted. After the operation, the monkeys became socially inept, markedly tame, and hypersexual, copulating with both animate and inaminate objects. They were unable to learn from painful experiences!

Subsequent operations on other monkeys, this time restricted solely to the amygdala, also transformed wild, unmanageable animals into tame, docile creatures. It soon became clear, however, that bilateral amygdalotomy performed on young male rhesus monkeys not only caused pacification but also had drastic effects on social behaviour. When Kling and others repeated the operation on other monkeys, returning them after recovery to their colony, the animals became fearful and fled from even neutral situations. They were, in short, unable to cope with the complexities of life in their natural habitat and either died of starvation or were killed by predators.

In spite of these reports, bilateral amygdalotomies have been performed on humans suffering from temporal lobe epilepsy, sometimes with drastic results. Humans with temporal lobe epilepsy have also been subjected to bilateral temporal lobectomy with, as should have been predicted from Klüver and Bucy's report, devastating effects on memory and general adaptability.

Amygdalotomies in humans continue to be carried out in the USA, India, the UK, Switzerland, Japan and Australia. We shall limit our attention here to a series of eighteen patients who underwent the operation in the Department of Surgical Neurology, University of Edinburgh, as part of a multi-disciplinary project which included careful psychological, psychiatric and neurosurgical assessment and follow-up. Only two of the patients did not suffer from epilepsy. Their ages ranged from eight to forty-six years. All manifested aggressive behaviour, but the neurosurgeon's criterion for accepting the patient was based on the judgement that the pattern of aggressive behaviour was detrimental to the patient's own well-being, not that it was detrimental to society. The aim of the surgical intervention was therefore to render the individual more psychosocially effective, rather than more manageable. The surgical procedure involved the bilateral stereotactic placement of electrodes within the amygdala, and its subsequent destruction by a radiofrequency current. An attempt was made, before destroying tissue, to obtain physiological localization.

Six patients underwent the operation under local anaesthesia, and were thus conscious throughout the procedure. One was a woman of eighteen who had no history of epilepsy, had a normal brain-wave pattern or EEG, but was severely subnormal and subject not only to violent outbursts but to self-mutilative behaviour. Another was a man of thirty-four, with a normal EEG and average intelligence, who had problems with both drinking and aggressivity. The remaining four all had abnormal EEGs as well as a history of aggressive behaviour.

On stimulation of the amygdala the patients' responses were aggressive. They swore, shouted angrily, and their behaviour became restless and destructive. Some tried forcibly to remove the stereotactic frame. One patient told the surgeon, 'I feel I could get up and bite you.' Another wished to 'escape'. Three had fits that resembled those that had previously occurred spontaneously.

Follow-up ranged from about six months to three years. The investigators, Hitchcock and Cairns, concluded rather cautiously that certain cases do benefit from amygdalotomy, and that improvements were not limited to a decrease in abnormal aggressive behaviour but also included a decrease in other areas of maladaptive behaviour. The results of the proposed annual reassessment of these patients will be of considerable interest.

Bilateral hypothalotomy has been performed by Balasubramaniam and Kanaka in Madras, India, to help in the management of fifty-four aggressive, destructive, restless patients whose maladaptive behaviour was associated in the past with encephalitis (infection of the brain), epilepsy, birth damage, schizophrenia and other conditions. Their ages ranged from three to twenty-five years. Two patients died within a day of the operation, but thirty-one out of the fifty-four became 'quiet', although still unable to live useful lives. The researchers claim that 74 per cent of the patients improved, and that not one was 'rendered wooden or inert'.

Personally, I feel that this operation is rarely, if ever, justified. In those rare cases when it is, it does, however, in contrast to the devastating effects of bilateral temporal lobectomy, leave memory undisturbed. This important finding was confirmed by the experienced Canadian brain surgeon Wilder Penfield in 1974. In Japan, Sano and co-workers have been performing hypothalamotomies since the early 1970s to treat patients for violent, aggressive or restless behaviour. They claim a 95 per cent success rate, but I'm inclined to take that with a grain of rice.

What then is the current position or relevance of psychosurgery? Bridges and Bartlett have summarized its position and its characteristics thus:

'We advocate that, as psychosurgery is a rarely needed treatment, it is best carried out at a few specialized centres where society can monitor the work, where research is facilitated and experience accumulated, and where patients can form a self-supporting group. The units should be the responsibility of both a neurosurgeon and a psychiatrist in close association, and referral to a neurosurgeon alone does not now appear to be the best practice, although it seems to continue to be the American custom. . . . It is to be hoped that [psychosurgery] will come to be unnecessary as psychopharmacology continues to advance to the point where illnesses that are now intractable will respond to future forms of medication, and psychosurgery will then no longer be needed. In the meantime some of the operations appear to have limited but uniquely important indications.'

Subcaudate and cingulate operations are recommended for depression, anxiety and obsessional neurosis. Symptoms should be both severe and chronic and have failed to respond to other treatments, including behaviour therapy. Amygdalotomy is only recommended where abnormal, severe and uncontrollable aggressiveness is associated with a psychiatric or neurological illness.

But whatever happened to Phineas Gage? He seems to have taken to the roads, visiting Valparaiso and Santiago, flitting from one idea and task to another. He eventually returned from South America and died in San Francisco in 1861, after a succession of epileptic fits, at the age of thirty-eight.

REFERENCES

M. H. Brown, 'Multiple Limbic Targets for Schizophrenia and Aggression', paper presented at the American Psychiatric Association, 10 May, 1973.

Stephan T. Chorover, 'The Pacification of the Brain', op. cit.

W. J. Freeman and J. W. Watts, *Psychosurgery in the Treatment of Mental Disorders and Intractable Pain*, Blackwell Scientific Publications, Oxford, 1950.

M. Scarf, 'Brain Researcher José Delgado Asks – "What Kind of Humans Would We Like to Construct" ', *New York Times*, 15 November, 1970, p. 46.

Desmond Kelly, 'Psychosurgery Today', in K. L. Granville-Grossman (ed.), *Recent Advances in Psychiatry*, Vol. 2, Churchill Livingstone, Edinburgh, 1976.

PART TWO

6

The Neurochemistry of Mood or Affect:

Mania and Melancholia

Melancholia, murder and self-murder are probably as old as the Nile. Man seems to have learned little over the past twenty-five thousand years about how best to love and cherish himself, or how best to care for and champion himself in his great grisly adventure towards the grave and whatever options, grisly or otherwise, may lie beyond it. 'Suicide is contrary to the inclination of nature,' comments St Thomas Aquinas, 'and to charity whereby every man should love himself'. Ideally, we should all be having a happy-go-lucky love-affair with ourselves from the uterus to the coffin. Sadly, however, few of us achieve this : we fall prey to depression and other psychiatric illnesses, and some of us are driven to take our own lives.

The relationship between mental illness and suicide has been elegantly demonstrated by Sainsbury and his team in a recent retrospective survey conducted in the United Kingdom. The relatives, friends and doctors of people who had committed suicide were interviewed soon after the fatality. The suicides' medical and psychiatric notes and hospital records were also consulted. Ninety-three per cent had been suffering from a mental disorder prior to their deaths; the majority (70 per cent) had an easily recognizable depressive illness, which could have been treated successfully had relatives or friends brought the condition firmly to the notice of the family doctor or to a psychiatrist. Uncomplicated addiction to alcohol, or alcoholism combined with depression and another drug dependency accounted for an additional 15 per cent.

In Britain, where – compared with countries like Denmark,

Sweden and Austria – the suicide rate is comparatively low, 1 per cent of all deaths are nevertheless caused by suicide. Though more elderly than young people die in this manner, it is the fourth most common cause of death in the 15-34 age group. Generally speaking, male rates are consistently higher than female rates. This pattern seems to hold good for most countries. It is of interest that national rates decline dramatically in wartime, when there is full employment and probably an increase in social integration and national morale. All the countries engaged in World War II showed this trend, whereas in neutral countries the rate of suicide remained static. Suicide rates increase in periods of social collapse, as in the economic depression of the 1930s.

Who then are the people most likely to kill themselves? How many are at risk on a global scale? Most surveys carried out in the USA and Western Europe have demonstrated that one out of every six people who develop manic-depressive illness will sooner or later die by suicide during the depressed phase of the illness. At least 1 per cent of all men and 2 per cent of all women will develop this illness at some time in their lives; in the United States Woodruff puts the incidence of this type of periodic, recurrent depression as high as 5 per cent for men and 10 per cent for women. Clearly the investigation of its causation, whether one deploys the neurochemical, socio-biological, epidemiological, behaviouristic, anthropological or any other reality-based approach, is far from being a mere self-indulgent academic exercise. On a global scale, if one takes the present-day human population at risk as approximately three thousand million, then over half a million people kill themselves each year.

Depression or melancholia may be a normal reaction in certain circumstances: for example, the death of a relative or close friend, divorce, a broken romance, or loss of employment. It is regarded as pathological either when there is no obvious reason or explanation for its development, or when its degree of intensity and duration is out of proportion to its cause. It may vary from a few weeks of bearable sadness to a devastating despair when no hope is seen for the future and the sufferer becomes actively suicidal.

Winston Churchill referred to his recurrent depressions as 'black dog' (luckily for Europe and the USA his mood was probably on an upswing towards hypomania when he was confronting Hitler during World War II), while Jacky Gillott, the talented English novelist, described her depression as a 'black owl'. 'Depression is a state of self-hate,' she wrote. 'It is the horror of feeling oneself inescapably bound within the body of someone you fear, loathe and despise. . . . Every depression is unique and each one is triggered off by a different factor, but there *are* common factors. One is an inexplicable sense of weight bearing the depressive down. Mine I call my great black owl; it roosts on my shoulders. The heaviness really does manifest itself physically. My whole face changes in a most extraordinary way, it goes *down*. All the planes and angles droop with apparent exhaustion. Every limb becomes so heavy, an arm or a leg is a real trouble to move. Simple things like making the bed or brushing my hair are such demanding, impossible ordeals that more often than not I don't bother. Occasionally, I will be violently angry and scream, but generally speaking it's hard to find the energy for anything so dramatic.'

It would be hard to better this description. Later she exhorts : '. . . all the time *know*, that the great black owl will tire of his perch eventually'. Tragically, Jacky Gillott eventually took her own life.

There are various different types of depression, defined both by their clinical symptoms and their presumed causes. *Manic-depressive illness*, which we shall consider in detail shortly, involves episodes of both depression and mania (or the less severe form of mania called hypomania).

The *neurotic* type of depression always has a psychological cause, such as stress, change of job, change of abode or the like. An individual should only be diagnosed as suffering from neurotic depression when the intensity of his disturbance and its duration is disproportionate to the degree of stress or loss involved. These individuals should always be helped because many eventually succeed in killing themselves.

It is crucial to bear in mind in this context that an analogous form of depression, which is reality-based, also exists. It too may lead to suicide or attempted suicide. Nevertheless, depression following the death of a loved wife, husband or child is natural. Many would argue that it is unwholesome to bottle up one's emotions and put on a stiff upper lip during the six months or year following such a serious loss. We must not confuse a normal period of bereavement or depression after such a loss with neurotic depression.

Occasionally severe stress may trigger off one or other of the phases of manic depression in people who are genetically vulnerable, but classically these two forms of mood disturbance develop out of a 'clear blue sky'.

Involutional (or *menopausal*) depression develops for the first time in women between the ages of about forty-five to fifty (appearing to coincide with the female menopause) and in men between the ages of fifty-five to sixty-five (when they may be going through the 'male menopause'). *Puerperal* depression, which sometimes resembles the clinical picture seen in schizophrenia, seems to occur in certain vulnerable females usually in the first month following childbirth.

Manic-depressive illness, as we have noted, involves episodes of both depression and mania. Since the mood of the patient swings at certain periods of his or her life to the pole of extreme excitement, or to the opposite pole of depression and retardation, this form of depression is known nowadays as 'bipolar'. In 'unipolar' depression there tend to be recurrent episodes of depression only. Untreated, these disturbances may last for weeks, months or even half a year or longer. Both types, unipolar and bipolar, are hereditary and involve deranged neurochemistry in the hypothalamus of the brain and possibly in other sites as well. These two variants breed true; that is, there are 'unipolar families' and 'bipolar families' and both variants have a genetic or inherited basis.

Any illness that can be proved to be inherited or genetic must have a biochemical origin, since each gene gives rise to an enzyme and, therefore, each abnormal gene to an abnormal enzyme. When we study the first cousins of unipolars and bipolars, about 10 to 15 per cent of these relatives have suffered from a similar type of illness. The incidence tends to be somewhat higher in the bipolar type, and so also the incidence of suicide.

Twin studies are even more revealing. The literature on the subject now includes 97 pairs of monozygotic or identical twins, and 119 pairs of dizygotic or non-identical twins. When one of a pair of identical twins (who carry the same genes), reared in the same environment, develops the illness – be it unipolar or bipolar – in 68 per cent of cases the other twin will also develop a similar mood disturbance at some time in his or her life. Where the twins are non-identical (i.e. have non-identical genes), and same-sexed, the concordance rate is only about 23 per cent. From these findings one can argue that genetic or biochemical events must be central to causation. Yet, since over 30 per cent of identical twins escape the illness, life experiences and environmental events must not be ignored. It is interesting that when twelve pairs of identical twins, reared apart in different environments from an early age, were studied, eight of these pairs were concordant for affective illness – that is, much the same percentage found in twins reared together.

In the depressed phase of unipolar or bipolar illnesses, some or occasionally all of the following symptoms occur against a background of depressed mood that varies from a mild degree of sadness to total despair and suicidal misery, at times going even beyond despair, suicide and hopelessness into a frozen, retarded, stuporose mental and physical immobility that resembles both physically and physiologically the period of hibernation in some animals :

loss of energy with easy fatiguability
loss of concentration, slow thinking or mixed-up thoughts
sleep disturbance (usually insomnia, sometimes hypersomnia)
loss of appetite
loss of libido
loss of interest in usual activities
low self-esteem and self-reproach
recurrent thoughts of death or suicide
diurnal mood swing (the depressed person often feels worse in the morning and gets somewhat better towards evening, or vice versa)

Delusions of worthlessness or of evil and wickedness may occur, or nihilistic delusions in which the patient denies his own existence or is convinced that his brain is absent from his skull. In addition, the patient may complain of weight loss, constipation, inability to weep, or a dry mouth. Men sometimes suffer from sexual impotence, and women from menstrual irregularity. On physical examination, the doctor may notice diminished pulse rate, lowered blood pressure, lowered body temperature, loss of facial flush and cold hands and feet.

By and large, these symptoms and signs are much less severe and less prominent in neurotic depression, when we often find a pre-depression history of neurotic, hysterical or childish dependency on others or a previous history of psychiatric illness other than depression, and where invariably a stressful event occurs before onset. In the neurotic variety, mood tends to change from hour to hour, or minute to minute, hypochondria and irritability are common, and suicidal attempts more often demonstrative than seriously intended.

In inherited depression many of the symptoms and signs result from alterations in the biological rhythms and body metabolism controlled by the hypothalamus. This centre, as we have seen, controls temperature regulation; the circulation of adrenaline and noradrenaline; thyroid hormone secretion, including the levels of sex hormones acting on the ovaries, womb or testes; the regulation of the brain centres controlling thirst, hunger and sexual behaviour; and, in conjunction with the limbic system, defensive or emergency reactions of fear and rage, as well as their opposite, the mediation of placidity. It is hardly surprising, then, that in severe depression not only is the internal environment disrupted but also the regulation of emotional mechanisms such as the expression of anger. The ability to relate appropriately and affectionately to close relatives or friends is also disturbed. A patient totally perplexed by this paralysis of feeling stated: 'I can feel no affection for anyone, not even for my own children.'

These hypothalamic changes may be causally related to an imbalance of neurotransmission in this part of the brain. The neurotransmitters that have been investigated in terms of mood disorders include noradrenaline (NA), dopamine (DA) and 5-Hydroxytryptamine (5HT). The first possible clues emerged during the early 1950s when reserpine, the active component of *rauwolfia serpentina* (a creeping plant used to treat illness in India for many centuries), was found useful in the treatment of schizophrenia and high blood pressure or hypertension. Two important effects of the drug were noted. It could produce a depression-like syndrome in animals, including sedation and motor retardation. In humans, a sub-group of patients who were treated with reserpine for hypertension developed severe depression. It was later discovered that the drug depleted the brain of all three neurotransmitters referred to above, NA, DA, and 5HT, now known collectively as the 'biogenic amines'.

This breakthrough observation was given added impetus when the drug iproniazid was synthesized for the treatment of tuberculosis. Clinically, it was reported to produce euphoria and over-active behaviour in some patients. Pharmacologically, it was shown to be a powerful inhibitor of an enzyme, monoamine oxidase (MAO), present in brain cells and elsewhere in the body. Inhibiting MAO leads to increased brain concentrations of NA and 5HT. In 1957 two reports appeared supporting the usefulness of iproniazid in the treatment of depression. Later another effective group of anti-depressants, known as the tricyclic group, was discovered. These drugs also increased the amount of biogenic amines available at the synapse or cleft between two neurons. Later still came the discovery that lithium, a drug effective in treating mania, decreased the quantity of biogenic amines at nerve receptor sites. (Rather paradoxically, lithium is also successful in preventing relapse into depression in both bipolar and unipolar patients, so the biogenic amine story is far from complete. In other words, simply linking mania with abnormally high levels of NA or 5HT may be naive. It is possible that mania and depression might reflect an altered balance between two or more neurotransmitters, rather than a change in activity of a single system.)

In spite of obvious gaps in our knowledge, the most popular hypothesis put forward by research workers has been that depression and mania are due to lack or excess of NA or 5HT or perhaps DA. In 1967 Shaw examined the brains of depressed patients after suicide and reported lower brain concentrations of 5HT and of 5-Hydroxyindoleacetic acid (5HIAA, the main breakdown metabolite of the neurotransmitter 5HT) when compared with a matched group of patients who had died from natural causes. Levels of 5H1AA and HVA (homovanillic acid, a metabolite of DA) can be measured in the cerebro-spinal fluid. Most studies have found low levels of 5H1AA in depression, as well as a reduced rate of 5H1AA accumulation, suggesting that brain 5HT metabolism is lowered in this illness.

In a study published in 1975 by Shaw, Johnson, MacSweeney and co-workers at the MRC Neuropsychiatry Laboratory, West Park Hospital, Epsom, a minute dose of radioactive L-tryptophan, the amino acid from which 5HT is produced, was injected into patients suffering from affective disorders (ill and after recovery). The results suggested that the total mass of tryptophan in the body is reduced in people prone to mania and depression, and furthermore that in depressed patients (ill or well) the turnover of tryptophan may be critically reduced. Thus, at least where tryptophan is concerned, these individuals may live on the brink of depression or mania even when well.

For descriptive purposes, sixty years ago, the German psychiatrist Kraepelin divided manic illness into four sub-types: hypomania, mania, delusional mania and delirious mania. These terms are largely self-explanatory. In the hypomanic phase the patient experiences a feeling of well-being and an increase in energy, so that he begins to take on more tasks and enjoys the challenge. Judgement is retained and distractibility does not seriously interfere with work. The patient looks well physically and may often feel not only 'on top of the world' but also that he could conquer it singlehanded. If the patient now progresses towards mania, increased assertiveness and combativeness may be noted. He becomes aggressive and irritable when challenged. His judgement is suspect. Later the patient's manner becomes overbearing, behavioural restraints are absent and there is often conflict with family, workmates and police. Later still, the patient may become over-active and thought-disordered – he talks almost non-stop nonsense and finally he may develop grandiose delusions (for example, he may be convinced he is the prime minister, or Christ, or some other figure his religious, political or social whims may cause him to regard as important).

The following symptoms were noted by Winokur and his colleagues when they studied manic patients who were hospitalized. The admixture of symptomatology observed is fascinating. Nearly all (98 per cent) overtly showed mood elevation seemingly varying from cheerfulness to exaltation, but in 83 per cent, totally belying the idea of the happy manic, the predominant mood was hostility. Over two-thirds experienced transient depression with morbid preoccupation and weeping. Two-thirds experienced diurnal variation of mood similar to that found classically in unipolar depression or in the depressed phase of manic-depressive illness. All were over-active and, of the most severe cases, 7 per cent developed the sort of physical posturing and stereotyped movements sometimes seen in severely disturbed schizophrenics.

Nearly all the subjects also developed pressure of speech and flights of ideas – jumping rapidly from one idea or topic to another. Almost half developed grandiose delusions. Twenty-one per cent developed auditory hallucinations and 9 per cent visual hallucinations. Behavioural disinhibition was common : increased sexuality in content of conversation and sexual demands on wife or girlfriend were noted in 65 per cent and 11 per cent became quite promiscuous. Increased alcohol intake occurred in 42 per cent and in 63 per cent insight into their condition and into their subjective feelings and way of thinking was lacking. On average, the illness – from onset of symptoms to their disappearance – lasted about eight weeks, and about half the manic episodes were preceded by a depressive episode lasting over one month.

My own clinical experience of manic patients and the mixed mood disturbances they suffer accords very closely with Winokur's. In many individuals symptoms of both mania and depression co-exist or alternate from moment to moment. Kraepelin, who formulated the concept of manic-depressive psychosis in 1896, also recognized that there are patients in whom 'the phenomena of mania and melancholia are combined with each other. . . . States arise which indeed are composed of the same morbid symptoms as these [i.e. mania and melancholia] [and] cannot without coercion be classified with one or with the other.'

I regard mania as a more severe mood disturbance than depression and one in which the neurochemical disturbance is probably also more severe. Indeed, some of the chemical derangements found in mania seem to be in the same direction as those found in depression, but of a more severe degree. It is also of interest that, before the advent of anti-depressant drugs and the major tranquillizers, ECT was used successfully in the treatment of both mania and depression. Furthermore, the manic patient usually needed more frequent ECTs to get him better than the depressive.

The apparently paradoxically mixed bag of symptoms found by Kraepelin and Winokur in manic patients may be resolved if we think of a continuum model, with normality at one end, mania at the other, and depression in an intermediate position. Thus the first indication of affective disorder would be depression, while a more extreme reaction could result in mania. It may be that not until depression has progressed to an intolerable intensity is a new, quasi-denial defence mechanism, i.e. mania, unleashed by those patients genetically loaded with bipolar genes. This continuum model was first proposed by Court in 1968.

It is of interest, too, in terms of this model, that manic patients have more pronounced disturbances in general arousal, in degree of insomnia and in severity of anorexia than do patients in the depressed phase. Also relevant to severity, and upholding this contention, are those reports in the literature in which more first-degree relatives of bipolar patients die by suicide that those of unipolar patients.

The eminent brain physiologist Professor D. G. Grahame-Smith reminds us that 'the brain is not a plastic bag filled with a solution of diffusing neurohumours'; with this caveat in mind, we shall now discuss briefly the more elemental chemical changes found in depressed and manic states and some possible brain mechanisms related to these changes.

In 1965 Shaw and Coppen used small injections of radioactive sodium, bromide and 'heavy' or tritiated water to study 'whole-body' water and electrolyte (sodium and potassium) distribution between body cells and the surrounding extra-cellular fluid. Since 0.02 per cent of the naturally occurring potassium in everyone's body is radioactive, there was no need to give radioactive injections of this electrolyte. They found a 50 per cent increase of intra-cellular sodium in depression and a 100 per cent increase in mania, when compared with normal volunteers; in other words, in mania there was the same type of shift as in depression, but the deviation from normal was much more extreme. With recovery, both groups of patients reverted to normal values. If these 'whole-body' changes also occurred in nerve cells in the brain, significant alterations in brain excitability would result. Both groups of patients would have 'less active' synapses than normal people : in depressed patients the average action potential would be about 7 millivolts less than in normal subjects, and in manic patients the action potentials would be even lower. Since the amount of neurotransmitter liberated by the nerve cell into the synapse is almost certainly proportional to the magnitude of the action potential, then depressed and manic subjects will have 'less active' synapses than normal people.

The severe, mixed emotional turmoil observed by Winokur in his manic patients may have demonstrated in behavioural terms the more serious degree of brain cell sodium abnormality found in this type of patient in Shaw and Coppen's electrolyte study. Similar findings were reported by Cox and co-workers in 1971.

Apart from the purely genetic-neurochemical, there are many other factors which might be implicated in the causation of affective disorders. Some writers have suggested that, in the past, melancholic and possibly even manic states may have had survival value. The German writer Lange considers that depression in man may be analogous to hibernation in certain animals and could in the past have served to reduce activity and food consumption during an unfavourable season. One type of depression, the retarded variety, is characterized by a reduction in physical and mental activity and often by agoraphobia, anorexia and loss of libido, all of which might be helpful under unfavourable seasonal conditions. It might possibly even be triggered off by appropriate but consciously unrecognized seasonal clues. Perhaps one could call this variety of depression 'stay-put' behaviour. John Price, the Maudsley Hospital geneticist, has suggested that in primitive times the seasonal migration of predators, for example, 'might have rendered invaluable a temporary mood of pessimistic caution; the death of the first family member would have been a late and cogent indication that the unfavourable season had begun.'

Similarly, the second major type of depression, characterized by motor restlessness, agitation and dissatisfaction with the environmental surroundings and general status quo, which has some features in common with manic illness, might have been of advantage to nomadic people occupying barren, unproductive regions for too long. 'Move-on' anxiety or manic restlessness might urge the community to uproot itself and move to a more favourable, better-appointed acropolis and more rewarding surroundings.

One English writer, Heymann, has suggested that depression was the natural state of primitive man until such time as he poked his nose into his own existential business to such an extent that he began to contemplate his origins and his future. At this point, it became necessary for him to evolve to our present state of relative elation to enable him to live with his awesome conclusions. Here we are almost back to 'denial' strategy, inherent in certain manic states already referred to.

Price has also compared the features of depressive illness with features relating to fall in 'peck-order' or dominance hierarchy that occur in baboons. A depressive behaviour pattern seems to occur in animals who are going down the hierarchy because age has taken its toll and/or younger animals have successfully challenged their position. The parallels between human and animal behaviour under these circumstances, illustrated in the table below, are striking and seem to me especially relevant to involutional melancholia, the type of depression associated with the male and female menopause.

Feature of depressive illness	*Feature of fall in dominance hierarchy*
Loss of appetite	Less access to food
Loss of libido	Less access to sex outlets
Avoids company	Must avoid animals who previously avoided him
Ideas of unworthiness and inferiority	More submissive behaviour
Selective forgetting of favourable memories	Must forget or forgo well-established habits of dominance
Average duration six months	Recovery from injury or illness allows resumption of former dominance
Commoner in later life	Commoner when powers waning, and more difficult to adjust
Commoner in females	Female status varies with harem (often monthly) and between harems
Associated with separation and bereavement	May follow loss of allies
Increase of anxiety and irritability	Increase of all 'dominance hierarchy' behaviour

As we have seen, there is a peak in the male suicide rate at the age of sixty-five, and in the female rate between fifty and fifty-five. These peaks not only reflect the increased incidence of depression in both sexes at this time of life, but also coincide with male and female involutional/menopausal stresses, associated in both sexes with a decline in physical, intellectual and reproductive capacity. It also coincides with other status-losing life events. At this age the male usually has to retire from his job or profession. His income and, as a consequence, his self-esteem and perhaps his domestic and social standing are reduced. The female may feel her age more acutely, accentuated by cessation of her reproductive cycle. She may also be less confident about her physical attraction. For married women this time also coincides with the youngest children leaving the house to marry or work elsewhere.

Perhaps depression at this time serves a purpose. Since the art of living seems to be to give up with good grace what must soon be given up perforce, involutional melancholia may make it less likely that the ageing human will fight (in vain) to regain his former 'rank'. Perhaps it is those who fight too hard, or who fail to resign themselves to a loss of status, who commit suicide at this time of life.

The contribution of psychosocial factors to depressive illness has recently been highlighted by a series of impeccably designed surveys of the social origins of depression in women in the UK. Professor George Browne and co-workers have identified four vulnerability factors : loss of mother before the age of eleven; the presence at home of three or more children under the age of fourteen; lack of a confiding relationship with husband; and lack of full or part-time employment. The first three factors are more common in the working class. These findings were confirmed by Dr Alec Roy in 1978. The importance of stress unmitigated by emotional support need hardly be emphasized, but one wonders whether these women were psychochemically programmed for depression by a major bereavement at a vulnerable age.

What practical steps can the lay person take in dealing with these illnesses, whether he himself or members of his family, friends, colleagues or acquaintances become ill? If someone feels mentally and physically exhausted and is suffering from some of the symptoms of depression already outlined, he or she should consult the family doctor. If his only advice is to 'pull yourself together', then I suggest a change of doctor. If the sort of picture we have outlined is obvious in the appearance and behaviour of others, firm, tactful advice is indicated. It is not easy to convince mentally disturbed people of what is best for them, or to muster the courage and tact to give advice, but it is important that one should try.

REFERENCES

Jacky Gillott, 'How I Learned To Live with Depression', *Cosmopolitan*, May 1976.

E. Kraepelin, *Manic Depressive Insanity and Paranoia*, 8th ed., Churchill Livingstone, Edinburgh, 1921.

John Price, 'The Genetics of Depressive Behaviour', in A. Coppen and A. Walk (eds), *Recent Developments in Affective Disorders*, Headley Brothers, Ashford, Kent, 1968.

7

Schizophrenia:

Why and How Do We Go Crazy?

> In future we will be allowed to exercise a direct influence by means of particular chemical substances upon the amounts of energy and their distribution in the apparatus of the mind.
>
> SIGMUND FREUD

> If I should return during my absence, keep me here until I come back.
>
> SCHIZOPHRENIC PATIENT

Schizophrenia is an inherited brain dysfunction which typically afflicts young people of both sexes, usually between the ages of fifteen and twenty-five. It often manifests itself in disordered thinking, emotional incongruity, auditory hallucinations and bizarre, gauche, and at times grossly disturbed social behaviour. The victim has little or no insight into his derangement. Schizophrenia causes worldwide devastation and misery. It spares no social class, no primitive group, no race, profession or subculture. It constitutes a universal health hazard of enormous and epidemic proportions. There are about 30 million people suffering from this illness throughout the world, and it is still responsible, on an international scale, for the bulk of patients in mental hospitals. In the UK, 40 per cent of all hospital beds are in psychiatric hospitals and nearly half of these are occupied by schizophrenic patients. The expectancy of developing the illness for members of the general population for England and Wales is 1.13 per cent for males under the age of fifty-five, for females the corresponding figure is 1.08 per cent.

On interviewing a schizophrenic patient, some of the following symptoms are likely to be noticed. There is a disorder of thinking which prevents the patient from following the determinative idea in a conversation; he misses the point, or fastens on details, and brings in irrelevant associations which divert him from the main theme of his original process of thought; as a consequence his thinking is incoherent, rambling and jumbled. Thought-blocking is common; the patient feels that his thoughts are suddenly taken out of his mind, or other thoughts, foreign to him, are put into his head. He may be convinced his mind is not his own or that some external power controls it. Here is a good example of schizophrenic thought-disorder: 'I have a lot of forced thoughts. My thoughts are all drawn-out words, they ought to be pin-pricks. There is an unnatural stoppage in my thoughts too. . . . I have heard voices say, "He is conscious of life." To get my feelings back to normal I feel like changing motor cars into battleships, to be superior to them.' Many patients have no insight into their thought-disorder, and consider their vagueness profundity, their deviant associations originality.

Another symptom which may be noticed at interview is emotional incongruity: the patient's affect (mood) is often inappropriate, so that when discussing serious matters his responses may be either fatuous or emotionally flat. Alternatively, given good news, he may break into tears. Hallucinations are frequently present and are usually auditory: the patient experiences voices speaking his thoughts aloud, or may hear two or more voices arguing or discussing him in the third person. He may hear voices commenting on his actions; a young housewife heard a voice making critical comments on what she was doing: 'She does not want that potato, she is putting it back because she thinks it has a knobble like a penis.'

Other patients report somatic passivity; they feel they are passive, reluctant recipients of bodily sensations imposed on them by some external agency; e.g. 'I feel X-rays entering the back of my neck, they pass down my back in a hot tingling strip and disappear into my pelvis which feels numb and solid like a block of ice.' Others, as we have seen above, report thought-withdrawal: 'I am thinking about my mother and suddenly my thoughts are sucked out of my mind by a phrenological vacuum extractor, and there is nothing in my mind, it is empty.' Patients may complain that they have alien thoughts imposed on them from some external power; e.g. 'It is not me who is unhappy. They are projecting unhappiness on to my brain.' Others feel that their impulses are controlled, also from outside, so that they carry out actions in response to these controlling influences as though they were the passive observers of their own actions.

Delusional perception can also occur. A young Irish patient, on being passed a salt cellar at breakfast, knew instantly and for certain that he must return home 'to greet the Pope, who is visiting Ireland to see my family'.

In spite of the symptomatology outlined above, intellectual defect does not occur and there is usually no clouding of consciousness, though intellectual laziness or evasion is often conspicuous. Generally speaking, in the majority of schizophrenics there is a dissociation, a splitting-up or fragmentation of the whole psychic life of the patient, emotional, perceptional and conative (the ability to take purposeful, competent, relevant action). The personality deteriorates and the sense of self-entity (or ego boundaries) often becomes vague or is lost completely.

The natural history of the illness is of considerable importance and interest. Before the introduction of the specifically anti-psychotic drugs like chlorpromazine in the early 1950s, only 25 per cent of patients made a complete or near-complete recovery; another 25 per cent never recovered. Of the remaining 50 per cent, the majority were left with a greater or lesser degree of residual personality damage as a consequence of each recurrent attack. As Sir Aubrey Lewis commented, 'Schizophrenia is always a serious condition. Though some recover, the tendency of this morbid change is to do permanent damage to psychic life. In the individual case however, pessimism is not justified. It is certainly never possible in the early stages of the illness to be certain that recovery is out of the question.'

The prognosis or outlook for the future of the schizophrenic varies with age of onset, type of illness and duration of illness. Prognosis is worse for younger patients, in cases without marked precipitating stress, when the onset of the illness has been insidious in development, and in cases with persistent hallucinations. The newer forms of drug treatment, together with improved administrative, nursing and social care, probably result in recovery in no more than 30 per cent of patients and some improvement in 60 per cent; many become chronic. In a recently published nine-year follow-up study by Simon and co-workers, only 20 per cent of patients improved in their psychiatric adjustment and work record; nearly 50 per cent were rated as worse, and the remaining 30 per cent were unchanged. The overall conclusion arrived at by these researchers was that (even though the new drugs had been available during the follow-up period) 'schizophrenia remains extremely resistant to treatment'.

Generally there are four main clinical groups recognized in schizophrenia. In the *simple* type, or schizophrenia simplex, the onset is gradual and the patient usually under twenty. There is a slow general deterioration with increasing lack of interest in the outside world, accompanied by an impoverished range of thinking and conceptualizing. The patient becomes idle and shiftless and cannot keep a settled job. Sometimes a highly intelligent and apparently stable student may become increasingly ineffective, solitary and apathetic. Such patients are often the victims of recurrent episodes of depression.

The *hebephrenic* type, which also occurs in young people, is acute in onset. Symptoms include thought disorder and emotional disturbance (including frequent giggling and excitement); auditory hallucinations with changeable, fantastical delusions often occur. Ideas of reference, in which the patient begins to believe that everything that happens in the external world has some special meaning directed at him, are often present, as is depersonalization or loss of that subjective conviction of the actual identity and congruity between oneself and one's body.

In the *catatonic* variety there are periods of high excitement alternating at other times with periods of stupor during which the patient may exhibit flexibilitas cerea, or waxy flexibility (e.g. if the patient's hand is raised in the air he may leave it there for hours on end). Stereotyped posture and mannerisms together with mutism, negativism and hallucinations are often found.

The *paranoid* form is generally rather late and insidious in its development, but probably less damaging to the personality than the hebephrenic variety. Paranoid delusions, usually persecutory, are present. There is generally thought disorder and, with the passage of time, steady deterioration. Occasionally hallucinations and delusions may be so luxuriant as to almost merit the old-fashioned title 'dementia phantastica'.

Only the predominating symptoms and features of these groups are cited above. Mixed and atypical cases occur and, at different times in the course of the same illness, features more typical of other categories of the psychosis may be seen.

There is general agreement amongst most clinicians and research workers that for schizophrenia to develop, an inherited or genetic predisposition is necessary. Other factors considered important in the aetiology are psychological, physical or psychosocial stress.

The expectation of schizophrenia in the general population, derived from investigations in six different countries, works out at 0.86 per cent. This rate varies between 0.4 per cent for Switzerland and 2.9 per cent found by Book for a population living in a remote and isolated part of Sweden, north of the Arctic Circle. The incidence found in the offspring of families where one parent is schizophrenic is 12.13 per cent. In the five reported studies on children born to families where both parents suffered from this illness, the risk of the offspring becoming schizophrenic ranges from between 36.1 per cent and 55.3 per cent. The American geneticist, Erlenmeyer-Kimling, reviewing these five reports most astringently, from both the diagnostic and statistical viewpoints, puts the overall rate at 25.2 per cent.

The evidence for a genetic component in causality becomes depressingly more impressive when we examine reports on monozygotic (MZ) twins and dizygotic (DZ) twins. Studies of MZ twins (whose genes are identical) show that if one twin develops schizophrenia, then in 57.7 per cent of cases reported, the other twin will also do so, whereas the concordance rates for the same-sexed DZ twins is only 12 per cent and opposite-sexed DZ pairs 5.6 per cent.

It should be pointed out here that twins *per se* are no more liable to develop schizophrenia than singletons, so that one cannot put down the heavy risk found in MZ twins to the twinship itself. If the shared family-environmental milieu accounted for the similarity within twin pairs, then the risk of schizophrenia should be the same for MZ twins and for DZ twins of the same sex brought up with the patient. The difference in concordance rates for MZ and DZ twins is, as we have seen above, quite a large one and has been confirmed in several studies. It is apt to mention here Rosenthal's 1963 study of a set of American MZ quadruplets, all of whom were schizophrenic.

Identical twins reared apart from birth or infancy are also of special interest. Reports in the literature from several countries, including Japan, Norway, Sweden and the UK, give a concordance rate for schizophrenia almost identical to that for MZ twins reared together – in fact slightly in excess.

In the USA, Heston followed up a group of forty-seven children born to schizophrenic mothers who were adopted into normal families at infancy. He found that 14 per cent of the adoptees developed schizophrenia, a proportion identical with that to be expected had they been reared with the schizophrenic mother. What exactly *is* inherited, however, still remains a mystery. It is well to remember too that schizophrenic offspring have been born to parents who are themselves completely normal. This could possibly be explained by gene mutation and is more likely to occur in older parents. In some cases the true paternity of the child may be concealed by the mother.

In spite of the above reports, which stress the importance of genetic factors, there is still a place for the action of environmental influences; after all, over 40 per cent of MZ twins escape becoming ill even when the co-twin breaks down. The carefully designed prospective studies into the life events of schizophrenic patients by Brown, Birley and Wing in the UK have demonstrated a significant excess of potentially stressful life changes and crises in the three-week period preceding the onset of an acute relapse. Furthermore, this held true for stressful events which could be considered quite independent of any change in the patient preceding his acute breakdown – for example the death of a relative from natural causes – as well as for events which could have been dependent on the patient becoming ill, for example, loss of employment. Brown and co-workers have studied the family relationships of patients on discharge from hospital and shown that those returning to so-called 'high emotional involvement' homes had a particularly poor prognosis. The role played by environmental influences with regard to actual causation, however, still remains to be clarified.

The possibility that a biochemical defect is a cause of schizophrenia is being investigated in almost all the developed countries. In a series of carefully designed experiments carried out at the MRC unit at Northwick Park Hospital, London, Crow and his team have offered evidence suggesting that the dopamine-utilizing system of the nucleus accumbens, part of the limbic system, is implicated in schizophrenia. More specifically, they suggest that the phenothiazines, drugs like chlorpromazine (largactil), thioridazine (melleril) and fluphenazine (moditen), all of which can sometimes cut short the persecutory delusions and other psychotic symptoms of this illness, exert their therapeutic actions by blocking the dopamine receptors in the nucleus accumbens (rather than in another dopaminergic region of the brain called the nigrostriatal system, which is concerned chiefly with adjustments of muscle and limb movements). Of these three drugs, fluphenazine, which exerts least effect on the nigrostriatal system, was shown to be as effective as the other two in its action on the nucleus accumbens.

It is relevant to mention amphetamine psychosis in the present context. The ingestion of large doses of this stimulant can cause a clinical picture indistinguishable from that seen in schizophrenia. Amphetamine causes stimulation by the release of dopamine from brain cells and thereby increases activity at dopamine receptors. If amphetamine psychosis is a true 'model' for schizophrenia, then we might argue that in the non-drug-induced psychosis, receptors in the nucleus accumbens, and perhaps in other related structures, are being bombarded by excessive amounts of dopamine, that these structures may be oversensitive to normal levels of this transmitter, or that the schizophrenic's brain is itself endogenously producing an abnormal substance which mimics the action of dopamine at these receptor sites.

Are the reward or pleasure centres referred to elsewhere involved in psychotic illness? Reports from Heath's laboratory at Tulane, USA, are relevant but controversial both from the ethical and methodological viewpoint. When depth electrodes were inserted into the 'pleasure sites' of schizophrenics' brains (including the medial forebrain bundle and septal region), no pleasurable responses could be elicited by stimulation, whereas in non-schizophrenic subjects the reverse was true. On the basis of electrical recording from leads, sometimes connected up to a hundred brain-implanted depth electrodes, and by other manipulations, including the injection of various chemical substances into several different sites in the brain, Heath concluded that the reward centres in the brain were defective in schizophrenia and that their destruction could be due to patients themselves making antibodies against these areas of their own brains. The Russians have been exploring this hypothesis for many years. Their research techniques are reputable but primitive. When Doniach, MacSweeney, Bottasso and Kushy explored this area, using fresh brain tissue carefully removed from the various anatomically defined reward centres of a normal young man (recently deceased) and 'treating' it with sera from the blood of thirty-five acutely ill schizophrenics, no positive antigen-antibody reactions were noted.

'Breakthroughs' in the biochemical investigation of schizophrenia have been reported over the years with regular monotony and boyish, well-intentioned enthusiasm and optimism. Even rats jumped on the bandwagon after they had been trained by an American lady called Smith to differentiate by smell between schizophrenic urine and normal specimens. Taraxein, a toxic claimed by Heath to have been isolated from the sera of schizophrenics; the 'pink' spot and the 'mauve' spot (at one time claimed to be found regularly on chemical analysis of the urine of schizophrenics); an imbalance of B group vitamins : all have had their 'crowded hour' of glorious life.

So when it comes to theorizing about the neurochemical defect that may be implicated in schizophrenia, there are almost as many hypotheses as neuroscientists. Nevertheless, researchers have in recent years learned much about the neuroanatomy, physiology and chemistry of the nervous system. Can we relate this knowledge to human learning or unlearning, to human pleasure and mood or affective states? It is quite likely that these complex phenomena are indeed mediated by interaction and integration of specific brain centres and their pathways, via 'messages' which ultimately impinge and rely on the subjective self for decoding and interpretation. In the final analysis, it is what the conscious self makes of these central neurochemical 'clues' regarding the inside-self-world and the outside non-self-world that is crucial. Human behaviour, be it cognitive/intelligent, fantasy/creative, conative/purposeful or hallucinatory/crazy, depends on how the individual sifts and filters these final-common-pathway 'messages' or central 'brain-clues'. If his brain chemistry is deranged, the person who is at the receiving end of the 'false' chemical clues behaves concomitantly in a deranged way, so that he may (depending on the type of prevailing brain aberration) become deliriously manic, psychotically suicidal or a floridly deluded, hallucinating schizophrenic who simply thinks, acts and is crazy.

A good analogy here is the very real pain which patients may feel in a 'phantom limb' long after the real limb has been amputated by the surgeon or lost in an accident. This pain may be experienced because the central brain mechanisms, including the thalamus, that would normally mediate painful and non-painful stimuli from the now amputated limb, are still firing off inappropriately, probably because they are no longer 'damped down' by incoming information or feed-back nerve impulses from the limb that no longer exists.

Let us now briefly discuss 'true' and 'false' brain messengers. Dopamine, noradrenaline and 5-Hydroxytryptamine are, as we have seen, highly respectable, well-established neurotransmitters. In their family trees, however, they have a number of pharmacological black sheep closely related to their 'parents' ' basic structures. The hallucinogen mescaline is very similar to dopamine; it is what chemists call an O-methylated derivative of this transmitter. Over a quarter of a century ago two Scots, Osmond and Smythies, pointed out this resemblance and suggested that if dopamine and other catecholamines were incorrectly O-methylated they would yield a 'mescaline-like' substance in the brain.

With the subsequent discovery of the indoleamine 5-Hydroxytryptamine in mammalian brains, and the identification of methylated indoleamines such as LSD, psilocybin, psilocin and DMT (or N, N-dimethyltryptamine, five times more active than mescaline), all acting as powerful hallucinogens in man, the original methylation hypothesis of Osmond and Smythies has been expanded to what is known as the 'transmethylation' hypothesis of schizophrenia. This postulates that schizophrenia might arise from the abnormal accumulation of psychotogenic, self-manufactured, aberrant O- or N-methylated derivates of the biogenic amines, dopamine, noradrenaline, adrenaline or 5-Hydroxytryptamine.

The amino acid methionine takes part in many of the body's biochemical reactions, including the donation of methyl groups. When Smythies and co-workers fed schizophrenic patients methionine in large doses it was claimed that it made their symptoms worse. Five other groups have claimed similar results for methionine. When Brune and Himwick fed schizophrenic patients with betaine, another methyl donor chemically quite unrelated to methionine, it also produced the same worsening of symptons, suggesting that these two substances' property of donating methyl groups (methylation) was responsible. In short, it is reasonably well established that if methionine is given to chronic schizophrenics, then in 40 per cent of cases it produces an acute attack superimposed on the chronic course of the illness. On the other 60 per cent, however, it has little effect, but no one really knows why.

Two Americans, Stein and Wise, have recently suggested that schizophrenia is caused by an enzyme deficiency which allows the production of the toxic substance 6-Hydroxydopamine, which then destroys noradrenaline pathways thought to be associated with brain reward centres. They consider these pathways essential for adaptive behavioural responses. In order to support their hypothesis, they have demonstrated that synthetic 6-Hydroxydopamine, injected directly into the brain of a rat, reduces the rate at which the rat presses a treadle to give itself a 'brain-rewarding' electric stimulus. Much of the evidence to date, however, suggests that dopamine, rather than noradrenaline, is the neurotransmitter involved in the mediation of reward.

It seems quite possible, therefore, that abnormalities in the brain-reward pathways, caused by either genetic or environmental factors, could lead to a permanent pathological mental state through the mechanisms already outlined.

Neurotransmitters other than dopamine, noradrenaline and 5-Hydroxytryptamine may also be implicated. In 1975 John Hughes and Hans Kosterlitz, working at Aberdeen University, made the exciting discovery that the healthy brain itself manufactures two substances, methionine-enkephalin and leucine-enkephalin. A group working at Johns Hopkins University in the USA soon confirmed these findings. The discovery of the enkephalins was extraordinarily important and has opened up whole new horizons in brain research.

Both these substances, and others discovered since, mimic the action of morphine and other opiates. Morphine, like its faster-acting derivative, heroin, can alleviate pain and cause euphoria. Such chemicals, the opiates, exert their effect on receptors which mediate the body's pain messages; they may also affect the centres which mediate the body's awareness of pleasure. These areas are found in the limbic system. It is probable that in man the naturally occurring opiates (known collectively as the endorphins) are turned on temporarily to alleviate severe pain or stress and that perhaps in other centres, like the tiny locus coeruleus or 'blue spot' (part of the limbic system), they themselves turn on nature's rewarding or motivation-enhancing mechanisms. The fact that morphine-like drugs act on the same centres is pure coincidence.

Whether or not we regard the endorphins as the 'pleasure substrate' in humans, they probably play an important role in the fine 'tuning-in' of sensory messages with mood or affect. Reports from a number of different research groups that the opiate antagonist naxolone – which can rescue opiate addicts from seemingly fatal overdoses in seconds – blocks auditory hallucinations in schizophrenics, suggest that further work in this field may prove tremendously rewarding and, most important in this context, that in psychotic illnesses the endorphin balance may be deranged.

It has long been known that the thalamus integrates sensation and sensory information reaching the brain. The medial part of the thalamus mediates poorly localized but emotionally-influenced, severe, deep pain, the type of 'emotional' pain best affected by drugs like morphine. It is of interest therefore that opiate receptor density in the lateral thalamus (which is adjacent to the hypothalamus) is very high indeed compared with other brain areas. Receptors are located in greatest abundance in the amygdala, an area we have seen to be very intimately associated with emotional behaviour. These receptors are specifically placed and designed to interact with the normally occurring morphine-like endorphins. Recent evidence, as has been emphasized by the American neuropharmacist, Solomon Snyder, suggests 'that the enkephalins are neurotransmitters or specific neuronal systems in the brain that mediate integration of sensory information pertaining to pain and emotional behaviour as well as serving other, still unidentified functions'.

By the use of enkephalin analogues that, unlike the naturally occurring substances, resist metabolic breakdown, it has been possible to show that enkephalins themselves have an intrinsic analgesic potency similar to that of morphine. This further supports the suggestion that, in schizophrenia, some of the reward centres of the brain might function abnormally or inadequately as a consequence of an imbalance in, or a relative deficit of these endogenously manufactured 'opiates'. We have already discussed the 'sham' rage and other intense emotional responses, including guilt, anxiety and jealousy, and the disorientation and 'electric shock' sensation that can be evoked when certain specific areas of the amygdala are stimulated in conscious humans undergoing amygdalotomy. It is not a far cry from these phenomena to the 'made' feelings and 'made' impulses, the incongruous affects and delusional perceptions often experienced and reported by schizophrenic patients.

Perhaps it is not so much the schizophrenic who acts, thinks and is mad or crazy, but rather that he is interpreting and mediating behaviourally, to the best of his ability, those false signals, clues and physiological 'mimickings' which, in all their unsymphonied chaos, bombard and bamboozle his conscious subjective self. It is possible that he has almost as little control over his moment-to-moment behaviour as the twitching, grimacing epileptic who is suffering a grand mal attack because brain cells are massively and inappropriately firing off in those areas which, under normal circumstances, would mediate purposeful, orderly and sequential limb movements and the subtleties of appropriate facial expression, as well as consciousness itself.

In 1979, Hare and Moran reported on their study of eight thousand psychiatric patients in the UK. (The patients had been diagnosed as suffering from a wide variety of disorders, including schizophrenia, affective psychosis, neurosis, and personality disorder.) One interesting discovery was that the mean age of the mother at the time of the patient's birth was found to be significantly above expectations for the general population. This observation was highly significant for the mothers of schizophrenic patients.

People use the phrase, 'the mad Irish'. Are the Celtic race, and in particular those people descended from the Celts who settled in Ireland, more prone to madness than other races? There is some evidence that we are. Hospital admission rates for mental illness in the Republic of Ireland are among the highest recorded anywhere in the world. Several surveys, including one by Kelleher, Copeland and Smith in 1974, confirm that Ireland has a very high first-admission rate for schizophrenia, at least twice as high as that in England and Wales. One explanation for this ties in with Hare and Moran's discovery. A recent report by Professor Per Dalen, a psychiatrist working at the University of Gotenborg, Sweden, suggests that the statistically higher incidence of schizophrenia reported from the Irish Republic may be due to the advanced age of the mother at the time of producing offspring. Other related factors may include the low marriage rate, the high rate of emigration (especially up to 1965), and the blinkered attitude of the Roman Catholic Church to contraception, which 'markedly influences family size and birth rates at high maternal age levels in Catholic populations'. Also relevant to Dalen's findings is H. B. M. Murphy's report that Roman Catholic males in Canada showed higher admission for schizophrenia than non-Catholics. This held true even when cases were subdivided according to ethnic origin.

A number of factors concerning ageing require brief consideration here. An age-related genetic or chromosomal change may have taken place in the elderly mothers referred to above, resulting in the production of poor stock in general, including offspring who later developed schizophrenia. The influence of maternal age on mongolism (which occurs in one out of every 650 live births) and certain other congenital anomalies is well known. The incidence of mongolism in children born to women in their late fifties is as high as 1 in 35.

Not only do ovaries and testes grow old, with a consequent deterioration in the quality of their 'offspring', but the 'offspring' themselves, the sperms and eggs, also age and deteriorate over time like any other living organism. Ovulation occurs in the human female on about the fourteenth day of the menstrual cycle, when the distended follicle ruptures and a ripened egg is extruded. Recent reports suggest that over-ripe gametes (eggs and sperms) are associated with human embryonic abnormalities. In 1972 Cohen studied fifteen cases of congenital abnormality; he obtained temperature charts indicating the time of ovulation and records of coitus for the cycle of conception. In five cases, ovulation and the fertilizing intercourse were separated by two days, in three there was a four-day delay and in one case, which resulted in the birth of a mongol, there was a five-day delay. In a study of mentally deficient children in the Netherlands, Jongbloet discovered that the greatest number of abnormal children had been born as a result of accidental conceptions to parents using the rhythm method, that is, during the 'safe' period, when, if conception occurs, it is likely to be associated with a delay in the interval between coitus and ovulation. Guerrero reported in 1974 that 30 per cent of conceptions ended in spontaneous abortion if coitus was delayed for three days after ovulation. The use of the rhythm method is also associated with ectopic pregnancy. Thibault, one of the leading authorities in this field, has strongly advised that when conception is desired, coitus should be planned to coincide as closely as possible with ovulation.

These reports suggest that there may be a relationship between high maternal age and mental illness, including schizophrenia, and that the rhythm system (or 'Vatican roulette') is associated with spontaneous abortion, monstrosity and ectopic pregnancy.

REFERENCES

Per Dalen, 'Maternal Age and the Incidence of Schizophrenia in the Republic of Ireland', *British Journal of Psychiatry*, Vol. 131, 1977, pp. 301-5.

Sir Aubrey Lewis, 'Psychological Medicine', in Sir R. B. Scott (ed.), *Price's Textbook of the Practice of Medicine*, 10th ed., Oxford University Press, London, 1966, p. 1192.

8

Schizophrenia:

Theories and Proposals for the Future

> Great Wits are sure to Madness near allied.
>
> JOHN DRYDEN

In the final analysis, only genetic studies into the epidemiology (incidence and distribution) of schizophrenia have stood the test of time and more sophisticated scrutiny. However, any genetic explanation of this disease must resolve the problem of how the gene or genes maintain themselves in a schizophrenic population, since it is well established that the fertility of schizophrenics is reduced to about half or three-quarters of the normal expectation. In 1964 Sir Julian Huxley and collaborators put forward the theory of schizophrenia as a genetic 'morphism', that is, that gene carriers had a selective advantage consisting of an increased resistance to pain and infection. This theory remains unproven. However, in 1971 Carter and Watts reported that relatives of schizophrenics appeared to be less vulnerable to some infections than the average population.

Gottesman's finding that normal individuals, unrelated to schizophrenics, who scored high on the schizophrenia scale of the Minnesota Multiphasic Personality Inventory (a scale derived from the responses of schizophrenic patients), were rated by those who knew them well as 'versatile, ingenious, inventive and imaginative', is interesting. It fits in with Heston's report regarding those children of schizophrenic mothers adopted into normal families soon after birth, who grew up to be normal adults. Among this group he found many who were more imaginative, spontaneous and colourful and had more interesting and creative jobs and hobbies than the normal or control group.

That strange thing called genius tilts the time-hallowed axis of perceptivity out of its mundane angle of observation. As a result, all modalities – thinking, seeing, hearing, sounding – may thereby acquire a primal freshness, so that a new, unthought-of, unseen, unfelt, unheard-of-before diaphorism may be created. Shakespeare talked about seeing 'sermons in stones', and the French Jesuit and palaeontologist, Teilhard de Chardin, celebrated these stones in *The Phenomenon of Man*. Picasso saw a fierce, behandlebarred bull in the saddle of the common bicycle and demonstrated this figuratively. Shelley wrote the history of *Homo sapiens* in a few simple lines after observing moths teeming outside his window on a summer night :

> 'The desire of the moth for the star,
> Of the night for the morrow;
> The devotion to something afar
> From the sphere of our sorrow.'

All three, de Chardin, Picasso, Shelley, were at some time regarded as crazy, mad, eccentric or dangerous. De Chardin, for instance, was rusticated to China by his religious superiors because of the originality of his philosophical and theological thinking; while Shelley was sent down from Oxford because he sincerely advocated atheism and refused to retract.

Three-quarters of a century ago, Havelock Ellis, in a book entitled *A Study of British Genius,* discredited the oft-held suspicion that highly intelligent and gifted people are more susceptible to psychotic breakdown than the more average in the population. Ellis's finding was substantiated in 1962 in a survey entitled *Cradles of Eminence*, by V. and M. G. Goertzel. Nevertheless, most observers in this field, including Ellis and the Goertzels, have noted a frequently-occurring mutuality of eccentricity and queerness among these talented individuals, many of whom were also generally regarded as far from stable or well-adjusted in terms of their prevailing mental status.

An account published by Barron in 1972 in the journal *Psychology Today* summarizes some of the resemblances between creative artists and schizophrenics. Both groups reported feelings of restlessness and a proneness to impulsive outbursts; both had a preference for solitude; both were subject to weird sensory and perceptual experiences including peculiar odours, ringing in the ears, and numbness in certain parts of the body. They both tended to reject conventional social values and had experienced a variety of 'mystical' thoughts and other experiences.

After completing a research project on allusive thinking in normal students and their parents, McConaghy and Clancy concluded that the type of thinking characteristic of schizophrenics may be found in a less exaggerated form in normal populations and be allied to high creative thinking. Karlsson's 1968 Icelandic study of the relatives of schizophrenics is relevant here; amongst this group he found a high incidence of individuals with superior intellect or leadership ability. After a careful review of the international literature on schizophrenia the experienced research worker, Claridge, concluded that the traits on which the creative thinker appears to deviate from the average person, are exactly those traits which, within the range of normal variation, may reflect an increased 'overloading' on a person with an underlying personality factor associated with schizophrenia.

The apparent similarity between creative people and schizophrenics has been explained in a number of ways. One explanation is based on the psychoanalytic concept of 'adaptive regression'. This model sees the psychotic breakdown as an involuntary and uncontrolled regression (back to childlike and primitive ways of observing and thinking) from a situation that had become too taxing for the schizophrenic's psychic resources. Likewise, the creative process is also considered to involve a regression to unconscious primitive levels of seeing and thinking, which allows the artist to free himself briefly from the conventional way of looking at something. Unlike the schizophrenic's, however, the artist's regression is under voluntary control and he is furthermore able to shape his trip back to primal, bucolic thinking and observing with his own more rational, better regulated, reality-based reasoning and observation. The artist is able to take advantage of his deliberate jump-back, to actually leap forward to a point more advanced than that where he stood initially; the psychotic is unable to accomplish this. The artist is in touch with, and is able to exploit, the fresh, ever-unconventional, unkeratinized eye of childhood which has not lost the 'vision splendid' of Wordsworth's ode 'Intimations of Immortality'.

Dellas and Gaier, more than anyone else, have refined our thinking in the area we are currently discussing : creative people, they argued, deploy their attention with a wider focus. Like schizophrenics, they are 'overinclusive'; but, unlike schizophrenics, they remain more aware of, and receptive to, and hold on to, more stimulus experience in usable form, while tending (like schizophrenics) not to phase out the irrelevant. Under the impact or 'input' of this wide, primitive, overloaded sensory-cognitive harvesting, the schizophrenic is unable to interpret or extrapolate. He over-elaborates, breaks down, goes crazy like an overloaded computer. To put it another way, the schizophrenic seems to have an inherited susceptibility to being the recipient of more incoming sensory stimulation than the average person. If, like the above-average creative person, he could cope with this high degree of stimulation, he might perform in an above-average manner; since, however, both the unusual intake and sensitivity of his receptive apparatus is not paralleled by an equally high-powered, central brain-processing apparatus, integration and interpretation break down and he behaves and talks in a way that is considered crazy. It is hardly surprising therefore that the major tranquillizers, which damp down sensory input to more negotiable levels, can benefit a high proportion of these disturbed psychotic patients.

The most impressive report relative to the area we are reviewing comes from Dykes and McGhie of Kingston, Ontario. They set out to explore the reported similarities between highly creative and psychotic thinking by testing the hypothesis that such similarities or correspondence lie in the fact that individuals in both groups, the highly creative and the psychotic, employ the common attentional strategies already referred to, which permit them to take in, or sample, a wider range of environmental stimuli or 'information' than a group of average subjects. They compared a creative population of highly intelligent normal people; a group of average subjects; and a schizophrenic patient group, using what were essentially three sorting tests.

Briefly, these tests assessed the subjects for unusual and idiosyncratic sorting, conventional ability, or a more convergent type of thinking required to sort the presented objects successfully. They were also tested for their ability to pair words correctly, while irrelevant as well as relevant material was simultaneously and independently played into each ear. The results, after careful statistical analysis, supported the hypothesis that both highly creative and schizophrenic individuals constantly focus on a wider range of environmental stimuli than the less creative or average group. In the patient group, this involuntary widening of attention tends to have a disruptive effect on performance, whereas the creative group is more successful at processing the greater-than-average input without incurring a performance deficit.

Forrest, now Professor of Psychiatry at Saskatchewan, Canada, considers that the gene or genes for schizophrenia may be expressed in terms of an heritable schizoid personality trait – solitary, aloof, introspective, distant and detached from others – which if allied to superior intelligence could then lead to unusual creativity in the intellectual and artistic spheres. He proposes the following model : an inherited schizoid trait might direct the individual towards intellectual pursuits, towards an interest in ideas and objects rather than in other people. Associated with this trait, especially in the presence of superior intelligence, could exist the tendency to an unusual or personalized use of language, the capacity to make unexpected connections between different ideas and concepts, and the potential for literary, artistic and scientific creativity. He suggests that this same trait, associated with more modest intelligence or adverse early family learning experiences, would predispose to schizoid personality disorder, to obsessional or hysterical illness, or to frank, manifest schizophrenia. He regards the schizoid trait as a necessary but not sufficient cause for schizophrenia. Whether it is these highly talented schizoid (but non-schizophrenic) genes or gene carriers in the general population who prevent the relevant genes, and therefore schizophrenia, from being bred out, is open to speculation.

The Freudian, psychoanalytic contribution to the understanding of schizophrenia has been of interest but, for the most part, unprovable.

The stage at which the infant distinguishes between himself and not-self, that is between himself and the various caring individuals who are in contact with him, has been termed 'the phase of object constancy' by Anna Freud. 'Person constancy' may be more readily understood. With this phase comes the differentiation of self-boundary, the slow dawning of self-awareness and self-entity and the recognition of the mother and other family members as 'constant fixtures' in the child's life. In many of the more regressional symptoms encountered in schizophrenia, self-entity and ego-boundaries are lost. This is typified in the schizophrenic symptom of diffusion or public broadcasting of thoughts, when the patient feels that his thoughts are escaping from the confines of the self out into the external world; it is also typified in the pathetic passivity the patient feels – 'You have no idea how terrible it is to laugh and look happy and know it is not you, but their emotions' – and by the thought-withdrawal, thought-insertion, 'made' impulses and volitional acts already described.

From the psychoanalytic approach, then, it is possible to conceive of schizophrenia as a massive catastrophic regression to a point in the patient's infancy when self-entity, and an adequate delimiting of self-boundary, failed to be achieved as a consequence of a poor relationship, especially between the mother and child. This notion has recently been expanded and explored by a number of research workers.

Family studies have cast some light on our understanding of the 'mad' family member and those features of his real or seeming madness which may be reactive to sick parental, or sick-making whole-family situations and pressures, muddlesome instructions or expectations, or unconscious scapegoating or labelling of the patient as sick; in other words, the patient is 'made sick', and is the representitive of a sick family unit.

It is worth reminding the reader here that as a psychiatrist (of one persuasion or another) a lot of one's efforts and skills, such as they are, are deployed in attempting to recast or retranslate the distorted language or the substitute or neurotic behaviour of the patient or of his family, into language that more readily lends itself to mutual exploration. Personally, I prefer to see a patient in his own home, with a close relative (or friend), and if possible other family members, present. A psychiatrist or psychoanalyst who sees any type of patient is, to a greater or lesser degree, dealing with a family or group on which several people, other than the patient, also impinge. The therapeutic scope of the psychiatrist in the formal, one-to-one setting is accordingly limited.

A somewhat extreme view regarding the patient's family and the phenomenon of psychotic illness is held by the medically qualified Glasgow psychoanalyst, Ronald Laing. In his book *The Politics of Experience*, published in 1967, he states, 'There is no such "condition" as "schizophrenia", but the label is a social fact and the social fact a political event. The person [so] labelled is inaugurated not only into a role, but into a career of patient, by the concerted action of a coalition (a "conspiracy") of family, G.P., mental health officer, psychiatrist. . . . The "committed" person labelled as patient, and specifically as "schizophrenic", is degraded from full existential and legal status as human agent and responsible person. . . .'

Frankly, the British Mental Health Act of 1959 was passed specifically to guard against this sort of hypothetical 'conspiracy' and abuse. In the UK, compulsory admission for any mental illness is nowadays permitted only if it is urgently and immediately essential on medical grounds for the patient's own safety and protection, or for the safety and protection of others. That said, occasional abuses, intended sincerely to be 'in the best interests of the patient', do still occur.

The real value of Laing's hyperbolical writing is that it jolted psychiatrists and other traditionalists in the para-psychiatric professions into re-examining long-established, somewhat osteoarthritic attitudes and procedures.

It is, as Forrest has suggested, unlikely that family disruption and family pressures *cause* the illness called schizophrenia. On the other hand, it is quite possible that a stressful, unwholesome family environment could quite unintentionally unmask such a serious illness in someone genetically predisposed, or indeed bring about an acute psychotic breakdown that might mimic and be misdiagnosed as schizophrenia in a person not genetically predisposed.

The anthropologist Gregory Bateson, and a number of psychiatrists including Alanen in Finland, Wynn in the USA and Leff and Hirsch in the UK, have studied interactional dynamics in families where one of the siblings was diagnosed as schizophrenic. Alanen investigated the mothers of 100 schizophrenic patients. He found a preponderance of women who were 'schizoid', 'emotionally defective' and 'lacking in empathic ability'. The mother-child relationships in this group also demonstrated a 'schizoid pattern of interpersonal relationships'; he described the mothers as 'dominating . . . they lacked understanding, and did not respect the child as an independent person'. Though aggressive, they were not rejecting. 'On the contrary, many of them had had a very possessive attitude toward the child . . . the child had clearly meant compensation for earlier frustrations . . . the child meant exceptionally much to the mother from the viewpoint of her own emotions and needs'. Most of the parents, including the fathers, were, after clinical assessment, and some dubious psychological testing, deemed to be suffering from disorders 'graver than neurotic'. Alanen's work is impressionistic, insightful but essentially unsupported by anyone other than himself, or by any objective psychological measurement other than the Rorschach (or inkblot) projective test.

Here is one of his thumb-nail sketches of a schizophrenogenic mother: 'She had an air of coldness about her . . . is fairly anxious but tries to conceal it. Attitude to patient is exceedingly possessive . . . the dominant spouse, father seems to be dependent on her. . . . Mother's approach to child rearing has been perfectionist . . . when patient was an infant, everything had to be done to the minute. Mother had fears of accident if patient not in sight. Despite her possessiveness something in the mother's attitude is suggestive of marked coldness.'

Bateson, like many other objective observers, noticed that much human communication is conducted by non-verbal methods, for instance, facial expression, tone of voice, shrug of shoulder or raising of eyebrows. The possibility thus arises that one person communicating with another may say one thing, yet at the same time communicate something quite different by using any of the non-verbal means of communication open to him; the second message may even contradict the first. This can give rise to a paradoxical situation for the recipient, especially if the messages are concerned with instructions about what to believe or how to act. Sometimes the 'emotional contradiction' may be purely verbal, for example, 'Trust me or I'll leave you forever.'

Having carefully studied the nature of schizophrenic communication, Bateson deduced the nature of the family environment that might lead to this form of faulty communication, and was led to formulate his hypothesis of the 'double-bind'. He asserts that a possible factor in the development of schizophrenia is the exposure in infancy and childhood to excessive 'double-bind' communication. We saw emotional examples of this in the aggressive-possessive attitude towards the patient of the mother in Alanen's study. According to the double-bind theory, rational thinking and rational conduct have to be learned by the child. They are not innate. The child learns them from the way in which parents order their daily lives. If the parents' world is confused and uncertain, with shifting, blurred meanings, and if the double-bind method of communication is constantly used, the child never learns to order or understand its world and schizophrenia may result. More especially, the 'double-bind' refers to instructions given; 'Do X' is said, and 'Don't do X' is at the same time communicated non-verbally by means which derive from ambivalent feelings on the part of the parent. The child is trapped in a hopeless dilemma, for he is too immature and powerless either to recognize his true position or to exit from the scene; whatever he does, he will be punished. For the child, one way of attempting to resolve his situation is to do nothing, or to behave in a totally ambiguous manner. This theory holds that the basic symptoms of the schizophrenic – disturbance in the form of thinking (and, as a consequence, speech), emotional incongruity and bizarre behaviour – derive partly from the patients' failure in the past to learn to think competently in a chaotic environment, and partly as a form of self-taught defence, devised in the past against the unresolvable demands of the double-bind.

While Bateson concentrates on the parent-child relation, Lidz, Fleck and co-workers concentrate on the role played by the family as a whole; that is, they view the entire family as pathological (or schizophrenogenic) and the schizophrenic in that family as the one who has been selected to play a particular role. This reminds us of the 'conspiracy' formulation of Laing, quoted earlier.

Theodore Lidz's team have placed particular emphasis on faulty 'age-sex' role-playing among the family members, and on the intrafamilial environment as a whole. Their stated aim is to take account of all family interaction, i.e. the ability of children to influence parents as well as vice versa. They consider the basic trouble to derive from psychological difficulties brought to the marriage by at least one of the partners. Most of their attention and reports seem to have centred on the parents.

Two types of families are distinguished: families with 'skewed' marriages in which there is one pathological parent, usually the mother, with the husband often tending to condone her aberrant ways. In the 'schismatic' type the husband-and-wife relationship is characterized by chronic hostility and tension, and typically by the disparagement of one partner by the other in the children's presence. Both types of families are seriously disturbed and none ever functions at any time in a way that could be described or characterized as normal.

In both these families, the skewed and the schismatic, the normal set of interpersonal relationships (that develops between the parents in families where there are two adequate parental figures) fails to evolve; consequently the set of interpersonal relationships that normally develops between each parent and the other in normal families, and between each parent and the children, is also missing. In both these sick family environments, the children become increasingly confused. This confusion is alleged to lead on to faulty personality development in the children, who are confronted not only by unsatisfactory parental models, but also with a disturbed model and distorting examples of interpersonal 'family-unit' behaviour.

The basic idea or hypothesis seems to be that, as a child, the future schizophrenic either learns inappropriate behaviour or fails to learn appropriate behaviour; in particular the sexual identity of the child is distorted by one or other or both parents so that it is very difficult for him to behave in a way appropriate to his age and sex. Both parents, in other words, have failed to observe (in their own behaviour) basic age and sex differences in their ways of relating to their children. For example, children may be treated by one parent as rivals for the attention of the other parent, or the mother or father may be involved in some sort of sexual association with the child. Indeed Lidz and his group believe that anxiety by parents and future patients about incestuous involvements is quite common.

It is furthermore suggested that the children in these families are often bound up in the parents' own conflicts, each parent competing for the child's support. All this conflict, skewing and schism (with its attendant intra-spouse 'undercutting', open hostility or cold hatred) is said to predispose to the development of schizophrenia in the offspring in these two types of families. It is said sons are more likely to break down in 'skewed' families and daughters in the 'schismatic' type.

Reading through the publications of Lidz and co-workers, one gets tied up in a variety of knots and binds, in fact one begins to feel, if not quite schismaphrenic oneself, certainly somewhat intellectually skewed and semi-schloshed. (Are Yale psychoanalysts schizophrenogenic?) Lidz himself, and I don't doubt the sincerity of his convictions for one second, tends to speak *ex cathedra.* Here is a typical quote from his paper, 'The Family, Language and Schizophrenia':

'Another major source of difficulty and distortion in a child's learning a consistent and coherent system of meanings arises in these families from the parents' needs to limit the environment and to force upon the family erroneous perceptions to maintain their own precarious emotional equilibrium. The child is taught erroneous percepts and concepts and is placed in a bind of being rejected unless he accepts the distortion. Perhaps, I first became aware of such difficulties many years ago when a schizophrenic youth said to me, "The one thing I can be sure of is that my mother loves me". Having heard the mother's qualified acceptance of her son and her bitter rejection of him unless he live to complete her frustrated existence, I know [*sic*] that for the patient to accept the axiom that his mother loved him, he needed to distort his entire grasp of interpersonal relationships, and to negate the emotions he perceived in his mother and felt in himself.'

To parody the English-fathered Irish patriot, poet and political martyr, Patrick H. Pearse : 'O Theodore, you are hard on mothers' – and on fathers too.

Bateson's double-bind hypothesis of schizophrenia is based on the emotionally disorganizing effect of the bind in which the children, and future patients, are placed by their parents. Lidz's group concern themselves with the transmission of unconsciously exploitative irrationality. Another American group, led by Wynn, have drawn attention to the fragmented or disruptive styles of communication of otherwise clinically normal-seeming parents of subsequently schizophrenia-developing offspring. Their studies have been distinguished by careful controls, i.e. a normal group is always selected for comparison with the experimental and possibly abnormal group. The research design used by the Wynn group is also impressive. Their hypothesis is that the types of thought disorder (manifested later by the schizophrenic offspring) are functions of the mode of family transactions and, more especially, of the parental styles of focusing attention and communication.

They recognize three types of schizophrenic thought disorder : amorphous(A), fragmented(F) and mixed(M). The A family group is characterized by amorphous and undirected forms of communication, with blocked or impaired use of language, vague and ill-structured interpersonal relations, and blunted emotional expression without nuances. The F group shows fragmentation of thinking and the M group displays a mixture of A and F.

Wynn and his colleagues took thirty-five families of young adult patients. These patients and their families were tested with Rorschach and other perception tests, but solely to provide samples of speech and 'test-taking behaviour'. These verbatim typescript records and protocols were rated 'blind' by another investigator (ignorant of the diagnosis of the patient from each of the thirty-five families being studied). From these tests carried out on the families, the diagnosis of the patient was then attempted. There were three diagnoses : schizophrenic (20), borderline schizophrenic (9) and non-schizophrenic (6 hospitalized neurotic patients). The results showed a correct prediction in twenty-eight cases out of the thirty-five, a truly impressive diagnostic performance.

In brief, this group of investigators were able to demonstrate, on the basis of carefully controlled investigations, that the families of schizophrenics tend to have forms of organization of thought and communication similar to the disorders of these modalities found in the patients; in other words, the schizophrenics could be placed 'blind' into their own families. They concluded that in schizophrenia we are dealing with an interaction between genetic factors predisposing to these types of disorder, and to learning experiences that exacerbate these predispositions; the pre-schizophrenic child is reared in a family environment where the 'baselines' of reference for communication are constantly and vaguely shifted, where those areas to which attention is directed are not crisp and clear-cut, but smudged, amorphous and fragmented over such a wide range of items that meaningfulness just cannot be properly deciphered. Wynn points out that 'many of these family members have severe disturbances for which there would be no psychiatric evaluation except on a research basis'. Commonly the relatives of the schizophrenics were found to have eccentricities to which a rather vague label such as 'schizoid' could be applied.

It is the overall impression of Wynn and his team that parents of schizophrenics, who are not themselves overtly schizophrenic, speak in communication patterns which are maximally befuddling to a listener who is trying to share a focus of attention or 'set' with those parents. (In 1971 a careful attempt by Hirsch and Leff to replicate the main studies of the Wynn group at the Maudsley Hospital, London, was relatively unsuccessful, whereas Lidz and his group claim to have replicated them successfully.)

One more interesting study relevant to this discussion will be examined before we try to arrive at some general proposals. Bower and associates interviewed schoolteachers regarding the school characteristics of male American adolescents who later became schizophrenic. The teachers had known the patients about five years before admission to hospital. They were ignorant of the purpose of the study and the interviewer was unaware during questioning of the identity of the patients or of the control (normal) children-group studied for comparison. The teachers had noticed the onset of personality disorders in the large majority of the future patients years before the overt onset of the psychosis. The most frequently reported characteristic in pre-psychotic children was shyness and withdrawal. Only a very small proportion of the children were seen by their teachers as actually sick emotionally. We seem to have returned once more to the 'schizoid' trait. If this American study were replicated by other research groups, then not only would the predictive value of the schizoid trait be established, but active prophylactic measures might be taken to protect these schizoid children from untoward stress, especially up till the age of twenty-five or thirty.

Even with the help of anti-psychotic drugs, more enlightened in-patient treatment, and a better understanding of the importance of community care, the long-term outlook and prognosis for schizophrenic patients still remains depressingly poor. This seems to hold true for the so-called developed and developing countries alike. Research in neuropsychiatry lags behind most other areas of specialized interest, while the staffing of most psychiatric hospitals in the UK and State hospitals in the USA, is either stretched to the limit or quite inadequate. Speaking at a meeting of the Royal College of Psychiatrists in February 1978, Sir Dennis Hill, then Professor of Psychiatry at the Institute of Psychiatry, London, said : 'We cannot be proud of our mental health services, because we know that the human and physical resources necessary to implement that ideal have not been made available; and quite simply because they were not sufficiently regarded, to be afforded. But this has not been admitted.'

But let us leave the parish pump of British medical politics for the dead, the half-dead-and-alive and those lucky few who manage to recover unscathed from psychotic illness. Because of the mortality rate from suicide (3-4 per cent), high morbidity and, on a global scale, the colossal expenditure involved in even half-caring for schizophrenic populations, it is suggested here that some international body, like the World Health Organization, in collaboration with the World Psychiatric Association, should consider recognizing the world-wide epidemic proportions and dimensions of schizophrenia as constituting a major health hazard and act efficiently, as it usually does in these circumstances, by providing money and, where required, personnel, for first-aid treatment and, hopefully, longer-term care of patients who are willing to accept treatment, and who are in urgent need of skilled professional care. If it is thought that I exaggerate, think of all the possibly ill-cared-for thought-disordered people in China, Russia and South America, not to mention the USA and the UK.

An alternative way of coping with this epidemic might be to get a plan of campaign drawn up by the United Nations, whose Secretary might persuade member nations to divert a small fraction of the money spent on military equipment towards funding a combined programme for clinical treatment and for research purposes. The wealthy international drug companies like Roche, ICI and others might also be persuaded to contribute. Not only would developing countries benefit from such support, but rapidly receding countries too, like the UK, USA and the USSR.

REFERENCES

Y. O. Alanen, 'The Family in the Pathogenesis of Schizophrenia and Neurotic Disorders', *Acta Psychiatrica Scandinavica,* Vol. 42, Supplement, p. 189.

R. D. Laing, *The Politics of Experience,* Penguin Books, Harmondsworth, 1967.

Theodore Lidz, 'The Family, Language and Schizophrenia', in D. Rosenthal and S. S. Kety (eds), *The Transmission of Schizophrenia*, Pergamon Press, Oxford, 1968.

9

Theories of Personality Development:

Sigmund Freud and Eric Homburger Erikson

Although man is essentially a cunning, self-aware learner, who can both profit from past experiences and make inferences about the future, heredity nevertheless plays a basic role in 'casting' or delimiting his adult personality structure in terms of the following measurable or near-measurable personality variables, each of which is intended to represent the more or less polar opposite of the other :

Intelligence	⟷	Subnormal intelligence
Extraversion	⟷	Introversion
Stability under stress	⟷	Neuroticism/childishness
Effective energy	⟷	Tense/obsessional/meticulous/easily tired
Caring for others	⟷	Psychopathicism
Truthfulness	⟷	Dissimulation
Non-vulnerability to psychotic breakdown	⟷	Psychoticism

What you are, and how you are reacting to an emotional or intellectual problem at any given point in time, are a product of genetic endowment (heredity) and the sum total of 'until-then' environmental experiences. These environmental experiences, as well as the genetic contribution, antedated not merely your birth, but conception itself.

Life 'proper' for the sperm that fertilized your mother's egg, as well as for its hundred million or more colleagues (who lost out in the egg contest and so petered out), began about seventy-five days before conception or fertilization, on the basement membrane of the seminiferous tubules in your father's testes. The primitive germ cell, or spermatogonium, that was to cause fertilization, began to develop into a mature sperm which would later – complete with motile tail, DNA and head aclutter with other chromosomal material – be capable of swimming off and, for a short time at least, leading a moderately independent, if limited, life of its own.

In contrast, the primordial follicle, containing the immature egg that was later to be fertilized into you, had been present in your mother's ovary at least from the time of her birth, together with about five million others. Only about five hundred of these follicles ever ripen into mature eggs or ova. No new ova are formed in the human female after her birth. Biologically speaking, therefore, your life-giving, life-enhancing environment – or, more accurately, pre-environment – is as old or older than mother herself.

Clearly, personality and psychic and somatic development are considerably influenced, for better or worse, by the intrauterine environment and intrauterine experiences. Paranatal experiences – for instance, normal labour followed by uncomplicated delivery, or prolonged labour requiring caesarean section or forceps delivery – are also of crucial importance. The human brain is already so large at the time of birth, in ratio to the maternal pelvic outlet, that the plates of the as-yet-unfused skull-bones have to mould and slide into each other during the baby's dangerous four-and-a-half-inch voyage down the maternal birth canal.

In man, the effect of maternal emotion on foetal behaviour has a long history of anecdotal support: in the New Testament (Luke 1:44) the aged but pregnant Elizabeth states, 'For lo, as soon as the voice of thy salutation sounded in mine ears, the babe leaped in my womb for joy.' Under more controlled conditions, Sontag demonstrated that pregnant women with labile (over-reacting) autonomic (not under voluntary control, such as one's heart-rate) nervous-system functioning, had the most active foetuses. These more active foetuses were also shown to have more gastric trouble and feeding problems as infants. Strean and Perr offered evidence implicating maternal emotional stress in the occurrence of cleft palate in some children.

Since the two maxillae that grow towards each other to fuse and thereby form the palate, normally accomplish this between the sixtieth and seventieth day of pregnancy, the timing of the emotional stress was crucial. Sixty-eight per cent of the mothers of offspring born with a cleft palate reported emotional stress during the first ninety days of pregnancy, compared with only 15 per cent of the same mothers reporting stress when their other children were born normal.

We have referred in a previous chapter to girls who grew up to become tomboyish in their teens as a result of excess androgen while they were *in utero.* Poor maternal nutrition may also affect the unborn child. It may affect the foetus directly, if the mother is unable to meet its nutritional requirements, or indirectly, by increasing maternal susceptibility to disease or by contributing to the occurrence of various disorders of pregnancy. Malnutrition can in addition have teratogenic effects on the foetus, rather like those caused by thalidomide.

In addition to intrauterine environmental experiences, genetic factors also play an important role in the development of intelligence and personality. Deliberate genetic experiments on humans are still, happily, guarded against in most countries, so researchers in this field have had to turn to nature, especially to twins. Most fascinating here are comparisons between MZ twins reared together in the same environment and MZ twins where each of the pair had been reared separately.

In 1962 Shields traced through the British Broadcasting Corporation 44 pairs of adult MZ twins brought up apart, 44 pairs of MZ twins brought up together (which he used as controls) and 32 pairs of DZ twins brought up together. More than half of those MZ twins brought up apart had been separated from one another since the age of three months. Shields assessed their personality and behavioural characteristics by personal interviews, intelligence tests and by self-rating questionnaires of extraversion (E)-introversion (I) and neuroticism (N)-stability (S) personality factors. As a measure of the resemblance between each member of a pair of twins, he used 'intra-class correlation coefficients'. For intelligence, identical (MZ) twins, whether reared together or in different environments, had almost identical scores. The correlations were 0.76 and 0.77 respectively. The correlation between non-identical (DZ) twins reared in the same home was much lower, only 0.51.

Personality testing, using the Maudsley Personality Inventory, yielded some intriguing results. When scores for the personality factors extraversion and neuroticism were compared, the MZ twins separated from each other in early life were more alike than the DZ twins, and even more alike (in their adult personality) than those MZ twins who had been reared together. A possible explanation for these findings, especially where E-I and N-S are concerned, might be that identical genetic programming tends to predominate, whatever the prevailing environment. A less simplistic explanation might suggest that when reared apart, identical genetic personality components develop and flower more fully when free of twin rivalry, dominance-submission competition, self-entity problems, etc. However, we mustn't ignore the fact that the MZ twins, whether reared together or apart, resembled each other in personality, including the intelligence factor, much more than the DZ twin pairs.

Lest genetic studies make us despairing of any positive environmental contribution towards intellectual or other development, let us briefly mention an investigation carried out by James Douglas in the UK. This was a prospective follow-up, over the course of many years, of all children born in England and Wales in one week in 1946. Their performance on scholastic tests was measured at the age of eight, and then again at the age of eleven. During the three-year interval those children who had performed well aged eight, and who had been living in homes of high parental interest in school work, improved their performance by an average of 3 per cent, whereas those of equal ability when aged eight, who lived in homes where the parents took little interest in school work, had deteriorated in performance by 6.4 per cent. Where 'streaming' had been carried out in the schools, children of equal initial performance ability gained 8.8 per cent if they had been assigned to upper 'streams', whereas those of equal ability, assigned to lower streams, deteriorated by 3.2 per cent.

One of the best-known theories of personality development is that of Sigmund Freud. He divided infancy, childhood and adolescence into five stages : oral, anal, phallic (including the Oedipal phase), latency and genital (or adolescent).

In the oral stage of psychosexual development, which predominates throughout the first eighteen months of life, the infant's needs, perceptions and modes of expression are primarily centred in the mouth, lips, tongue and related organs. Oral sensations include thirst, hunger, pleasurable tactile stimulations evoked by the nipple or its substitute and sensations related to swallowing and satiation. Oral drives or instincts have two separate components : libidinal (pleasure-seeking) and aggressive. States of oral tension are said to lead to a seeking for oral gratification with the resulting quiescence, e.g. at the end of being breast-fed. The oral triad during this period of development consists of the wish to eat, to sleep and to reach that sense of resolution or relaxation which occurs at the end of a good sucking-feeding session just before the onset of sleep.

Libidinal needs, that is, oral eroticism, predominate in the early part of the oral phase but later become mixed with more aggressive components or oral sadism. This aggression may express itself in biting, chewing, spitting or crying. Oral aggression is said to be connected with primitive wishes and fantasies of biting, devouring and destroying utterly. Ideally, during the oral phase, a trusting dependence on nursing and sustaining objects is established and a comfortable expression and gratification of oral libidinal needs is achieved without excessive conflict or ambivalence from oral-sadistic wishes.

At this stage of a child's development, either excessive oral gratification or excessive deprivation by the mother can, it is held, lead to oral fixation and contribute to the development of pathological personality traits in later life. These may take the form of excessive optimism/narcissism, or pessimism, depression-proneness and demandingness. 'Oral' personalities are often excessively dependent and require that others should give (in) to them and look after them; they want to be 'fed' so badly that they may become inordinately and exceptionally giving themselves simply in order to elicit from others a return of 'being given to'. They are often extremely dependent on material possessions and objects to maintain their self-esteem. Envy and jealousy are said to be associated with oral traits. A successful negotiation and resolution of the oral phase lays the foundations of a future personality with capacities to give as well as to receive graciously from others; this person grows up without either excessive dependence or envy, but with a capacity for trust in others as well as a sense of self-reliance, self-acceptance and self-trust.

The anal stage lasts from about one to three years of age and is said to be prompted, or indeed determined, by the maturation of neuromuscular control, particularly over the anal sphincters, thus permitting the infant more scope for voluntary control over retention or expulsion of faeces. This stage is said to be marked by an intensification of aggressive drives and sadistic impulses associated with conflict over anal control and the struggle with the mother over retaining or expelling faeces during toilet training. According to Freud, this struggle and conflict over anal control gives rise to increased ambivalence, not only over retaining or expelling faeces, but also in relation to the child's own drives towards separation, individuation and independence of others.

'Anal eroticism' refers to the sexual pleasure in anal functioning both in retaining the 'precious' faeces and in presenting them as a precious gift to the parent. ('Parcelling' of faeces is a well-recognized clinical phenomenon in child psychiatry; some children may believe that the faeces are actually part of themselves and hide their parcels away carefully.) On the other hand, anal sadism refers to the expression of aggressive wishes connected with the expulsion of the faeces as destructive weapons; such urges are often displayed in childhood fantasies of bombing, shooting and killing.

The anal phase is said to be intimately tied up with the child's striving and longing for independence. Ideally, during this period the child acquires anal sphincter control, which is paralleled by his attempts to achieve personal autonomy and independence. If he fails in his efforts too often – either by exhibiting over-control, which could result in faecal retention, or by failing to gain reasonable control, which might result in messing – excessive shame, self-doubt and feelings of loss of control over himself prevail. The personality that may later develop in the 'anal' character who has fixated his development at the anal phase (either because his toilet training has been over-controlled but the child has not rebelled against this; because he has rebelled out of feelings of frustration and aggression with the parent; or because his experiences during this phase have left him ambivalent) may include traits of excessive orderliness, obstinacy, stubbornness, wilfulness, frugality and stinginess. When the adult's defences against anal traits are not effective, then ambivalence, messiness, defiance, rage and sado-masochism may become manifest. Anal traits, and the individual's efforts or defences to enable him to cope with the ancient, long-forgotten anxieties associated with unsuccessful negotiation of the anal phase, are classically seen in obsessive-compulsive neuroses.

Succesfully negotiated, the anal phase establishes a baseline for personal autonomy, independence and initiative without feelings of guilt, a capacity for showing initiative unaccompanied by shame or self-doubt, a lack of ambivalence and a capacity for co-operation with others without conceit and overconfidence or self-diminishment and defeatism.

The phallic phase, which includes the Oedipal phase, begins during the third year and has usually ended by the time the child is six. It is characterized by a basic focus of sexual interest, stimulation and excitement in the external genitalia. The penis is now the organ of chief interest for both sexes. It is suggested that the little girl considers her lack of a penis is evidence of castration. This phase is associated with an increase in genital masturbation, said to be accompanied by predominantly unconscious fantasies of sexual involvement with the parent of the opposite sex. For both sexes, the imagined threats of castration and parental retaliation arise in association with guilt over masturbation and Oedipal wishes and fantasies.

During the phallic stage the objective is to focus erotic interest in the genital area and in genital function. This lays the foundation for gender identity and integrates the residues of the previous stages of development into an overall genital-sexual orientation. The establishment of the Oedipal situation is important because ultimately it enables the child to construct from the experiences of its Oedipal conflicts an internalized parent image or 'conscience', which Freud called the super-ego; these conflicts also enhance gender and sexual role identity and enable the child to resolve his Oedipal strivings and fantasies and adjust to more realistic sexual goals in the future. In short, it is said that the influence of castration anxiety and penis envy, the child's repressive defences against both of these, and the patterns of gender, sexual and age-role identities that emerge from the phallic-Oedipal phase are the very primary determinants for the development of the future adult's personality.

If he negotiates it successfully, the child emerges from the Oedipal-phallic phase with a secure sense of sexual identity, a sense of sexual curiosity without embarrassment, of initiative without guilt, and a sense of mastery over the external environment as well as over disruptive internal processes and impulses. The resolution of the Oedipal conflict at the end of the phallic period is said to give rise to powerful internal resources for the regulation and rechannelling of drive impulses towards constructive goals. This internal source of control is the super-ego, based, as we have seen, on an internalized image derived from 'good', non-punitive parental figures.

The pathological traits that may arise during this phase encompass nearly the whole gamut of neurotic personality types and include those aberrations due to gender identity and sexual role confusion : inadequate personality, frigidity, multiple personality and trans-sexualism.

The latency period lasts from the sixth year until puberty and is characterized by a temporary repression of sexual interests. Pleasure is now more than ever before derived from the outside world, including school experiences which offer scope for exploiting and satisfying natural curiosity and provide substitute gratifications for the earlier sexual interests. This period, which coincides with the elementary school age, is very important for the child's social development and for his acquiring the knowledge and skills required to negotiate the workaday world. Lack of self-control at this stage may lead to failure on the part of the child to sublimate his energies in the interests of learning and the development of social skills. Excessive inner control, however, may lead to a premature closure of personality development and the development of obsessive character traits. Ideally, during this phase the child continues to develop a sense of industry and a capacity for mastering problems and concepts that enable him to function autonomously without feeling he has always to run the risk of failure or defeat. This period provides a basis for a mature adult life, with a sense of satisfaction in work and a capacity for forming meaningful emotional attachments to others.

Finally, the genital or adolescent phase, which extends from the onset of puberty (11-13 years) until young adulthood, includes the physiological maturation of sexual function with an attendant intensification of drives, especially libidinal or sexual. This intensification is alleged to produce a regression in personality organization which reopens and reinaugurates conflicts of previous psychosexual stages, and thereby provides a new opportunity for a more satisfactory resolution of these conflicts, with renewed hope of achieving a better, more mature gender, sexual and adult identity.

The primary goals and objectives of this period are the ultimate separation from dependence on and attachment to the parents and parental figures and the establishment of mature, Oedipal-free, non-incestuous, heterosexual 'object' relationships – that is, the ability to relate as an adult to people of the opposite sex, coupled with and augmented by a mature, reality-based sense of personal identity in the acceptance and harmonious integration of adult roles and responsibilities. Acceptance of the need to adapt to social demands and values should also be gained.

Pathological traits that may derive from failure to negotiate this period are legion. Erikson, whose reinterpretation of classical Freudian psychoanalytic conceptualizations will be discussed next, summarizes failure to resolve adult issues during this phase as 'identity diffusion.'

It is easy with hindsight and our smattering of new information to find fault with the Freudian formulation of personality development, just as it is easy for a modern aviation engineer to criticize Da Vinci's design for an aeroplane. Both men were heroes, both ahead of their time and contemporary thinking, both admittedly flawed, but flawed in the grand tradition of the Homeric. Professor O. L. Zangwill, the Cambridge University biologist and neuropsychologist, simply points out that as a result of Freud's researches, psychology today is as different from the psychology of sixty years ago as biology before and after Darwin.

In brief, although the causation of neurotic illness and neurotic personality development is still far from clear, after Freud there can be no doubt whatsoever that the neurotic is a person who has failed to come to terms with those instinctive, unconscious attitudes, desires and emotional relationships which played an important part in his early life, but which have not been integrated adequately into adulthood. More specifically, he has failed to abandon wholly the emotional ties which in childhood bound him to his parents and family.

Erik Homburger Erikson, a Dane born in Frankfurt and reared by his mother and Jewish stepfather, brought the Freudian os, anus and phallus, id, ego and super-ego out of the rather cloacal and fusty confines of the Jewish-Viennese-Victorian family closet. He thereby extricated the murderous, guilty, castration-fearing three-to-six-year-olds from the exasperations of the Oedipal triangle and placed them in the more expansive milieu and flux of the psychosocial world outside, where they would have daily contact with other children and teachers from ethnic, religious and national backgrounds different from those of their parents and where expectations and aspirations could differ radically from those that prevailed in their own homes. He rejected Freud's rather Calvinistic notion of predestination – that the personality and its subsequent development is almost irrevocably laid down in the first five or six years of the individual's life – reasoning that 'if everything goes back to childhood, then everything is somebody else's fault, and trust in one's power of taking responsibility for oneself may be undermined'.

Of nuclear importance to Erikson's essentially psychosocial theory of personality development are the concepts of identity, identity crisis and identity confusion. Identity is the sense of one's continuous being, in spite of surrounding change, as an entity distinguishable from all others – *inter mutanda constantia.*

Unlike Freud and the majority of psychiatrists in the UK, USA, Russia and elsewhere, Erikson escaped the indoctrinations of a medical training, making his way into psychology and psychoanalysis via teaching in a kindergarten. As a child he had his own identity problems, which he was resilient enough to overcome and from which he derived personal benefit as well as insight and sympathy into the problems and privations of the young. At school in Frankfurt he was teased by his Jewish classmates because of his Nordic appearance, whilst at other times he was mocked by his gentile companions because he was a 'Jew'. Danish by origin, yet having to live in Germany, this paradoxical 'displacement' could not but have exacerbated his own identity confusion and sense of not belonging. (He referred charitably and kindly to his parents' deception of him regarding the real identity of his biological Danish father as their 'loving deceit'. His real father had left his mother while she was pregnant with her only son.)

A great deal of what Erikson studied was concerned with how group values are inculcated in the young by culture-bearing mothers and how, in the apparently endless limbo or moratorium between childhood and adulthood, the young hanker for and try to grasp on to group identity.

In *Childhood and Society,* his first book, published in 1950, he states that 'the study of identity . . . becomes as strategic in our time as the study of sexuality was in Freud's time'. He regarded the sense of one's identity that emerges at the end of adolescence as a psychosocial phenomenon preceded in one form or another by an identity crisis that may be conscious or unconscious, acute or long-drawn-out and which is either concluded successfully, only partially resolved, or not resolved at all.

Erikson extended and broadened Freud's theory of infantile sexuality by studying the child's development beyond puberty. A leitmotiv of optimistic common sense runs through his writing. By concentrating on healthy development and showing that the ego can usually develop in a healthy way, if given the right environment, he moved the focus of psychoanalysis from pathology to health. In fairness to Freud, it was perhaps the experience of living in a place and time where sexual taboos were savagely excessive that drove him to concentrate so heavily on sexual conflict as the exclusive source of all neurosis.

In the healthy personality, Erikson regarded the ego as the mediator that organizes and adaptively deploys information from the outside world. (Freud's ego was less at ease – 'like a man on horseback who has to hold in check the superior strength of the horse', i.e. the id, or the instincts demanding immediate gratification. The Eriksonian ego was less in thrall to the id than Freud's.) When the ego functioned aptly the individual was positively aware of and enjoyed a purposeful sense of well-being and calm contentment. He was on good terms with himself – unfrustrated, unselfwracked, unshortcircuited by neuroses. He was not having to waste time and energy on unproductive psychic pain.

While Erikson placed more positive emphasis on the healthy functioning of the ego than did Freud, his formulation of the super-ego, 'the oppressive force of conscience', is almost identical, deriving, as they both agreed, from the internalized or introjected prohibitions and restrictions of parents, parent figures and society.

Unlike Freud, Erikson did not set out to prove a theory, but rather to act as a bridge between psychoanalysis on the one hand, and the social sciences (including social anthropology) and the broader historical issues on the other. Although he did not regard the erotogenic zones – mouth, urethra, anus and genitalia – as the actual biological defining and determining agents of instinctual activities and experiences at each psychosexual stage of development, sucking and biting, elimination and genital stimulation nevertheless have great symbolic significance in Erikson's theory, being closely associated in the child's mind with the differing types of emotional and social experiences that impinge on him as he slowly discovers and tries to master his anatomical, physiological and emotional modalities.

Erikson divided life into eight stages of social and emotional ego development, which are summarized in the table below.

These eight stages of ego development, which roughly parallel Freud's five stages of psychosexual development, cover the in-

Stages	*Psychosocial crises*	*Psychosocial radius*	*Psychosocial modalities*	*Favourable outcome*
Oral-sensory (birth and 1st year)	Trust v. mistrust	Maternal person	To get To give in return	Drive and hope
Muscular-anal (2nd year)	Autonomy v. shame, doubt	Parental persons	To hold (on) To let (go)	Self-control and willpower
Locomotor-genital (3rd –5th year)	Initiative v. guilt	Basic family	To make (going after) To 'make like' (playing)	Direction and purpose
Latency (6th year to onset of puberty)	Industry v. inferiority	'Neighbourhood'; school	To make things (competing) To make things together	Method and competence
Puberty (adolescence)	Identity v. identity diffusion	Peer groups and outgroups; models of leadership	To be oneself (or not to be) To share being oneself	Devotion and fidelity
Young adulthood	Intimacy and solidarity v. isolation	Partners in friendship, sex, competition, co-operation	To lose and find oneself in another	Affiliation and love
Adulthood	Generativity v. self-absorption	Divided labour and shared household	To make be To take care of	Production and care
Maturity	Integrity v. despair	'Mankind' 'My Kind'	To be, through having been	Renunciation and wisdom

Adapted from Erikson, *Childhood and Society.*

dividual's entire journey or life-adventure from the womb to the tomb. They have both positive and negative features, are punctuated with emotional crises, and are considerably affected by the individual's culture and by his interaction with the society in which he lives. Personality continues to be shaped and moulded throughout each stage.

In each stage the psychosocial opposites or polarities see-saw as they strive for ascendancy. Thus during the first stage the infant learns either to trust or to mistrust; in the second stage he acquires the basic attitudes of autonomy on the positive side or shame and doubt on the negative side. How a person fares in one stage will determine how well he copes with the problems of the next. These polarities, fortunately, are not so firmly fixed that they cannot later be modified. For example, the child who has learned mistrust during his early months of life experience may, if the quality of his mothering improves and parental care becomes more supportive, reverse this to trust at a later stage. All is not lost; there is always hope.

Erikson's first stage of ego development coincides with Freud's oral phase and extends throughout the first year of childhood. During this year the child discovers and gradually learns whether he can rely on and put trust in the prevailing environment in general and in himself in particular. The trust/mistrust ratio depends on how he is handled, mothered or foster-mothered and generally cared for. As we have seen, whether the end result for the child is good, bad or indifferent, experience during subsequent stages may alter the end result of the first year for better or worse.

In the infant's first months the mouth predominates as the most sensitive and most vital zone in the whole body. It is the crucial expressive/introjecting, pleasure/pain-inflicting area of rapport with the (as yet) uncharted world outside and the vague, booming, mysterious, subjective world within.

The oral phase is never superseded because throughout life the mouth and tongue continue to be essential for sucking, drinking, and eating, continue to be used in aggressive and non-aggressive verbal behaviour, and are also employed in adult life as part of the individual's sexual repertoire – kissing, licking, sucking, biting, fellatio, cunnilingus, etc. Every man, every woman remains a suckling child, a fellatrice, till death intrudes.

The muscular-anal phase, during which a family/social crisis may arise in the area of autonomy versus shame and doubt, lasts throughout the second and third year of life (Freud's anal phase), during which the child learns to walk, feed himself and to speak to and for himself. It is not till the child is about two years old that he gains control over the anal sphincter muscles so that he can voluntarily let go, that is, release, his faeces. (Bladder control is mastered earlier.) Socially speaking, he now has two alternatives – to hold (on) or to let (go). The society in which he lives decides what degree of bowel and bladder behaviour is permissible, and on this in turn depends the child's anxiety levels regarding his degree of competence in sphincter control. A more generalized, more metaphorical struggle over keeping or letting go also occurs in relation to anality. If at this stage the parents are tolerant enough and flexible enough to rely on the child's ability to manage and control himself, and if they remain supportive without being over-indulgent, the child usually gains confidence in his abilities to regulate his bladder by the age of two and his bowels by the age of three. This permits him to experience and feel a balance of tolerance and love over anger, self-hate and parental punitiveness, of easy and spontaneous expression as opposed to stifling suppression. He gains confidence in himself as a result of increasing mastery and a sense of manly independence overbalances shame and self-doubt. He feels not only that he can control himself, but that he has some degree of control over his own outside world. If, on the other hand, it is indicated to him, and he is regularly reminded, that his faeces are bad, if he is over-controlled, and over-restrained, he becomes angry at his lack of mastery and feels foolish and ashamed of himself. As a consequence he may generalize this shame into mistrusting his own basic goodness and thus fall victim to self-doubt, self-harassment, even despair.

The locomotor-genital stage, when initiative versus guilt are in the balance, coincides with Freud's genital stage and runs from the third year through to the fifth. The child now experiences the excitements of nursery school, street and playground. He learns to initiate activity. Whether or not this innovativeness is reinforced depends on the scope of physical freedom permitted him and on how well his burgeoning curiosity is satisfied. If it is conveyed to him that his behaviour or interests are dangerous or bad, this may cause him to accumulate a sense of guilt about these adventures and exploratory activities.

It is a difficult, exciting stage for the child, who is already avid to experience the world as an adult. At home, children of both sexes get involved in the Oedipal family romance, expressing great passion, usually but not always, for the parent of the opposite sex. The boy is refused sexual intimacies with his mother, so he often feels he may have done something wrong or bad, and thus feels guilty. To augment his anxiety and guilt, he also realizes he is too small to take on his father. Sibling jealousy and sibling rivalry add to his discomfort. A conflict arises between his desires and lusts and what his parents permit him to achieve. Parental values and restrictions are now transmuted by the child into a conscience or super-ego. If parental restrictions have been too severe or are too strictly interpreted by the child, his own super-ego may become cruel and too uncompromising, so that from this time onwards he too may tend to over-control and over-constrict himself. The super-ego remains partly infantile throughout life and therein may lurk human tragedy, for the infantile super-ego can be (and may continue to be) primitive and cruel to the point where the child (or adult) over-controls himself to near self-obliteration, especially when an over-obedience, even more literal than the parents ever wished to inculcate, has been learned. An alternative tragedy may also occur; according to Erikson, one of the deepest conflicts in life is the hate for a parent who has served as the model and executor of the super-ego, but who was discovered by the child trying to get away with the very transgressions which the child, because of his own strict super-ego, can no longer tolerate in himself. He is left feeling morally or emotionally humbugged, ruled over strictly by a super-ego acquired under bogus circumstances.

Later on in this stage the child's 'crush' on the parent gradually lessens and he may now entertain the notion of becoming a parent too. Usually the child gains more initiative than guilt from these domestic conflicts. Since sexual desires and their satisfactions are taboo he now turns happily outwards from the home scene. The boy is said to enjoy the excitement of being on the make, on the attack, enjoying conquest. While he becomes dominant in the intrusive mode, the girl may turn to modes of 'catching' in more aggressive forms of snatching, or in the milder form of making oneself attractive and endearing. All this time the world is slowly opening up its mysteries to the child's boggling, voracious, exuberant mind.

The stage of latency is the school-age period from about six to eleven and incorporates Freud's latency period. Now the battle and its outcome lies between industry and inferiority. Family conflicts and their Oedipal complexities and anxieties are put to one side. Industry is now the child's preoccupation – the use of language, implements, machines. By industry, Erikson means a 'sense of being able to make things and make them well and even perfectly'. If at this stage the child's efforts are frustrated, a sense of inferiority may accumulate in place of a sense of accomplishment, industry is forsaken and the child comes to the conclusion that he is, in fact, inferior.

The issue, the outcome, is now not (as Freud implied) solely in the hands of the parents. The child's teachers too may also help him to raise his self-esteem. At the age of ten this self-esteem may be well established. It will then provide the fulcrum from which further exploration is initiated.

During the stage of puberty and adolescence the conflict lies between ego-identity and role-confusion. The young person now begins the struggle to develop, to eke out, a personal 'identikit'. Searching for this, he falls in love with heroes and ideologies and develops 'crushes' on members of his own, and sometimes of the opposite, sex. If individual identity remains smudged, group identity becomes much more necessary. Youth at this period finds itself in what Erikson calls a 'moratorium', suspended between 'the morality learned by the child and the ethics to be developed by the adult'. Most adults remain aware of the excruciating self-consciousness, social and physical insecurity and frustration that frequently prevail during this time. How the teenager has fared in attaining trust, autonomy, initiative and industry in the earlier stages, now has an important bearing on how well a sense of personal identity is establishing itself.

With the advent of puberty childhood proper comes to an end. Youth has now truly begun. In puberty and adolescence, Erikson points out, all samenesses and continuities relied on earlier are more or less questioned again, not only because of a rapidity of body growth, which equals that of early childhood, but also because of the additional development of genital maturity and adult libido. In their search for a new sense of continuity and sameness, adolescents have to re-fight many of the old battles. Much depends now on the ego's ability to integrate all previous identifications with the vicissitudes of the adult libido and sexual identity, with the skills and aptitudes developed out of natural endowment and with the opportunities offered in finding a satisfying social role. The young adolescent has the daunting task of finding out who he is, and introducing himself respectfully to that reality that is he, or alternatively of discovering or becoming aware to some extent that he is a nobody, trying to be somebody, or everybody. If instead of identity, role-confusion is the outcome, this may have arisen out of strong previous doubts regarding something as fundamental as sexual identity itself.

In the stage of young adulthood the outcome rests between emotional intimacy or emotional isolation. This period of development was ignored by Freud. It extends from late adolescence and lasts until early middle age. If the young adult has successfully resolved the identity crisis, he can now become involved with other people without fear of losing personal identity. He is not afraid of the intimacy inherent in sexual relations, true friendships and other deep relationships which scare off those who are still the victims of role confusion, and continue to be emotionally out of touch with themselves, lurking away to indulge in self-absorption and inordinate narcissism. Such people may end up unmarried, unloved, unloving, friendless, isolated forever in their negatively constructed menagerie of despair.

Sexually, the young adult should be capable of making love in such a way that the experience is shared with the partner. In true sexual intimacy there is mutuality. Ultimate genitality for Erikson meant orgasm with a partner of the opposite sex who is loved, trusted, and willing to share life's work, play and procreation and to provide for the healthy development of the offspring. This genitality must be mutual.

The stage of adulthood spans the middle decades of life when the outcome is either generativity or stagnation. By 'generativity' Erikson means a generous and vital interest in events outside the home, in bettering society and guiding the oncoming generation. Childless people can be generative too. Adults living only to indulge personal needs and comforts, concerned only with pleasuring themselves, are the victims of self-absorbed stagnation. The up-and-coming generation rely on adults for guidance, so too do adults rely on youth for regeneration and true viability.

The outcome of the stage of maturity may be either a feeling of reality-based satisfaction and integrity derived from a life productively lived, or the despair felt on contemplating a life led with little unselfish regard for others. Maturity can be a satisfying period, a time to contemplate and savour one's major efforts, and to enjoy the company of grandchildren and other young people. The person with integrity knows 'that for him all human integrity stands or falls with the one style of integrity of which he partakes. The style of integrity developed by his culture or civilization thus becomes the patrimony of his soul, the seal of his moral paternity of himself. In such final consolation, death loses its sting.' The lack or loss of this maturity, this accrued ego integration, is signified by despair and fear of death, when that individual's one and only life cycle is not accepted by him as the primordial gift of life's bounty.

There is a poetic logic, a felicitous and impeccable sense of metaphor in Erikson's formulations, and his theory of personality development is as imaginative as it is speculative, as inspiring as it is unprovable. It is hoped that his conceptualizations will become more relevant and applicable when we discuss the concept of emotional maturity in more detail.

Only a few examples will be given of those areas from which Erikson considered abnormal development and functioning might arise. In *Childhood and Society* he considers that a pathological absence of basic trust may be observed in the lack of self-boundaries experienced in infantile schizophrenia; a lifelong underlying absence of such trust is apparent in adult personalities in whom withdrawal into schizoid and depressive states is habitual. The infant is born helpless and uncomfortable; he has no knowledge of what is real and outer and what is imagined and inner, and so cannot distinguish between (reality-based) fear and anxiety (for no good reason). If 'anxiety-fears', which are appropriate and understandable in childhood, persist into adulthood they then must be regarded as neurotic. As the infant fears not being fed, being left empty, so too does the drug addict who longs to take in through mouth or skin something that will give him, like the well-fed baby, a sense of infantile satiation. At the weaning/biting stage, the infant, incensed with his painful teeth, with his mother when she withdraws and with himself for his own lack of power, may develop a state of sadistic-masochistic self-confusion, or what Erikson calls 'an evil dividedness'. At this time too, sudden weaning and loss of the mother, without an adequate surrogate mother, can lead to infantile, and sometimes to a life-long, depressive state.

If bowel and bladder training are not accomplished in an atmosphere of mutual give-and-take between mother and child, if control of these sphincters is demanded too early or too aggressively, the child may become so angry with the way in which he is manipulated that he himself may later retaliate by trying to control everyone and every event, and so develop into an obsessive compulsive neurotic. Under the assault of a brutally strict developing super-ego he may so repress his sexual fantasies and wishes regarding his mother that he is unable to accept having ever had them and resort to hysterical denial. If this pattern is carried into adult life, sexual inhibition or impotence may result, or the child may try to resolve his anxieties by scapegoating them onto his own body and so develop psychosomatic disease. A young man or woman who reaches adulthood without resolving his or her sexual identity and sexual role may find it difficult to settle on a career and to plan for the future. If adult identity is not secure, the person may shun close relationships and retreat into self-absorption and isolation.

If in late or middle age the person feels that nothing he accomplished was meaningful or worthwhile, that he never acquired the things he wanted, never felt that his life related to some sort of universal order, he may fall victim to severe panic and anxiety attacks as he sees his time run out, his uneventful life cycle come full circle as it sadly tolls out its final hollow anticlimax.

Jung said that a physician's main function was to prepare people for death. The art of living and dying is to give up – calmly and with good grace – what we must soon give up perforce.

REFERENCE

Erik Erikson, *Childhood and Society*, Imago Publishing Co., London, 1951.

10

Self-Deceit and Psychic Lies

> . . . and the state of man, like to a little cosmos,
> Suffers then the nature of an insurrection.
> WILLIAM SHAKESPEARE, *Julius Cæsar*

How does the potentially crazy, partly self-aware, narcissistic, self-humbugging, somewhat psychoneurotic, anankastic, occasionally altruistic ape defend himself against the thousand natural and unnatural shocks that flesh and soul is heir to? How does he defend himself not only against the ambushing world outside, but also from the rancorous, potentially traitorous, ill-construed, often poorly-integrated, parental-ancestral-archetypal vestiges and imagos and long-forgotten introjected figures that lurk within, and may at any time attack their host? How he copes depends on the resilience and quality of his personality, the state of his physical health, the amount and quality of the support and understanding he gets from others, and on his degree of anxiety control. It is on this last capacity, and in particular on the defence mechanisms, wholesome or unwholesome, which he uses to enable him to feel less anxious, less life-frightened, less self-intimidated, that we shall be concentrating in this chapter.

As we have seen in our brief survey of Freud's theory of personality development, parental authority is, as it were, 'internalized' or introjected by the child in the course of his development, partly by means of restrictions imposed on the child during the Oedipal stage. This 'internalized' authority, or super-ego, is believed to form the nucleus of the adult conscience. The super-ego derives from the ego, but acquires a certain autonomy. It may be regarded as a conglomerate formed within the ego out of an early, primitive and complex process of indentification with parental figures. In Freud's words, the super-ego is (for better or worse) 'the heir to the Oedipus

Complex'. Its function is a restrictive and punitive one, and unlike the ego, the super-ego is essentially unconscious. It is best conceived of as the instrument of primitive morality, and as a primitive control system it may be excessively strict, moderately strict, or almost totally non-existent, as in the psychopath.

The ego embraces those parts of the personality most closely concerned with consciousness. It is the active agent in perception (seeing, hearing, sensing) and exercises a dominant control over language and voluntary motor activity. Its activities and functions are characterized by consciousness and constant adaptation. It must not, however, be equated with consciousness only, for it owns forces that may operate independently of the will and without the subject's knowledge or awareness.

The ego's strength and cohesion as a dynamic system has to be maintained by effective transactions with the environment, as in personal relationships and in the psychosocial activities of work and leisure. These relationships and activities are mediated in the normal personality by the imagos or 'internalizations' of good parental figures and others from later experiences. These imagos or unconscious 'parental/object' representations, distilled out of early experiences of key figures in the developing child's life, constitute a pattern of what feels 'ideal' for a person. Thus when they are matched, reflected or approximated in others, they give rise to satisfying emotional qualities in childhood and adult relationships. The good conduct and satisfying behaviour associated with these good figures of long ago, create in adulthood a set of self-values or an 'ego ideal'.

The id is wholly unconscious and comprises that nucleus or residue of instinctive forces or superseded or half-superseded attachments that prevailed in infancy. It is a basement repository of those remembrances of early psychic experiences which have not been incorporated into the ego or drawn into the super-ego. Psychic events at id level can only be deciphered through their indirect impingements on current behaviour. They can never become directly available as objects of introspective scrutiny or assessment.

The super-ego and the id share an unconscious two-way structure and are in fairly free communication. The ego has to mediate to the best of its endowment between the two. Indeed, speaking metaphorically, the severity which the super-ego sometimes manifests towards the ego may derive from the access it has to aggressive impulses and primitive hankerings at the level of the id. In a mature personality the ego and super-ego function harmoniously together to form that selective unity of perceptual and unconscious behavioural focalization known as 'character'.

Although Freud's topography of the mind is crude – and we must remember that he was chiefly concerned with the exploration of unconscious mechanisms, or motivation, in the interests of clinical medicine – it is nevertheless useful. Some important aspects of inhibition or control, which make possible a high level of ethical conduct and personal integrity, rely in no small way on mechanisms that operate and prevail outside the field of rationality and consciousness.

Freudian concepts still pervade current psychiatric thinking, whether or not the commentator subscribes wholly or partially to Freud's teaching. These concepts are especially valuable when one attempts to decipher what motivates the individual, consciously or unconsciously, as he tries to 'problem-solve' the ineluctable quandaries of his life-cycle.

Intra-psychic conflicts may arise between one's instinctual or id impulses and one's conscience or super-ego; such conflicts may remain wholly unconscious but can nevertheless give rise to anxiety which acts as a danger signal. How these conflicts are 'metabolized' or dealt with depends largely on the individual's ego functions. These functions include ego-synthesis, the capacity of the ego to unite, organize and bind together drives and tendencies within the personality, thus enabling the person to think, feel and act in an organized, appropriate and self-directed manner. Generally, the underlying conflicts, if sufficiently conscious, and the accompanying normal anxiety, are dealt with by realistic action, by sublimation, or by postponing gratification and tolerating normal degrees of frustration, anxiety, guilt or depression. In some cases, however, ego-synthesis may bring together various forces in a way that, while not completely adaptive, is the optimal solution for the person in his particular state and predicament at a given time. Thus the formation of a symptom that represents a compromise of opposing tendencies may, although unpleasant, be preferable to yielding to a dangerous instinctual impulse or alternatively trying to stifle that impulse completely.

Let us take the example of an eighteen-year-old filing clerk, of low average intelligence, who was referred to me because her eyes had become paralysed in the 'upward-gaze' position. On being given a sedative drug she could move her eyes about normally. She then admitted that she 'could kill' her boss, who gave her too much work. She would have liked to have given in her notice, but her parents 'would have been furious'. Having found herself in what was, for her, an intolerable position, which she was unable consciously to verbalize, she unconsciously contrived her hysterical conversion symptom, which meant, of course, that she was unable to do her job. Although her symptom must have caused her some inconvenience, it did enable her to escape from the anxiety caused by the 'murderous' instincts which she could not decipher or negotiate, and the parental anger that would have been visited on her had she resigned from her job.

This case is but one example of the many complex, unconsciously-deployed devices that are resorted to, to a greater or lesser degree, by the normal individual, but most especially by neurotic or immature personalities, at times of crisis. What such defence mechanisms or 'psychic lies' have in common is that they limit or constrict awareness, so that threatening, anxiety-provoking cues from the inner and outer environments are excluded. Most of these self-manipulations, the major forms of which we shall now consider, are carried out at the unconscious level; that is, they are dissociated from consciousness.

Repression is generally considered to be the basic defence mechanism, other defences coming into operation only when repression fails to prevent unacceptable drives or instincts from intruding into consciousness. It is a manoeuvre for dealing with unbearable aspects of inner life, excluding from awareness unacceptable sexual wishes, aggressive urges, fantasies, emotions and memories. For example, a prim and proper spinster repressed from conscious awareness her desire or instinct to be sexually promiscuous. Her repressed desire later found symbolic expression in her symptom, which manifested itself as an hysterical loss of sensation in the lower half of her body, with inability to move her lower limbs.

In contrast, *suppression* means being conscious of inner impulses – for example, the desire to steal – but consciously controlling the outward expression of these impulses.

Repression presupposes a repressing agency – either the ego or the super-ego – and a stimulus – the anxiety which unacceptable instincts, desires and wishes may cause. It is to Freud's great credit that he demonstrated that apparently unreasonable anxiety ('free-floating' anxiety) is a true danger signal. The danger is not external but internal. It is the danger that repressed urges and tendencies will break through the defences of the ego and so disturb the delicate mental balance on which peace of mind and even sanity ultimately depend.

Denial is the involuntary and automatic refusal to accept a reality situation or fact. It may enable the person to comfort himself or herself with an illusion, as in the case of a mother, who abused barbiturate drugs, refusing to consider that her child, who had choked in his cot by inhaling his vomitus, might not have died had she not been stuperose from drugs at the time. People who suddenly lose their eyesight may deny this for days or weeks. A young schizophrenic patient whose parents had died many years before believed quite firmly that they were still alive and came to hospital to visit him every day.

Reaction formation enables the person to deal with an unacceptable impulse by allowing expression of that impulse in its opposite, antithetical form. A child of parents unduly intolerant of aggression may (unfortunately) have to deal with his healthy assertiveness by becoming a model or angel-child to please his parents. Similarly, being excessively clean and perfectionistic may be a reaction against the urge to make a mess; being non-aggressive and submissive may be a reaction against the repressed urge to destroy and dominate.

Displacement is an oft-resorted-to manoeuvre and consists of the displacing of an inner impulse, urge, or affect (emotion) to an external person, situation, object or animal, which is then regarded as the source of the impulse or threat. Had repression been used, it would have pushed down the inner urge to unawareness; but by using displacement the person then has to avoid the feared 'substitute' situation or object. A classical and interesting example is Freud's case of Little Hans, who feared horses at a time in childhood when he was apprehensive of his father. Hans's anxiety over wishing harm to his father was displaced to and so became associated with horses, the proximity of which he then had to avoid. Thus he was able to reduce his anxiety levels but at the cost of avoiding horses. We see more prosaic examples of displacement in everyday life. A person may refrain from reacting aggressively to a senior bully but later allow himself to attack an inferior associate; a man may meekly accept his boss's abuse and unfair criticism at the office, only to contrive idiotic pretexts for becoming angry with his unfortunate wife or children when he returns home.

We have all at some time or another resorted to *rationalization.* Who, for example, has not lost his temper and lashed out excessively at someone and then later on grossly enlarged on the degree of provocation? Rationalization essentially consists of explaining one's behaviour and attitudes by distorting the facts and being dishonest with oneself in an effort to maintain self-esteem.

Introjection, when resorted to in adult life, is more pathological than rationalization. It may, for example, be used to deal with the loss of someone's affection by taking in or introjecting his attitudes and personality: a bereaved person may acquire the characteristics of the close relative who has died, and thereby feel that the dead person has not been completely lost forever. *Identification* involves a similar process but extends to actually becoming like the other person. Hysterics may develop someone else's symptoms by identification. This process may, however, play a part in normal mourning or in depression following a bereavement, when for a time the person bereaved feels identified with the deceased.

Projection means viewing a mental image as objective reality. It has been the subject of much speculative writing and analysis. According to the child analyst Melanie Klein, all fear of the mother in infancy and all paranoid or persecutory ideas in later life, ultimately stem not from the infant's real or actual experiences of having been hated, rejected or maltreated, but from projection onto the mother's breast (which is the object of oral wishes, impulses, fantasies and anxieties for the infant) of his own self-destructive death wishes, thereby getting rid of them. Projection of internalized (or introjected) aspects of others (i.e. imagos) consists in attributing to someone in one's environment those feelings towards oneself which derive historically from people one has introjected in the past. While introjection involves internalizing, projection involves the splitting-off of painful, dangerous or persecutory internalized imagos and their projection on to others (i.e. 'external objects'), whereby they are banished from the mind in which good experiences and imagos are being integrated. A paranoid schizophrenic, persecuted and terror-stricken from within by the bad imago of a feared father, which has re-irrupted, may project that imago on to the outside world, and so develop delusions of persecution he attributes to others.

Regression entails returning, under stress, to earlier childlike stages of development, and behaving accordingly. A child of five who has been dry and clean for two years may regress to soiling and bed-wetting after the birth of a sibling because of anxiety due to real or imaginary parental neglect. We all tend to regress when we are physically ill. Some of my students take to thumb-sucking when stressed by a patient's bizarre behaviour during a clinical case conference. Regression can be quite normal under certain circumstances, for example when adults pleasure each other sexually. This, as we all should know, may include sucking at each others lips (kissing), licking or sucking the penis (fellatio), licking the vagina and clitoris (cunnilingus), mutual sucking of the breasts (mamillare est orare), not to mention the sort of childish ventriloquistic babel that passes for romantic pillow-talk.

Only a few more mechanisms will be mentioned before moving on to discuss the more mature defence mechanisms. *Acting-out behaviour* is really a tantrum; it may be the direct expression in 'substitute' behaviour of an unconscious impulse or wish in order to avoid becoming aware of the accompanying emotion. Thought is replaced by action, which implies that either the impulse being acted out has never acquired verbal representation, that the impulse is too intense to be dischargeable in words, or that the person is so immature as to lack the capacity for inhibiting or resisting tantrum behaviour. *Magic undoing* is commonly seen in obsessional neuroses but also occurs in superstitions and in religious ceremonials. If a person believes that his aggressive thoughts could, by magic, lead to another person's death, magic undoing might consist of carrying out some ritual, in the belief that this would magically protect the object of his aggressive thoughts from danger. *Schizoid fantasy* is a tendency to use fantasy and to indulge in autistic retreat or narcissistic self-admiration for the purpose of reducing stress, or conflict-resolution or for gratification. In *hypochondriasis*, reproach or resentment towards others, arising perhaps from loneliness, bereavement or unacceptable aggressive impulses, are transmuted into self-reproach and into complaints of pain, for which no organic explanation can be found. Headache, back-ache, facial pain and abdominal pain are common complaints, together with neurasthenia, a condition characterized by lassitude, irritability, pressure headache on top of the head and disturbed sleep. The hypochrondriacal person tries to solve his subjective wretchedness by opting out unconsciously into the invalid role. Genuine existent illness may also be overemphasized, exaggerated and exploited for its evasive and regressive possibilities.

Isolation is a defence mechanism used typically by obsessional neurotics. When something unpleasant happens to the subject, the experience is not forgotten but instead is deprived of its emotional component, and its associative connections are suppressed or interrupted, so that the experience remains as though isolated from the ordinary processes of thought. This may enable the person to have aggressive thoughts without the accompanying stressfulness of feelings of anger.

What then are the mature defences used by the well-integrated personality to cope with dangerous impulses or with undue anxieties? *Suppression* may be used, consciously or semiconsciously, to postpone attention to a conscious impulse or conflict until a more appropriate time, or to deny that impulse gratification indefinitely if it is regarded as morally wrong. *Sublimation* involves gratification of an impulse whose goal is retained but whose object is diverted from a socially objectionable to a socially valued one. Sublimation of aggressive impulses, for instance, can be mediated through competitive sports. It differs from the neurotic defences by allowing instincts to be channelled rather than repressed or dammed up. Feelings too are acknowledged, modified and directed towards a significant person or goal, so that instinctual satisfaction results. The well-integrated person uses *anticipation* – realistic anticipation of, or planning for, future inner discomfort – as, for example, when death of a close friend or relative is soon inevitable. *Altruism*, vicarious but constructive and instinctually gratifying service to others, brings pleasure and helps alleviate his own tensions and stresses. A *sense of humour and self-irony* allows the expression of real personal discomfort in a way which does not actually cause discomfort or make others feel ill at ease. Finally, *asceticism* allows the elimination of directly pleasurable emotions attributable to an experience. It is directed against all those 'base' pleasures perceived consciously, so that gratification is actually derived from their renunciation. Great saints are as tough as nails, normal as bread, wholesome as the earth, and fewer than established religions would have us believe, as few as the number of great poets that have enriched world literature – but we can all aspire.

11

Pathological and Non-Pathological Personality Types and the Concept of Emotional Maturity

Over the years, a number of systems have been devised to measure certain dimensions of personality scientifically. One of the most successful has been that of H. J. Eysenck, Professor of Psychology at the Institute of Psychiatry, London. The Eysenck Personality Questionnaire has acquired considerable popularity as a useful clinical research tool.

Applying the statistical technique of factor analysis, Eysenck identified various dimensions of personality. His introversion-extraversion dimension derived from the psychology of Jung, while the other major dimension in his scheme, neuroticism-stability-under-stress, owed much to the work of E. and P. Slater on neurosis associated with prolonged combat stress, carried out during the last war. Although Eysenck's theory of personality originated in research involving both normal and neurotic subjects, it applies to every individual. Everyone can be allotted a position on each of Eysenck's dimensions, on the basis of his answers to a questionnaire. Eysenck is himself in no doubt that his theory of personality is an over-simplification. Since he first proposed it in 1947, he has enlarged and expanded it regularly, and this process will no doubt continue.

Introversion, as such, should not be regarded as pathological. The introvert is typically quiet, retiring, introspective, prefers books to people and is reserved except with intimate friends. He keeps his feelings under control. He is reliable, pessimistic and moral.

Extraversion is made up of two main traits – impulsiveness and sociability. The extravert craves excitement, takes chances, acts on the spur of the moment; his feelings are not under tight control and he is not always reliable.

If someone develops a neurotic breakdown, his degree of extraversion/introversion is said to determine which specific condition he will show; the interaction between the two personality factors is important. Introverted neurotics show one group of symptoms – for instance, anxiety states, phobias and obsessions – while extraverted neurotics are more likely to develop a different form of breakdown, exhibiting hysterical and psychopathic features.

Eysenck's theory and definition of personality also take into account the person's general ability or intelligence in the performance of mental tasks. He feels that this is closely related to mental speed. Generally speaking, intelligence or cognitive ability refer to a purposeful series of activities in which the person tries to provide solutions to problems posed during his day-to-day existence. His more or less permanent 'problem-solving-ability' score might therefore be placed on a continuum somewhere between the polar opposites of high and low intelligence (or alternatively genius and subnormality).

Eysenck defines personality as 'the more or less stable and enduring organization of a person's character (will), temperament (emotions), intellect and physique (bodily configuration and nervous system/hormonal endowment).' His personality factors are scored from the Eysenck Personality Questionnaire, which the subject completes alone, and from which the dimensions of personality (except intelligence) can be calculated mathematically.

The Eysenck Personality Questionnaire was first published in 1975, superseding various earlier models. For the first time, it gave parity of esteem with the previous factors of extraversion (E) and neuroticism (N) to a more recent factor, psychoticism (P). This factor was supposed to measure the individual's degree of vulnerability to psychotic breakdown into, for example, schizophrenic or manic-depressive illness, but it seems that since it was first postulated in 1952 the concept of psychoticism has been modified to indicate, in its most extreme form, 'psychopathicism'. The P factor seems more aptly to describe the psychopathic individual often found in prisons: 'The high Psychoticism (P) scorer is cold, impersonal, hostile, lacking in empathy, unfriendly, untrustful . . . unemotional and lacking in human feeling. . . . It is interesting that criminals have an unusually high "P" score. . . .' We shall be looking at psychopathicism in more detail later in this chapter.

Much speculation and theorizing on personality structure has also centred round Freudian theory. If we accept Freud's theory, then the oral personality (who has failed to master very early infantile impulses) tends to be passive, clings to others for support, while at the same time being grasping and demanding. He wants to greedily possess other people and other things.

Psychoanalysis has given us one of the few really coherent theories about the early development of the depression-prone or anal personality (sometimes described alternatively as obsessional-compulsive, depressive or anankastic). In adult life he is excessively neat and tidy, suppresses emotion and tends to be pedantic, obstinate, stingy and punctual. This person develops, during the second year of life and later, an insatiable need to be loved, wanted, approved of, combined with an extremely unhealthy form of emotional dependency towards parental and other authority figures. This insatiable need to be loved and cherished is increasingly frustrated as the child grows up and is expected to become less demanding and more emotionally self-supporting. As the psychologist Metcalfe points out, this frustration would generally lead to anger against others, but in the case of the 'love-addicted', depression-prone person, the fear of alienating those people whose love and help he dearly needs makes him feel angry and then guilty. He has to turn this anger inwards – on himself. Each recurring frustration causes him increasing anger and despair.

Using Eysenck's questionnaire, Coppen and Metcalfe tested a group of depressives long after they had recovered from a severe depressive illness. They closely examined the group's responses to those questions indicative of a tendency to worry, repetitive thinking and feelings of tension. Scores were consistently higher than normal. On the other hand, the responses to questions indicating a tendency towards a variable mood, a capacity to daydream and to fantasize were negative and consistently lower than normal. In short, their responses indicated a tense, worrying attitude to life, a denial of fantasy and imagination and a rigid, limited, habit-bound personality. They had over-learned how to inhibit the expression of emotion.

The phallic personality, according to Freudian theory, came a cropper during the Oedipal phase, because the child could not negotiate the sexual rivalry, guilt and castration anxieties of that period of psychosexual development. As a result, the adult is impeded emotionally, has to repress sexual impulses and deny more mature erotic needs, while at the same time attracting or wanting to attract others sexually. Relationships are kept superficial, for there is little capacity for a healthy intimacy. Women with phallic personalities are usually frigid, while men associate with several partners but rarely contrive an enduring liaison.

In 1835 an English psychiatrist, James Cowles Prichard, described a personality type (now known as psychopathic or sociopathic) in terms of 'moral insanity', emphasizing, however, that there was no defect of intellect or reasoning, nor any insane illusion or hallucination. This unfortunate individual's permanent state consisted of a 'morbid perversion of the natural feelings, affections, inclinations, temper, habits, moral dispositions and natural impulses'. A black sheep, you might add by way of summary.

It is generally agreed that the psychopath has a serious defect in feeling and empathy. He cannot take in how his impulsive behaviour damages others, nor can he understand, even in the most elementary way, the feelings of others. He has a poorly developed, defective or undeveloped super-ego or conscience. He is almost totally affectionless. Remorse is well outside his affective repertoire and rarely, if ever, becomes part of it. His impulsiveness, and his compulsiveness to manipulate and cheat others, are the keys to his understanding. For these reasons he cannot form satisfactory relationships and he repeatedly fails in his marriage or love affairs, in his work and in his social life. Though his intelligence may be well above average, he is constantly in conflict with the norms of social behaviour and custom and with the law. However catastrophic his failures, he never learns from them for the simple reason that he is unable to postpone immediate gratification : his impulsivity is such that he must grab at whatever he wants in the here-and-now. Like the infant, he obeys Freud's 'pleasure principle' because he is at the mercy of his own primitive, asocial id, which tends to maintain him in a state of painful tension, demanding to be gratified or, for a short time at least, alleviated. His uncontrolled destructive outbursts, often in the absence of sufficient provocation, dismay his associates. He is sometimes aware of the build-up to these outbursts and will often admit that after the aggressive outburst he feels calmer and relieved of tension. His anti-social patterns are often monotonously repeated but he never learns. Physical assaults, kleptomania or gambling may provide the excitement he repeatedly craves. He rarely seems to notice that his behaviour can be very destructive to others.

The wild, crazy behaviour of the aggressive psychopath has always fascinated and preoccupied society. Do we perhaps envy his seemingly free-and-easy, swashbuckling, buccaneering way of life, reminiscent of the Elizabethan pirate or the outlaw gunman of the Wild West, who had no need of others and could travel light, free of commitments, family ties and feelings of guilt? Probably a better explanation might be that we all have within us a psychopath too timid to break out of his cocoon and purge himself of his socially imposed inhibitions and frustrations by running amok with an axe or gun.

The second variety of psychopath is known as the passive type. He is seriously inadequate and unable to adapt to social requirements, chronically inept, passive, pathetic, and dependent. In contrast to the aggressive type, many passive psychopaths are placid and responsive. Others among them are withdrawn, emotionally cold and apathetic. Some are drifters who may repeatedly end up in prison because of some minor theft or other transgression, others survive in hostels and Rowton Houses, or may be supported at home by indulgent family members. They are the product of inadequate personality development and poor or negative parental influence.

That Nature should genetically programme, and thus predestine, the personality development of a certain group of individuals for hell and damnation, or at least for a blistered life of compulsively self-imposed purgatory, seems not only horrific but downright unsporting. Nevertheless, most authorities agree that there is a genetic predisposition which does play a part in the causation of psychopathicism.

An investigation in Denmark by Mednick and co-workers, of impeccable design and published in 1974, demonstrates quite convincingly that criminal propensities are inherited. (Denmark is a small country with a stable population, a national population register and centralized police and psychiatric registers. As a result it seems to have become a sort of ultra-Arcadian human game reservation for American and European psychiatric research workers.) Out of a population of 1,145 male adoptees followed up by Mednick and his team, they were able to show that where the biological father had a criminal record, the adoptee was also significantly more often criminal than was the case in the comparison group. They then selected two carefully matched adoptee groups, each numbering 143. Members of one group had criminal records, whereas the other group had none. When the biological fathers of both groups were traced, 49 per cent of the fathers of the criminal adoptee group had records, compared with only 28 per cent of the fathers of the non-criminal adoptee group. The degree of criminality found among the fathers of the criminal adoptees was considerably worse than that of the comparison group. These findings are both impressive and depressing.

In another study carried out in Denmark, Christiansen examined a whole generation of twins. He found that if one twin is criminal, the other is significantly more often found to be criminal in MZ (identical) twins than in fraternal twins. More recently it has been shown that men with an extra Y chromosome (the XYY constitution) are found in great excess in the special hospitals to which mentally abnormal aggressive offenders find their way. (It is highly unlikely, however, than an extra Y chromosome *invariably* leads to crime.) Gibbens has reported a high proportion of sex and other chromosomal abnormalities in delinquent women.

In an attempt to delimit an organic explanation for criminal behaviour, Williams found that the EEG, or brain wave patterns, were abnormal in 49.5 per cent of a large series of men committing violent crimes, compared with only 12 per cent of the general population. Of those in his population of prisoners who had committed isolated acts of violence, such as murder, a very high proportion (24 per cent) showed EEG abnormality, as did 65 per cent of those with a persistent history of serious aggression.

(It is relevant to mention here that as we approach senility our EEG tracings may demonstrate a deterioration in brain function. With due respect to law and order, it would be interesting to carry out EEGs on High Court judges in the UK and elsewhere where there is no specified retirement age, and where a small proportion of judges not only regularly doze off, but also sound off in court as though they were well into their septuagenarian or octogenarian dotage.)

Other factors which have been alleged to contribute to sociopathic behaviour in adult life include maternal stress during pregnancy or at the time of birth, deprivation or rejection by the mother in the early years of life, the absence of the father, or the effects of early institutionalization. The psychoanalytic interpretation stresses the psychopath's immature personality and emotional development and describes him as fixated at the pregenital phase (i.e. before the third year), when sexual identity has not developed and there is no super-ego and hence no castration fear. Some authorities suggest that whereas the neurotic expresses his unconscious conflicts in his symptoms, the psychopath does so by stereotyped, irrational or socially inept or hostile behaviour. Most experts stress the importance of an unfavourable early environment and disruptive sociocultural learning experiences, without which some individuals' genetic predisposition might perhaps have remained dormant. All authorities agree on the difficulties involved in treatment, some going so far as to consider most, if not all, forms of treatment to be useless.

Two centres, however, have shown some success in treating psychopathic patients. At the Henderson Hospital in the UK treatment is based on the therapeutic community. This is essentially a living-and-learning situation in which the subject can shed the social conventions and any resulting inhibitions, regress to early social and environmental situations and therein explore and reconstruct more productive ways of interacting with others. This is done in the company of peers who are also participating in the same healthy process.

Herstedvester in Denmark, an institution run by G. K. Stürup in a penal setting, also has a good track record. Treatment follows the therapeutic community principles modified to fit into a prison environment. In one sense the therapeutic odds are somewhat in favour of the prison authorities and, by extension, the prisoners. The court commits the prisoner to confinement at Herstedvester on an indefinite sentence. The prisoner may be allowed to sit alone and 'brainwash' himself in solitary confinement. He remains there until he decides himself to ask to see one of the senior prison administrators. They then work out practical goals for the future. Plans are totally reality-based and parole or discharge depend on the prisoners' progress. As we noted earlier, among the options open to habitual sexual offenders is old-fashioned agricultural castration, enhanced cosmetically by the intrascrotal transplant of two comely artifactual testes (Stürup is said to carry about and rattle a pair in his pocket, rather like Captain Queeg of *The Caine Mutiny*). In some ways his offer is more humane than the hormonal castration with oestrogens available to similar offenders in the UK. Of 900 psychopaths treated at Herstedvester, 87 per cent were finally able to leave the prison and to function in the outside community. This indicates that in the right setting the psychopath can indeed relearn, especially when this entails working out and towards his own personal social salvation in a captive setting.

Less damaged than the psychopath is the schizoid personality. Unlike the psychopath, he or she may ask voluntarily for psychiatric help in a social crisis, or because of psychosomatic illness. Walton, Professor of Psychiatry at Edinburgh University, considers the core of this type of deviation to consist of social detachment, avoidance of close relationships, and mistrustfulness. Sometimes, however, the schizoid's remote exterior may hide strong emotions which he may be able to express only to a sensitive, receptive psychiatrist, in a closely-guarded diary, or while daydreaming. Many psychiatrists consider this personality deviation as predisposing to schizophrenia. Time of onset varies. Parents may describe schizoid deviation beginning in the preschool years and becoming worse when schooling commenced and the child became even more preoccupied with his own idiosyncratic ideas and activities.

Most of us will have met the hysterical or histrionic personality type. These people are usually 'on heat' for attention; generally, but not always, female; and usually, but not invariably, phoney. The hysteric is a show-off, theatrical and histrionic in manner and dress. The exhibitionism is intended to impress or indeed to shock others. Nearly all hysterics have a compulsion to appear to themselves and others as superior to their true selves. They are often miserable when alone, but when in company usually contrive a sort of antic, gushy gaiety. They frequently lie in order to impress others and gain attention, and would prefer even the reassurance of insult, which they may provoke, to the anxiety of being ignored. Sometimes they tell major untruths; this is known as 'pseudologia phantastica'. The female hysteric is often frigid, although she may invite seduction by her sexy behaviour. Both male and female rarely sustain lasting friendships or meaningful relationships with others. They are resistant to therapy. A proportion may at some time in their lives develop hysterical conversion psychoneurosis – for example, hysterical blindness or paralysis – in order unconsciously to manipulate their escape from what is to them an intolerable life situation.

The normal personality is much more difficult to describe than the abnormal. Indeed, in one sense there is no such thing. Different societies, different psychiatrists, in fact each and every person will have a different concept of normality. That said, I would regard as normal anyone with near average intelligence who copes fairly consistently with his family, his work and his social commitments and enjoys being alive. He will show the following healthy adult characteristics, which arise from satisfactory experiences at the earlier stages of his development : a satisfactory sense of identity and self-image; a reasonable capacity for adapting to society's requirements without undue conformity; a reasonable enjoyment of life and concern for family, friends and others; an ability to tolerate losses, frustration, conflicts and anxiety; an ability to control aggression but to display, nevertheless, justifiable anger; an ability to enjoy the mutuality of an on-going sexual relationship, together with a capacity to care for and enjoy working to provide for the offspring that may result.

Related to the concept of normality is that of emotional maturity, but in the mature person you look for much more than in the normal person. Mature behaviour is as much the polar opposite of psychotic/crazy behaviour as indeed it is of neurotic/childish behaviour. Paul Vispo has listed the qualities which have been ascribed to the mature person by twenty-one authors who have written on this subject. They are as follows :

Harmony with environment and/or oneself
Independence
Acceptance of reality
A system of moral values
Acceptance of responsibility
Adjustment to genital level of psychosexual development
Adaptability
Parental and creative abilities
Capacity for object relationship based upon differentiation of the object
Insight or self-knowledge
Consistency in personality
Tolerance
Outreach
Periodic regressions
Management of aggression
Management of anxiety

Self-expression

Ability to delay action

Inner freedom

Capacity for the primordial act of wonder

To this list I should like to append two more qualities :

Outrage

Global kinship

Most of the writers Vispo considered include the first six items on this list; few consider any one particular quality the essential one, except Boelem, who listed only one item, the last. It is surprising that only three of the writers refer to what I consider one of the more important qualities, management of aggression.

Before elaborating further on these qualities I should like to stress that human maturity is essentially a concept of the total personality. The observation of one isolated performance does not tell us much about what the actor is like backstage. Thus the more or less consistent life-style of the person must be taken into account. It is abundantly clear that psychological, intellectual, emotional and physical development do not proceed at the same pace in any given individual; any or all of these areas may become either temporarily or permanently arrested. A person with a brilliant intellect may be pathetically inadequate in coping with human relationships. A brilliant surgeon may be embarrassingly naïve socially. A schoolboy of fifteen may have the IQ of a boy of nineteen, but the 'emotional age' of a boy of fifteen, an adult of twenty, or indeed a child of ten. A psychiatrist may be a first-rate clinical diagnostician and a competent psychotherapist, but at the same time be incapable of maintaining an adult emotional relationship with his wife. When assessing emotional maturity, therefore, it is essential to observe both the social and external behaviour and the internal or intra-psychic behaviour or state. The qualities listed by Vispo relate to both these aspects.

Harmony with the environment and with oneself means that the mature person is not only on good terms with himself but also with the people he works with, with the other members of his family and with his friends. This does not mean that he is submissive, but that he does possess a degree of general adaptability.

By independence is meant that he is able to arrive at his own conclusions and not just present an amalgam of the opinions he has heard expressed by others; in other words he is sufficiently self-confident to think things out for himself having listened critically and selectively to the opinions of others.

Acceptance of reality means to be able to see one's abilities, faults and achievements, to be able to distinguish wishful thinking from the feasible, to be able to confront the ineluctable drabness of life as it is with its haphazard joys, its frequent frustrations and its very occasional jigs of happiness.

A system of moral values means that the person maintains ideals and permanent standards of behaviour in his dealings with others. He accepts responsibility for his actions, his decisions and for those under his care. He never runs away though he may often feel like it.

Adjustment to genital level of psychosexual development simply means that a mature person has a capacity not only for receiving love on a permanent basis from a person of the opposite sex but is also capable of returning that love in a generous, wholehearted manner. He is capable of enjoying the physical side of sex for its own sake but also recognizes in it the symbolic total giving of two people in a simple physical manoeuvre of mutual trust.

According to Erikson, the Utopia of genitality should include mutuality of orgasm with a loved partner of the other sex, with whom one is able and willing to share a mutual trust and with whom one is able and willing to regulate the cycles of work, procreation and recreation, so as to secure for the offspring, too, all the stages of a satisfactory development.

A mature person is adaptable. He is not rigid and stereotyped in his behaviour. He is not a 'stuffed shirt'. He is good company in any company. He is rarely condescending and then only consciously so and only to the intellectually pompous.

Parental and creative abilities mean that he is able to pass his knowledge on to the young in an interesting way. If he is a parent he permits his children to explore the world about them without fretfully curtailing their every adventure. He can on occasion find new ways of evoking his offspring's interest and of expanding the repertoire of those interests.

'Capacity for object relationship based upon differentiation of the object' simply means that the mature person is able to take an interest in and to love others and not be permanently wrapped up in narcissistic self-love. He is able to forget himself appropriately in the interests of others.

Insight or self-knowledge is most important; it means that a person is aware of the chinks and kinks in his own psychic apparatus. He has a fair degree of understanding of his own personality type, and of his ambitions, which are realistic and related to his natural endowment and special training. His personality is consistent; he does not have major mood swings so that at one time he is elated by minor good fortune and at another time depressed by an equally minor 'catastrophe'.

Tolerance, Vispo points out, means two things. Firstly, to be able to tolerate tensions, frustrations and failures without panic or intensive depression. Secondly, it means that we are tolerant of others and their ideas, even when they are different from ours, but that we do not permit ourselves, in spite of this tolerance, to be pushed around intellectually, morally or physically.

Outreach is an Americanism which means that life for the mature person is always increasing in range and in importance. He is constantly extending the horizons of his interests and he can reach beyond himself, so that he is sympathetic to and capable of putting himself in touch with the aspirations of others.

Periodic regressions simply means that he retains some childlike curiosity for play and fantasy and is not above doing his own bit of clowning on occasion : *dulce et decorum est descipere in loco* – it is good to have a jug of wine now and then.

A minimum of floating anxiety and aggression is permissible even in the mature person. However, he does possess the ability to relax at appropriate times and to permit his mind to wander over the various topics which interest him. With regard to aggression, this has to be sublimated in the right direction so that its energy is rechannelled into activities which are professionally and perhaps artistically acceptable. It also means that he is capable of using aggression when indicated without cover for defence purposes, or alternatively withhold his aggression until the right moment. It is related to outrage which I shall comment on later.

Self-expression means to be able to communicate our feelings and our ideas to others. Ability to delay action means that the mature person has long-term values in mind and does not invariably resort to short-term ones – Freud's reality principle versus the pleasure principle.

The mature person has inner freedom. He is at peace with himself, he accepts himself as he is and is not trying at all times to project a false image of himself. He is confident enough in himself to admit his own failings without making a boring fetish of declaiming them to others. From this internal peace and inner freedom he develops an unsmug serenity, an acceptance of the good, the indifferent and the bad which he must confront daily. He is pleased he was born – he is a good animal.

Capacity for the primordial act of wonder simply means that the world about us constantly intrigues our interest, that we are capable even in old age of being astonished and delighted by the variety and ingenuity of the things we see and hear and feel, that life never becomes a chore and we never become blasé in the drab, hope-castrating implication of that word.

By outrage I mean that sensibility to injustice or humbug – at local bar or international level – which prompts you to strike a practical well-directed blow to redress the wrong rather than merely abreacting – 'unpacking your heart with words'. It is related closely to management of aggression.

By global kinship I mean an unromantic feeling of biological and social empathy with people of every race (or racial mixture), colour or creed and the imagination at least to try to extend this kinship not only, for example, to white South Africans, bigoted or non-bigoted, but to ineffectual white and coloured people all over the world :

> 'See the unhealed grief
> in every mean and selfish act,
> finding sweetness even in the mealy mouth.'

It implicates a responsibility to give unobtrusive practical help, not charity, whenever possible, and the wit to realize you are only doing your brother a small favour and that you don't deserve any thanks.

Must we possess all the above qualities in order to be mature? Certainly not. What I do regard as fundamental is insight or self-knowledge or 'self-objectification'. As Allport says : 'The man who has the most complete sense of proportion concerning his own qualities and cherished values is able to perceive their incongruities and absurdities in certain settings.' He goes on to specify a very important aspect of this quality, 'a sense of humour' – the ability to laugh at ourselves and the things we love, to see behind some solemn event the contrast between pretension and performance. (Psychiatrists are notoriously humourless and when they jest their jokes smell of the midnight oil.) Vispo writes: 'If we cannot or are afraid to face ourselves, our motives, our limitations and possibilities, how can we imagine that we are not going to distort external reality to our taste or needs? If we take ourselves too seriously we will lose sooner or later our sense of proportion, and then criticism will not be accepted in good faith and only adulations will satisfy.'

Some of the qualities listed above are obviously related to the external world. The mature person accepts reality, is in harmony with the environment and though he is independent (because he is able to arrive at his own conclusions), he is nonetheless maturely dependent on others. He is capable of love at a truly genital heterosexual level. He is tolerant but does not suffer from a 'professional nice guy' complex. He is consistently responsible. He is able to express his ideas, feelings and emotions to others competently and he is not afraid or embarrassed to do so. He is creative; he uses his energy successfully for achievement and does not burn up his free energy in neurotic fumblings. He continues throughout life to be delighted by the things about him – even in old age he continues to wonder like a well-informed child.

The person who has arrived at maturity is also at peace with himself – he accepts himself as he is, warts, beauty spots and all. From internal peace will derive a contentment with life. Vispo has summarized internal qualities by saying that a mature person will show a continuity or consistency in his personality, 'he is essentially genuine or congruent, he has a character structure'. This consistency in personality does not mean that he will be perfect or that he will not suffer moments of regressive behaviour – sudden expressions of unjustified anger, a selfish reaction, momentary delusions of grandeur – but rather that the mature person will rectify his behaviour and recognize his mistakes without feeling that he is losing self-respect. (The immature cannot do this.) He must be able to be alone – to be able to be at peace with himself while alone and at the same time to be in full communion with life. When the immature are alone they are ill at ease; they are lonely. They have a continuous need to receive the unquestioning support and busy reassurance of others. Being able to be alone is to accept that our strength needs to come essentially from the quiet well of our own spiritual resources.

The social (external) and intrapsychic (internal) qualities discussed above may join to express in the mature individual what Allport calls a 'Unifying Philosophy of Life', a system of goals and values that will give shape and reason to our existence. For some this may take the form of altruism, for others a religious approach to life, a true morality, or a sense of informed sincerity and a sense of truth. The word 'wisdom' best summarizes this quality.

Does religious belief exclude one from arriving at maturity? Far from it. The mature person not only confronts his own personal reality and the stark reality of his outside world, but he does both with calm ulterior optimism. The Christian believer has Pope John Paul II, Dag Hammarskjold, Teilhard de Chardin and T. S. Eliot quietly at his side. Charles Darwin was a mature and deeply religious man but lacked the *joie de vivre* of the true Christian. Religion or faith is, to me at any rate, a humble, joyous, optimistic act of imagination and trust in the unknowable.

(Personally, I find myself in the embarrassing position of being a lukewarm agnostic, a chronic doubting Thomas; if Jesus were kind enough to visit me, I would not only want to put my finger into his wounds but also to check his pulse and blood pressure and take a full psychiatric history.)

To sum up, in the mature personality I would expect to find at least the following: self-knowledge (insight), peace with oneself, independence, only a minimum of floating anxiety (i.e. anxiety for no obvious reason), integration in one's social group, a system of ethical values, acceptance of reality, a sense of humour, possibilities of self-expression and of wonder, outrage and global kinship.

I shall end this chapter with a mournful cheer by quoting Bertrand Russell, the most brilliant child who ever lived to be nearly a hundred:

'It does not do to live in memories, in regrets for the good old days, or in sadness for friends who are dead. One's thoughts must be directed to the future and to things about which there is something to be done. This is not easy; one's past is a gradually increasing weight. It is easy to think to oneself that one's emotions used to be more vivid than they are and one's mind more keen. If this is true it should be forgotten, and if it is forgotten it will probably not be true.'

REFERENCES

G. Allport, *Pattern and Growth in Personality,* Holt, Rinehart & Winston, New York, 1961.

H. J. Eysenck, *Dimensions of Personality,* Routledge & Kegan Paul, London, 1947.

Bertrand Russell, *Portraits from Memory and Other Essays,* Allen & Unwin, London, 1956.

Paul Vispo, 'On Human Maturity', *Perspectives in Biology and Medicine,* Vol. IX, 1966, pp. 586-604.

12

Of Masks and Motivation

> We are all disturbed personalities and life consists in learning to deal with one's own problems and those of other people.
>
> PROFESSOR KATHLEEN JONES

> O wad some Pow'r the giftie gie us
> To see oursels as others see us!
> It wad frae mony a blunder free us,
> And foolish notion.
>
> ROBERT BURNS, 'To a Louse'

Are psychiatrists, if only because of the 'irrationale' of their professional aspirations, crazy? Indeed, are psychiatrists people? Does the practice of psychiatry lead inexorably to a chronic (or acute) unselfdiagnosable erosion, repression or depersonalization of the psychiatrist's own entity or individuation, so that he becomes a sort of self-maintaining, jargonizing, tautological, cybernetic machine, migrating the ill-charted Sargasso of a medically-biased speciality that has not even yet worked out its own psychopathology with any degree of precision? Does the psychiatrist's professional persona or mask, essential up to a point for the efficient conductance of his specialist deployment, malignantly and almost invariably absorb into its own mechanizing, perfunctory substance that erstwhile real character who put on the mask in the first place? Where did that real character come from, and what was his conscious and unconscious motivation for setting out on the long, perhaps ambivalent and self-seeking journey towards Epidaurus, Mount Cithaeron, Thebes, Denmark Hill or Bethesda?

These questions first occurred to me in 1971 in Mexico City, at a reception held to welcome those who had come from all corners of the world to attend the Fifth World Congress of Psychiatry. Over the next six days we were to have the opportunity to select from and listen to a list of 1,205 papers on topics ranging from military psychiatry and suicide (non-military) to cross-dressing and transsexualism in the American male toddler. (This paper, seductively entitled 'Forty Boys Who Want To Be Girls', was by far the best I managed to hear.)

Almost every subject under the sun was on the official menu, except a paper drawing attention to the reasons why our Russian colleagues – and some of those guilty were actually present at the reception – were abusing psychiatry for political purposes in order to lock up dissidents in psychiatric asylums, after they had found for the ruling junta by diagnosing schizophrenia.

Suddenly the vast reception seemed unreal: thousands of male and female members of my own professional species were milling about like a vast swarm of robots, and psychiatric patients, political or non-political, seemed very, very far away. Perhaps instead of sounding off about the abuse of heroin in the UK, I should instead have given a paper on 'The Therapeutic Value that Patients Provide for Their Psychiatrists'. Here we all were in Mexico – but for what, and from where, and why? Or, as Dr David Cooper once put it, more succinctly, more pertinently and in a much broader context: 'Why am I here, why have I put myself here, who is paying for me for what, what should I do, why do anything, what is anything and what is nothing, what is life and death, sanity and madness?'

Some of the same questions returned at the opening of another conference in Amsterdam in 1973, as we all stood for one minute in silence to pay our last respects to one of the senior organizers who had committed suicide the previous day. It was the Seventh International Congress on Suicide Prevention. I soon lost all interest in attending the eighth. Who wants to attend psychiatric conferences that carry a mortality rate?

It is easy to debunk psychiatrists: corny old jokes get recycled – two psychiatrists meet on their way to work in the morning, one says to the other, 'You're feeling good today, how am I?' But because we are at least of marginal value to our patients and occasionally provide a lifeline of vital necessity, as on those occasions when we prevent a severely depressed patient from killing himself, we must therefore pluck up the courage and the ability to take ourselves both more and less seriously. With all our imperfections on our heads, most of us, nevertheless, in the words of Bernard Shaw, 'want to be of use'. In order to achieve this as a clinician working in the patient's best interests, it is essential for the psychiatrist to remain aware both of his professional mask and the strengths and limitations of that real character behind it. The surgeon, at the very least, has useful professional utensils; alas, for a large proportion of his patients, the psychiatrist is reduced to himself – he is, in the best sense of the term, playing the prostitute with all the resources of his psyche, in the interest of his patients.

What motivates us? Freud's psychology is essentially the psychology of unconscious motivation or, put another way, of unconscious hankering after psychic self-salving or self-reparation for real or imaginary Oedipal and pre-Oedipal frustrations. Bearing in mind famous world tyrants – Napoleon, Mussolini, Hitler, Stalin, Nixon – all of whom were physically of small stature, in Freudian terms we may all, whatever our profession or job, be trying to compensate or indeed over-compensate for what Alfred Adler was the first to call an 'inferiority complex' : a complex or cluster of ideas and feelings relating to our real or imagined social, physical or psychological inadequacies. According to Adler, these universal inferiority feelings derive from every infant's sense of helplessness, and they supply the motivation for all subsequent compensatory strivings for superiority, mastery and perfection; if successful, these then lead to the achievement, and hopefully the maintenance, of self-esteem. This may be accomplished in a healthy way – 'compensation' – or in an excessive, distorted and pathological manner – 'overcompensation'. Therein lie the pitfalls for the person seeking either political power, 'merely' political and social acceptance, or subjective self-acceptance. These pitfalls, as we shall see, are open to the psychiatrist lacking in self-knowledge just as much as they are to his potential patient whose aspirations continue to remain pitifully unfulfilled.

Put briefly and simply in Adlerian terms, the growing child, whatever his professional calling turns out to be later on in life, forms his life goals and life-style (that is, his normal or distorted adaptation to his social milieu) by weaving outer and inner experiences into a consistent pattern or map of the world and of the self. Although some of his hankerings remain in the background of awareness and therefore unconscious, they may nevertheless influence his life ambitions and strivings after non-neurotic compensation and self-esteem, or alternatively his highly neurotic, disruptive overcompensations.

With these Adlerian notions or 'models' in mind, let us now consider that person (male or female) of slightly above average intelligence, who is consciously unaware of what inferiority feelings power and drive him inexorably on towards a resolution, or a 'super-resolution', of harrowing, ill-deciphered, personal tensions. One tempting way to strive to resolve these difficulties, or at least partially to raise his self-esteem, is to become a psychiatrist or psychoanalyst or both.

Two avenues are open to him. He can enter psychiatry via a medical training, and without necessarily undergoing a prolonged personal analysis. Or he can undergo what may be an expensive training analysis (e.g. Freudian or Jungian), which can take three or more years, after which he may then become a psychoanalyst or analyst and enrol as a bona fide member and practitioner of the relevant association.

If he takes the first avenue, receiving a medical and surgical training and later a broad-based, eclectic training in general psychiatry and neurology, but not undergoing a training analysis, he may be less likely to misdiagnose and 'psychologize' a patient with an organic disease that 'announces' itself by causing psychiatric symptoms. (Multiple sclerosis, for example, often presents for the first time as severe depression; a psychosis due to low circulating levels of thyroxine may present as 'myxoedema madness', a syndrome that may closely mimic schizophrenia.) Unlike the psychoanalyst, however, or the psychiatrist who *has* undergone analysis, he will be less aware of those 'anxiety-echoes' and long-ago-repressed frustrations and aggressivities which some patients may innocently evoke in him. His handling of patients may thus at times lack that professional objectivity and concerned detachment which is the hallmark of the good psychiatrist. To put it more bluntly, the non-analysed psychiatrist may at certain times, and with certain patients, tend unconsciously to scapegoat, or counter-transfer, or get rid of his own repressions onto his patients and at their expense.

It is my belief that the physician embarking on a career in psychiatry should first be treated himself during a training analysis. At the end of even the most mediocre training analysis he would emerge at least partially aware of his previously unconscious motivation for wanting to become a psychiatrist. Consequently he would be less likely to use his future patients unwittingly to enable him to adjust, modulate or alleviate his own anxieties or personal aspirations for power, 'mastery' and an acceptable level of self-esteem.

If a training analysis proved too expensive, two other courses are open to the trainee psychiatrist. He could undertake a supervised self-analysis, with access throughout to an experienced, analytically-oriented senior colleague with whom he could discuss regularly those problems deriving from his professional self-scrutiny and any personal difficulties that might be impinging on his therapeutic relationships with patients. Alternatively, he could undergo a behaviouristic analysis from an experienced behaviour therapist. This could not but help to put him in touch with himself – his drives and goals, his motivation, his controlling and manipulative tendencies – and his life-style, revealing any overcompensatory or other hankerings in his own personality that might otherwise go totally unnoticed throughout his entire professional career. In terms of time and money, since behaviour therapists rarely spend more than twenty hours taking a clinical case history, this latter option might prove the least expensive and perhaps not the least rewarding. The opportunity of being observed directly by a behaviour therapist during real therapy sessions with patients, and having practical and professional advice on how better to control his own or the patient's anxiety levels, or how to improve his therapeutic skill by being made aware of his shortcomings, would not only be of enormous help to the psychiatrist but would also benefit his patients.

Where do psychiatrists come from? There is some evidence that psychiatry may attract the most emotionally unstable from the ranks of the medically qualified. The work of several investigators in the United States, including Blachly and co-workers, Freeman and Thomas, has demonstrated that physicians as a group have one of the highest suicide rates among all occupations and, furthermore, that under the age of forty, suicide is the leading cause of death among physicians. More specifically, of all the medical specialities, psychiatry, taken pro rata, has the highest suicide rate of all. Blachly's report showed that paediatricians had the lowest rate, with 10 suicides per 100,000, and psychiatrists the highest with 61 per 100,000. I agree with Blachly that 'the high rate in psychiatrists is undoubtedly influenced by preselection'. In addition, I would speculate that many physicians who specialize in psychiatry are unconsciously, or perhaps consciously, attracted to psychiatry in the hope of resolving some of their own emotional difficulties. The same holds true, to a lesser extent, for all medically qualified individuals. There is nothing wrong with this provided these resolutions are not achieved at the patient's expense. Indeed, the physician who has brought to psychiatry a healthy awareness of his own idiosyncrasies is in my opinion a more potentially sympathetic and insightful therapist than that psychiatric war-baron who has never, at any time of his life, had a good old dent kicked into the shining armature of his own impeccably modulating ego. I would certainly be reluctant to take my troubles to such a tin god.

In a lecture delivered in February 1979, Sir Denis Hill, Professor of Psychiatry at the Maudsley Hospital, London, drew his listeners' attention to that distinguished American psychologist, David Shakow's analysis of the functions of the psychiatrist as observer; these were: 'objective, participant, empathic and self-observing'. These abilities are, or should be, used by all physicians, but they should be most highly developed in the psychiatrist and constitute the very core of his clinical skills. John Romano pointed out, in a paper in *California Medicine* in 1972, that it is the patients who teach us most, and the clinically mature psychiatrist knows that throughout his career he will, if he remains open-minded and unsmug, continue to learn from his patients.

Professor Hill then outlined the characteristics of clinical maturity: personal and emotional maturity, which means freedom from personal neurotic nostalgia about one's own past; protection of the patient from the negative aggressive aspects of one's self, but also the ability to acknowledge the fact when one does not like a patient; the capacity to empathize with the mentally ill, but to remain objective about the significance and meaning of the various manifestations of illness; and to be kind but not to indulge oneself or the patient in excessive compassion.

Hill especially emphasized the hazards to patients that can arise from the psychiatrist's own personality, and which can be traced to his inadequate or biased training: 'The well-known risks of excessive identification with the patient and neglect of the phenomena of transference and counter-transference, [are] inherent in every doctor-patient relationship. Ignorance and neglect of this can bring pain and damage to both.' He noted the limitation on psychiatric skills that results from total, blind acceptance of one ideology – one type of explanation only, for all mental illnesses. At the end of his lecture he frankly warned his listeners, the majority of them psychiatrists, of the serious hazard for patients that arises when the psychiatrist, especially if he embraces one clinical ideology, is intensely motivated to cure at all costs, 'when he has a passionate and excessive zeal to treat, and the unfortunate inability to accept that in the present state of knowledge we are not infrequently therapeutically impotent'. Out of this narrow and blinkered attitude have come, in Hill's opinion, some of the abuses of psychiatry – excessive and unselective use of ECT, multiple leucotomy operations, excessive use of drugs, and the legal methods of restraint, which even under the present Mental Health Act in the UK, designed (ironically) to protect patients from just such a danger, may nonetheless through its small loopholes, still permit a pyschiatrist, 'acting of course honestly although ignorantly, to impose excessive treatment' on his patients and without their consent.

What then is my operational definition of what constitutes a person? Or, more specifically, are psychiatrists people?

A person is an individual who competently uses at least two principal masks or personae. *Persona* is the Latin for the actor's mask. In *Archetypes and the Collective Unconscious* Jung comments: 'The persona . . . is the individual's system of adaptation to, or the manner he assumes in dealing with, the world. Every calling or profession, for example, has its own characteristic persona. . . .' It is this persona that helps a person effectively to negotiate his professional or job role. The second, social persona is more akin to a 'non-mask' or rather a near-transparent mask that is readily, easily and suitably adjustable to fit each informal situation when the individual is professionally 'off-stage'.

A person is essentially someone who shows an appropriately sensitive awareness of others on all occasions, professional or otherwise, whatever their age, job, sex, or social or intellectual status. A person is someone who can do this easily, readily, naturally, intuitively.

During the last fifteen years, while attending a dozen or more international conferences, it has often occurred to me that an alarmingly high proportion of the psychiatrists I met at such gatherings, and more especially on informal occasions during these meetings, were incapable of taking off their professional masks even hours after we had all gone officially 'off-stage'. They appeared so loath to doff the professional stance or posture, so determined to cling to their formal 'costumes', that their rejection of the natural mask seemed complete. As Jung goes on to say in the passage from which I quoted above, '. . . the danger is that individuals sometimes become identical with their [professional] personas – the professor with his textbook, the tenor with his voice. . . .' The professional becomes so closely identified with his own persona at all times that he becomes 'personavized' – socially, even professionally burlesqued – and lives what Alfred Adler called a 'life-lie'.

In fact, after many similar experiences at international gatherings, from Tokyo to Mexico, Reykjavik to Athens, it suddenly occurred to me that perhaps, for many of my colleagues, the natural 'non-mask' never truly existed in the first place.

How so many psychiatrists got into such a state, how they became so woefully 'personavized', one can only speculate. Nearly all had had a tough, drudging, prolonged medical indoctrination and training, had passed their searching final examinations after which their success had been substantiated in degree ceremony, passing-out ball and sundry parties. In spite of all this, were anxieties and emotional vulnerabilities still so pursuant and clamorous that they were compelled, by some exorbitant and irresistible machination of the unconscious, to perform a sort of primal somersault and opt out into psychiatry as a means of escaping into a socially acceptable, potentially self camouflaging defence mechanism called 'doing psychiatry'? Perhaps the less timid and more romantic among them might even have fantasized that by so doing they would automatically get themselves reborn, reparented, refurbished, would shed their self-haunting nobodyness and start really existing at last in the grand existential style of Ludwig Binswanger ('*Dasein*'), at last getting on with becoming their new, true ultimate selves, the way the acorn busily gets on with becoming an oak.

Unfortunately, this process whereby the psychiatrist (or any other physician) loses his natural mask and becomes totally identified with his professional persona, affects not only himself but his patients. If being a general physician tends to make a person aloof, becoming a specialist can make that person even more aloof. Doctors and people in the para-medical or 'helping' professions – social workers, health visitors, midwives, nurses, even hospital administrators – also tend to be absurdly self-important at times, putting their own interests above those of their patients. Professor Kathleen Jones, a social administrator at the University of York, expressed this very succinctly to members of the Royal College of Psychiatrists in November 1977 :

'The patient's view of what is happening to him is as valid as that of the therapist, and therapists ought to listen as well as to prescribe. The so-called helping professions do often serve their own professional interests rather than the true interests of their patients or clients – a fact that troubles many thoughtful medical and social-work students. Psychiatrists can create mental illness by labelling those who struggle with impossible human situations as "sick" and "treating" them with drugs and ECT. Social workers can perpetuate social injustice by offering casework to people whose basic need is for enough to live on, somewhere to live, and a little personal dignity. Of course it is not always true, and it is not the whole truth; but there is enough truth in the critique for it to be taken seriously.'

When patients come to their doctors they are often anxious or fretful, or even downright terrified. This reduces many of them to a state of near-sycophantic beholdenment towards us. (Added to this, of course, is the fact that some of us see them literally with their trousers down.) They thank us fulsomely for our ministrations, as though we were giving this professional help for nothing, as though we weren't being rewarded not only in cash but in several other lucrative, esteem-enhancing, neurosis-salving currencies. If we don't keep our tongues respectfully and firmly in our cheeks we not only come to expect their excesses of gratitude as a right, but we ourselves begin actually to believe what they think and say of us while under our well-intentioned duresses.

Why is it that some of us behave like this towards our patients and towards ourselves? One possible explanation may be found in Freud's concept of 'reaction-formation'. This, as we have seen, is an unconscious defence mechanism resorted to when an instinctual impulse from the id, which is (consciously) unacceptable, is overcome or kept in check by substituting in its place an exaggeration of the diametrically opposite instinctual urge or impulse. So, for example, a helpless underling may be ultra-civil to the boss he hates.

Showing solicitude and concern for a humanity may be a reaction-formation against strong, instinctual, deeply-rooted urges to be cruel and sadistic. Perhaps some of us in the helping professions are paradoxically spending our professional lives reparatively and vicariously making amends to our unconscious selves for that anger and aggression within us that derives from long-forgotten real or imaginary punishments or neglects. These ancient wounds we now metabolize not by venting this long-lost, disremembered anger and sadistic grudgement directly on ourselves or others, but instead by discreetly deploying ourselves and 'taming' these urges in the silent, satisfying and socially acceptable aggression of 'doing good'. But all the while, deep down, or maybe not so deep down, the primitive urge is still there.

The Adlerian formulation we considered earlier in this chapter is also relevant here. By playing 'big brother' to others who have fortuitously come under our administrative or therapeutic jurisdiction, we may be trying to resolve or compensate for our own feelings of inferiority. In addition, the small pomps (which of course we magnify), the kudos, the secondary rewards and gains of having our self-esteem burnished by patient and underling, are also quite addictive, especially for those amongst us who are least self-critical and most in need of fulsome ego-support and reassurance. This puts the court jester as well as the devil's advocate out of court, and so some of us drift along having gelded ourselves of corrective, of feedback, having lost all sense of self-irony and abandoned ourselves to the slow, horrific fate of being nuzzled to death by a claque of grateful 'sick lambs'.

The observations of Henry Miller MD are relevant here. In January 1970, Miller, then Vice-Chancellor of the University of Newcastle upon Tyne, admitted to a resounding stroke of genius: in the late 1960s he had inaugurated a Society for the Abolition of Psychiatrists. He remains secretive about the possible extent of its masonic power, the strength of its membership, or the number of applications for membership he received from psychiatric patients. In his public confession he made a few courtly, good-humoured but extremely perceptive suggestions: that the psychiatrist should remain first and foremost a true physician, skilled in the diagnosis of somatic as well as mental illnesses or illnesses that are a combination of both, rather than spend his time preventing world wars, pretending that he is the ultimate authority on bringing up children, or 'misusing his jargon to confuse any and every topical issue in an incessant series of television appearances'. He pointed out tactfully that 'the psychiatrist is of course encouraged in his universal pontification by the inexplicable veneration with which his views are regarded by many who ought to know better. . . .' In Miller's opinion, this unjustified veneration springs 'in part from the priest's loss of prestige and from the collapse of religious values'.

Referring to insight, that is, a person's insight into his own neurotic or psychotic behaviour, the subject of so much discussion at psychiatric meetings especially among 'those psychiatrists who lay great store on introspective data, that one might imagine it would be carefully cultivated as well as highly valued by those psychiatrists themselves', Miller said : 'I have no hesitation in saying quite categorically that this is not so. My careful personal observations confirm the rather unexpected finding that the practice of psychiatry in any of its forms does not necessarily confer any insight whatever.'

Is Miller overstating his case? Is he – and indeed am I, in the argument I am advancing in this chapter – being a little too harsh on my psychiatric colleagues? Where insight is concerned, it might be useful to look a little further and consider the behaviour of psychiatrists 'in the field'. And why not go straight to the top, to Sigmund Freud and Carl Jung, the founding fathers of modern psychiatry? Both, of course, are exceptional, in that they possessed that monstrous thing called genius – Freud might be regarded as a major genius, Jung as a minor exemplar – but neither's forte could be said to include logic, self-insight or emotional maturity.

Freud, an Austrian Jew (the most unorthodox Jew since Jesus Christ), in terms of sheer intuitive creativity makes Mount Olympus and all its divine, self-absorbed alumni seem as flat as Denmark Hill. He himself quite openly acknowledged his Olympian qualities and happily compared himself to Copernicus (who demolished the belief that the earth is the centre of the universe) and to Charles Darwin (who put the ape back into man by offering scientific proof for the ancient theory of evolution).

Even Freud's blunders were Homeric. He not so much put the cart before the horse as put the driver's rear-end before his head. His descriptions of the oral, anal and genital stages of emotional development indicate that he literally believed the erotogenic zones themselves – the mucous membranes of the anus, mouth, urethra and genitalia – to be the actual biological determinants of instinctual behaviour and of the different childhood experiences at each stage.

Yet, in spite of this biological clanger, he was still right in the sense that sucking, biting, elimination and genital stimulation all acquire great symbolic significance as each becomes associated in the child's mind with the different types of socio-emotional experiences that envelop him as he discovers his own physiological functions.

Freud himself was quite unaware of his own aggressive orality and, more especially, his own resounding anality. He hoarded and retained many of his ideas and beliefs against all reason, as obsessively as he hoarded the collection of sculpture (symbolic faeces, by his own terms) that cluttered his study and allowed him to enjoy 'retention pleasure' to his heart's content. He was an ergophobiac, an obsessive-compulsive worker. 'I cannot imagine life without work as really comfortable,' he wrote to the Swiss pastor Oskar Pfister in 1910. 'With me, fantasizing and working coincide; I find amusement in nothing else.' Sexually too, he was obsessive to the point of being seemingly incapable of adding to or subtracting from his harem of two – his wife and her sister Minna.

Regarding what might be interpreted as Freud's own oral aggression and anality, Theodor Reik, an early colleague who eventually broke with Freud and emigrated to the United States, noted that during the 1910s and 1920s every critic appeared to Freud himself as a moral hypocrite, every honest and serious judgement was considered as 'resistance'. The late J. A. C. Brown, a psychiatrist and social psychologist, described how, about this time, one disciple after another disagreed with the Master and left, 'not at all with the tacit agreement to differ but rather in an aura of heavy disapproval and the sort of invective that was once heaped upon the heads of heretics'. Jung commented: 'There was one characteristic of his that preoccupied me above all: his bitterness.'

The break between Freud and Jung in 1913 reveals much about the character of both and is especially illustrative of the blind spots, peevishness and craziness even of men of genius. They really fell out over sex and bog corpses. Jung couldn't accept Freud's teaching that, if regarded from within, sexuality included spirituality and had an intrinsic meaning of its own. Jung felt that Freud's concrete terminology was too narrow to express the concept of spirituality. He became bored with the master's 'monotony of interpretation', invariably sexual: 'Freud never asked himself why he was compelled to talk continually of sex, why this idea had taken such possession of him.' One might argue here that Freud's obsession with sex was a reaction-formation not only against accepting the mystical side of his own unconscious nature, which he seems to have become aware of at times, but also against the greatest Oedipal crime of all, Freud's own murder of God the Father by writing him off to Limbo as a mere fiction that man had created, or invented, out of his own feelings of helplessness and despair.

The first of a series of leaden last straws in their relationship was when Freud said to Jung: 'My dear Jung, promise me never to abandon the sexual theory. That is the most essential thing of all. You see, we must make a dogma of it, an unshakeable bulwark.' Jung asked, 'A bulwark against what?' Freud replied, 'Against the black tide of mud – occultism.' In other words, against everything that philosophy and religion had learned about the human psyche.

About this time, too, Jung became interested in peat-bog corpses. This annoyed Freud. As they discussed them one day over dinner, Freud suddenly fainted. He afterwards accused Jung of having death-wishes towards him. Freud fainted again under somewhat similar circumstances on another occasion. The conversation had turned to more glorious mummies than those found in the bogs of Northern Europe, more particularly to that of King Amenophis IV, a member of the pharaoh dynasty who had destroyed the inscriptions on his father's steles because of his negative ('Oedipal') attitude towards the late king, who was venerated as a god; it was said that behind Amenophis' creation of a monotheistic religion there lurked an unresolved father complex. Freud fainted during the discussion and, always a gentleman, Jung, rather like Aeneas, carried his 'father' to safety and laid him on a couch. Jung comments, 'In his weakness he looked at me as if I were his father. Whatever other causes may have contributed to this faint, the fantasy of father-murder was common to both cases.' What a Dantesque scene. Was Freud living out in real life the fictions of his own personally-created mythologies, had he never really resolved his own Oedipal guilt, or, as I have suggested above, was he in part his own guilt-laden scapegoat, haunted by the consequences of having exterminated God the Father and all He symbolized? Had he in fact symbolically killed a father twice over?

The crazy behaviour of these two great explorers of the mind is impressive. Both cheated when they interpreted each other's dreams. Freud had a dream, the contents of which Jung has kept secret but which he interpreted as best he could. Then during 'free association' he asked Freud for some additional details from his private life. According to Jung, Freud responded with 'a look of utmost suspicion', before replying, 'But I cannot risk my authority.' Jung comments: 'At that moment he lost it altogether – the end of our relationship was already foreshadowed. Freud was placing personal authority above truth.'

What an odd couple. Freud the spoilt philosopher, who indulged in cocaine and allowed himself to be killed by nothing more heroic (or less phallic) than a cigar (which he habitually suckled). Jung a spoilt anthropologist, brilliant, but with somewhat of a hint of the gombeen intellectual cockalorum. A resilient Swiss, with a most inventive mind, he recovered from his own devastating Oedipal rift with Freud and went on to prove himself one of the most spiritually and intellectually solvent physician-psychiatrists Europe has so far produced. Both acted under a major delusional system in that both were convinced they were creating a new science which they both, for a time, called psychoanalysis. In his obituary of Freud, who died of oral cancer in London in 1939, Jung referred to his work as 'epoch-making' and 'probably the boldest attempt that has ever been made to master the riddles of the unconscious psyche upon the apparently firm ground of empiricism'.

As a boy, Jung found spiritual liberation in a dream in which he saw God defecate on the roof of the local cathedral (he hated going to church and was conscious of the aridity of organized religion from an early age). Freud had a similar dream once, when, as Gargantua, he pissed on the roof of Notre Dame. As Shakespeare says, 'We are such stuff as dreams are made on.'

If you consider these two great men to be somewhat mad, what of these who have followed them? What, for instance, does one make of Dr Thomas S. Szasz, Professor of Psychiatry at the State University of New York and a well-known member of the American Psychoanalytic Association? Szasz has written a brilliant book called *The Myth of Mental Illness*, which, as the title suggests, sets out to prove beyond all shadow of doubt, that there is no such thing as mental illness. He succeeded, but rather ruined this spectacular achievement by staying on in his old professorial chair.

Are doctors really guilty of doing society more harm than good, of creating diseases rather than eliminating them? In his well-documented, civilized and well-reasoned book, *Doctors on Trial,* John Bradshaw, himself an experienced physician, poses these very pertinent questions. He bases his answers and opinions on recent research papers written by doctors themselves and published in *The New England Journal of Medicine, The Lancet, The British Medical Journal* and *The Journal of the American Medical Association.* In the final chapter of the book he concludes: 'We must look for hope, not to doctors, but to those, whether or not they are medically qualified, who see the need to create a new society, of which health will be an integral part (as ill-health is of ours); and who will search for the philosophy, the religion, needed for the establishment of such a society.'

REFERENCES

J. S. Bradshaw, *Doctors on Trial*, Wildwood House, London, 1978.

David Cooper, quoted by Kathleen Jones in 'Society Looks at the Psychiatrist', *British Journal of Psychiatry,* Vol. 132, 1978, p. 321.

Sir Denis Hill, 'The Qualities of a Good Psychiatrist', *British Journal of Psychiatry,* Vol. 133, 1978, p. 97.

Kathleen Jones, op. cit.

Carl Jung, *Archetypes and the Collective Unconscious,* Routledge & Kegan Paul, London, 1959.

Carl Jung, *Memories, Dreams, Reflections,* Collins and Routledge & Kegan Paul, London, 1963.

Henry Miller, 'Psychiatry – Medicine or Magic?', in T. Silverstone and B. Barraclough (eds), *Contemporary Psychiatry,* Headley Brothers, Ashford, Kent, 1975, pp. 462-6.

PART THREE

13

Girls Will Be Boys:

Sexual and Gender-Role Identity

Any attempt to understand man's behaviour which does not take into account his sexuality, 'normal' or 'deviational', is of very limited value. In the two chapters that follow we shall be looking at the more common deviations – male and female homosexuality – and at the less common ones : paedophilia, sado-masochism, exhibitionism, zoophilia, transvestism, transsexualism and the like. First, however, it is essential to consider how the fundamental determinant of male and female sexuality develops, and how in some individuals gender is wrongly assigned at birth.

The human primate, as we have seen, is an outrageous anatomical congruency of two sexes and several brains, all wrapped up in one body. Thus, whether we are predominantly male or predominantly female, we live our lives, almost by definition, in a state of greater or lesser psychosomatic/somatopsychic flux and ambivalence. The majority of us are essentially specialized hermaphrodites, that is, either heterosexual males or heterosexual females, each bearing the organs of the opposite sex in attenuated form. It seems only logical to assume that this somatic duality is also paralleled in the psyche and that at times the resulting ambivalence may lead to sexual and non-sexual behaviour that may range from the merely eccentric or deviationalist to the frankly psychotic or delusional. Jung formulated this duality in terms of the 'anima' in the male and the 'animus' in the female, these terms describing the unconscious image of the other sex we carry about in us, both as individuals and as members of the human species.

We must all, whether we are homosexual, ambisexual, heterosexual or neuter, live our lives in a world geared for, and run by, heterosexuals for heterosexuals. To make things slightly more complicated, the natural form of the human, whether male or female, is in fact female; the male is essentially the result of biological 'interference' with natural foetal development. Man's estate, the estate of the human ape, is far from being nice and simple. Indeed it would seem almost specifically designed to lead on to madness.

For the first six weeks after conception, male and female embryos look exactly alike. Both boys and girls develop a primitive gonad which does not yet indicate whether it is to become an ovary or a testis. Indeed, every foetus has two complete sets of sexual ducts, the male or Wolffian system, and the female or Mullerian system. The female embryo, however, has XX chromosomes in every cell of her body, which will eventually programme her into becoming a female, while the male has XY chromosomes that will programme him into becoming a male. Basically, therefore, sex depends on the arrangement of the sex chromosomes. If this is XY then usually the foetus will develop testes and male internal and external genitalia; if XX, it will develop ovaries and the female genitalia. An XX arrangement of chromosomes is associated with the presence in various body tissues, including the white blood cells, of a small 'drumstick' of chromatin projecting from the nucleus of the cell. This Barr-body, as it is called, is present in the cells of the female (XX) but not in the male (XY). This discovery was made only about thirty years ago by Barr and Bertram.

If the embryo has the Y chromosome, the primitive gonad develops into a testis, and the male or Wolffian system differentiates into the testicular duct systems of the epididymis and sperm duct (vas deferens). The female or Mullerian structures meanwhile undergo regression until only a few rudimentary structures, like the uterus masculinus, remain. (On rare occasions a 'true' human 'male' hermaphrodite is born with a normal testis on one side and a normal ovary on the other, together with a tube, a unicornate uterus and variable penis. This child is genetically male.)

If, on the other hand, the embryo has XX chromosomes, the opposite occurs. For another three months or so the gonad remains undifferentiated, then it develops into an ovary. The female or Mullerian system develops into the fallopian tubes, uterus and part of the vagina, while the male or Wolffian system remains in a rudimentary state.

It is important to keep in mind that the basic mammalian state is female. If the ovaries are removed at the early stages of embryonic development, growth still follows the female route; if the testes are removed during the development of a male (XY) embryo, then development switches back to follow the female route.

If the foetus is to develop anatomically as a male, androgens must be present. It is the androgens or male hormones that are secreted when the primitive gonad becomes a testis which regulate the development of the genetic (XY) male foetus into a male. In the female embryo, the Wolffian duct degenerates because there is no male hormone to sustain it. This critical period can be extremely short in some mammals. In the classical experiments of the French scientist Jost, carried out on the rabbit, castration of the genetic male before embryonic day 21 was early enough to ensure the complete feminization of all the remaining reproductive system. On day 23, castration of genetic males arrested masculine differentation in favour of resumption of feminine differentation, but hermaphroditic anatomical features were produced. By day 24, however, it was already too late for castration to interfere with the masculine differentation already under way.

Mammalian masculine anatomy, as Jost's experiments show, is 'turned on' by something added by the presence of the male Y chromosome, without which the more basic disposition of the embryo towards the feminine asserts itself. Psychosexual development and differentation is achieved in utero along analogous lines, since the brain – and more especially the hypothalamus – seems to be basically female in both male and female mammals. Goy demonstrated in 1968 that male hormones, quite apart from their masculinizing effects on the external genitalia, influence the behavioural system as well. Intrauterine exposure of the (unborn) female monkey to large doses of the male hormone testosterone results in subsequent adult behaviour akin to the male's. Postnatal administration of androgens has no such effects.

Postnatal administration of female hormones or oestrogens, however, can affect sexual behaviour. Castration of adult rats followed by treatment with a female sex hormone can release typical female sexual behaviour patterns. The male hamster behaves likewise after similar manipulations are carried out. These observations are of importance with respect to the long-term effects of prenatal and neonatal hormonal influences on sexual development and behaviour in humans.

The major work on the development of gender identity in humans has been carried out by Dr John Money and his colleagues at the Gender Identity Clinic at Johns Hopkins University in the USA. Especially relevant here are their studies of two major syndromes of prenatal androgen excess, in which the human genetic female foetus, carrying a full complement of two X chromosomes, is masculinized.

In the 'adrenogenital syndrome of the female hermaphroditism' the adrenal glands of the female (XX) foetus produce a pathological excess of androgenizing (male) hormones, so that the foetus undergoes a masculinizing differentation of the external genitalia. What should be the clitoris resembles a penis, and the labial folds, which should have been the vagina, are fused and resemble an empty scrotum. At birth or later on, the appearance of these females may resemble that of a boy with undescended testicles. However, the internal genitalia managed to differentiate as female (womb, fallopian tubes, ovaries) before the excess of androgen produced by the abnormal adrenal glands could affect them.

In laboratory animals like the rat, which periodically come on heat – that is, have oestrous cycles – prenatal or neonatal androgen excess permanently defeminizes the female's hypothalamic-pituitary cycle-controlling mechanism in the brain. In species which have menstrual cycles, evidence from rhesus monkeys, provided by Goy in 1970, and from humans, observed more recently by Jones and Verkauf, demonstrates that prenatal androgenization may delay the onset of puberty by about a year. In some cases, however, the delay is longer, indicating the possibilities of amenorrhoea or a permanent failure of menstrual cycles to occur. Apart from this special group, women with a history of the androgenital syndrome are able to menstruate, gestate and lactate.

The syndrome of 'progestin-induced hermaphroditism' occurs rarely as an untoward side-effect in female foetuses of mothers given synthetic progestin by their doctors as a treatment to preserve the pregnancy from a threatened miscarriage. It has also occurred in pregnant mothers who have inadvertently taken androgens by mouth, and in women who themselves produce pathological amounts of masculinizing hormone secreted by an ovarian or adrenal tumour during pregnancy. When used as pregnancy-saving agents, synthetic progestins act biochemically like androgens.

In cases of either of these syndromes, counselling of the parents and early surgical feminization of the child are equally important. In addition, females suffering from the androgenital syndrome are given cortisone, in order to suppress the adrenal gland's production of an inappropriately large amount of male hormone.

There are, however, cases of 'false hermaphroditism' where the child was assigned to the wrong sex. Some of these girls (all carrying XX chromosomes) were wrongly assigned and reared as males. Their external genitalia were extremely masculine at birth so they were surgically masculinized shortly afterwards. A comparison of this group with those reared correctly as females is of great interest. The 'male' group showed a masculine gender identity concordant with their sex of rearing, and subsequently, in their teens and young adulthood, manifested romantic and erotic behaviour typical of males.

Do they or their female sexual partners qualify as homosexual? As Dr John Money points out, the answer depends on which of the criteria of sexual dimorphism one uses to assess such a partnership. On the criterion of chromosomal sex, or on the criterion of true internal gonadal sex, the relationship would be homosexual, but on the criterion of hormonal sex, external genital appearance and gender identity, it would be heterosexual. On the grounds of common sense, a copulatory relationship between a person with a penis and a person with a vagina is heterosexual, regardless of any possible discordancy among the other hidden variables of sexual dimorphism.

Girls with a history of prenatal androgen excess (from any cause) typically identify themselves and develop behaviourally as tomboys. This tomboyism does not rely on the continued postnatal availability of androgen excess. It occurs even when the hormone imbalance was corrected from birth onwards and manifests itself regardless of the sex of rearing. In those children who were reared as boys, it is part of their typically boyish gender identity. The two dominant traits of this tomboyism are vigorous energy expenditure in athletics and indifference to the rehearsal of maternalism in childhood doll play, when compared to a carefully matched control group. The tomboy girl, assigned to the correct chromosomal sex, might, if given the chance, have elected to have been born a boy, but she never has the transsexual's compulsion for sex reassignment or the child transvestite's abhorrence of the clothes of her assigned sex (although she will probably have a preference for plain, utilitarian clothes, especially shorts and jeans). She dislikes jewellery, cosmetics and fancy hairstyles, and shows a preference to combining a non-domestic career with marriage in preference to only a domestic career as housewife and mother.

Girls whose androgenization was terminated at birth reach the boyfriend stage later than their age mates. They do not, however, tend to be lesbian or bisexual in their erotic behaviour and love affairs. On the other hand, androgenital females who reach adulthood still under the influence of high levels of their own adrenal androgens, which in childhood had induced an early puberty that was unsightly, disfiguring and virilizing, present a somewhat different picture. In one study reported by Ehrhardt, Money and Evers in 1968, ten out of twenty-three of these women reported bisexual imagery in their dreams and daydreams, and three reported lesbian as well as heterosexual behaviour.

Finally, there is evidence to suggest that girls whose mothers were treated with synthetic progestins during pregnancy are more aggressive than girls whose mothers were not so treated. A recent study by Reinisch, comparing progestin-exposed girls and boys with their unexposed siblings, showed that exposure in utero to synthetic progestins has a definite effect on child's potential for physical aggression, as measured by a psychological test designed for this purpose.

As we have already noted, for masculine differentiation to occur in the foetus, something – i.e. androgen – must be added. It is this added androgen (more specifically, dihydrotestosterone, a product of testosterone) that allows the foetus to differentiate in external morphology as a male. If androgenization fails to occur, or if the cells of the foetus are insensitive to the stimulatory effects of the male hormone, a genetically male foetus, with XY chromosomes, will develop neutrally or, in other words, will follow the female path. Normal female differentation represents the end result of non-androgenization. Without androgenization, the brain maintains its basic feminine 'disposition', in spite of genetic maleness.

De-androgenized genetic XY males are rather less common than androgenized females. They possess two testicles, which are undescended, a penis which resembles a small clitoris and a somewhat shortened vagina. Outwardly, therefore, they look like females, but they lack a uterus, ovaries and fallopian tubes. This is because the Mullerian-inhibiting substance secreted by the testicles acts normally, preventing the differentiation and development of the Mullerian ducts, but the lack of androgen prevents the development of male external genitalia.

If they look like females, these de-androgenized genetic male babies are usually assigned to that sex and their subsequent gender identity and sexual orientation is female. In cases where the external genitalia are ambiguous in appearance, the sex of assignment has sometimes been male, sometimes female. Either way, the individual's sexual aspirations almost invariably coincide with gender identity and upbringing.

If he is reared as a male, the missing androgen ingredient of long ago is deciphered in the information he gives about erotic functioning. He is heterosexual but seems less responsive to erotic imagery than the average male. He does not have wet dreams. He may even be able to have multiple, self-induced orgasms in the female manner, especially if he cannot ejaculate. He is less active than most men in making a sexual approach to a woman. These men know that their penis is very small and possibly inadequate when erect for effective sexual intercourse. In non-erotic aspects of gender identity these de-androgenized males may be entirely masculine, even to the point of overcompensation in the tradition of the rugged masculine stereotype. This, however, does not include competitive fighting, nor are such men noted for their general aggressivity.

The genetic male who is reared as a woman presents a rather touching contrast. The predominant image that derives from Money's data is that of a woman who gives priority to marriage over a non-domestic career, who likes the domestic life and is prepared to rear a family by adoption. 'She' is usually realistic about her infertility and does not tend to daydream about pregnancy or child-caring. She has already anticipated the maternal role in her childhood play and was definitely not tomboyish. She seems more than averagely affectionate. She is satisfied with the female role and follows feminine fashions in clothes and cosmetics. She is totally heterosexual in practice and in fantasy. (Her partner, typically, has no knowledge of her genetic and gonadal diagnosis.) She has average libido, reaches climax during sexual intercourse, is not sexually experimental nor particularly inclined to take the lead in initiating sexual overtures. Her breasts, 'clitoris', vulva and vagina (which may have required surgical lengthening to aid comfortable intercourse) are erotically sensitive. In summary, she more or less conforms to the ideal stereotype of femininity in pre-World War II society and does so gracefully and spontaneously, whether or not she knows the facts about her chromosomal and gonadal sex. When she and her husband adopt children, she proves an exceptionally good mother.

I hope that by now it has become clear that correct sexual assignment at birth, and gender-role identity at any age, are not as cut and dried as they seem on the doors of public lavatories. Until it became possible to sex a baby with ambiguous genitalia by looking at its cells under the microscope, the gender identity of the unfortunate child often depended on the whim, guess or wish of the parents, the grannie or the family doctor. Thereby arose some tragedies. Generally, however, genetic sex (whether XX or XY), or even gonadal sex, are completely insignificant in determining sexual identity. This, at least, is the classic psychosocial theory of how maleness and femaleness, in terms of sex-gender-role identity, develop in humans after birth. First proposed by John Money, it has been accepted by many social psychologists, physiologists and psychiatrists for nearly a quarter of a century.

Briefly, Money suggested that once a child had learned its sex-gender role, it could not, with few exceptions, be changed thereafter. Money and his associates found that when attempts were made to 'convert' adults who had been assigned to the wrong (genetic) sex at birth into accepting their true gender-sex roles (i.e. the role in which they could be fertile), most were reluctant to accept this and some became quite disturbed at the prospect of having to relinquish their role of assignment and upbringing. This suggested to Money that between birth and the age of two, the male or female child could learn to be either sex; after this period it became fixated in the sexual identity in which it had been reared.

This theory may have to be modified in the light of some recent discoveries made by investigators who studied spontaneous female-to-male sex changes which occurred at the onset of puberty in some of the children of twenty-three families living in a primitive village on one of the Caribbean islands. Other preliminary reports on work currently being carried out on animals and human volunteers will also be touched on briefly since they, too, are relevant to our discussion.

The parents of one Caribbean family, Mr Batista Belarminico and his wife, Benilda, have ten children. Four of them, born and reared as girls, have already changed into strapping, well-muscled young men. For example, the eldest child, now in his early thirties, began life as a girl called Antonia; a girl called Isobel is now a young man called Chichi. Virgilio only recently (1979) began the change from female to male. The metamorphosed children were born with normal female external genitalia, but at puberty, when aged about twelve, the labia of the vagina of each child fused to become a scrotum and two testes descended into it, while the clitoris enlarged to become a normal penis. Of the twenty-three affected families in the village, at least thirty-seven children have already changed sex, a process which began in the early 1930s. Only in the early 1970s did these individuals become the subject of scientific research. The major question to be answered was why did these girls, who were reared as such, change over to men at puberty, and not only do men's work, but also have normal sexual intercourse and relationships with women, and become accepted by their neighbours as real men?

One of the investigators, Dr Julienne Imperato-McGinley, and his co-workers, undertook the formidable task of putting all the family pedigrees together and tracing them back for seven generations to one common ancestor, a lady called Altagracia Carrasco, who lived round about the 1850s. She carried a mutant gene; that is, one of her own genes changed its character spontaneously by a process called mutation, a chance happening that occurs about once in several million times. This mutant gene was non-dominant, so that it only became manifest in a female offspring when both parents carried it, probably located on one of their sex chromosomes.

In the case of these 'changing' children, the 'tainted' mother's egg is fertilized by a 'tainted' Y sperm and develops into a foetus with normal testes. As usual, the testes early on secrete a substance which absorbs the female sexual ducts (present as we have already seen in all male embryos). The testosterone also secreted by the testes, preserves the male sexual ducts. However, in these (male) children, the external genitalia do not change to male because, as a result of their genetic defect, they are unable to convert the sex hormone testosterone to another sex hormone, called dihydrostestosterone, in sufficient amounts; as we have noted, it is in this hormone that the development of the male external genitalia depends. However, with the onset of puberty, the surging rise in the production of testosterone forces the dihydrotestosterone levels up and so the changes that should have occurred long ago in utero now begin to take place.

But why should they adopt the male gender role with such apparent ease and alacrity, in contrast to the XY 'females' described by Money? Unlike Money's 'females', the 'changing' children's brains were exposed to a normal male level of testosterone in utero and also after birth. Their brains were masculinized or, in other words, normal male levels of testosterone had programmed masculinity into their brains. This suggests (contrary to established scientific belief) that the male brain and the female brain are different at birth, whereas most scientists would hold, like Money, that the differences in sex-role behaviour between boys and girls are learned socially.

It is relevant to mention here some recent work on copulatory behaviour in rats by Professor Roger Gorski. The typical receptive female rat automatically arches her back as the male mounts. Gorski has demonstrated tha he can give a male rat the female copulatory behaviour response by injecting it with a testosterone-neutralizing substance during a critical period just after birth, thereby depriving it of its testosterone. The treated (male) rats look exactly like normal male rats, but they demonstrate no male libido and behave sexually like females. More recently Gorski has demarcated the 'sex centre' in the rat brain, using special staining techniques on post-mortem slices of tissue. This centre is bigger in the normal male rat than in the female, but in the 'terminated' male it is exactly the same size as in the female.

In 1979, Allerand, working at Columbia University, New York, dissected out the sex centres from the brains of foetal mice. She grew half of each centre in fluid containing testosterone and the other half in fluid to which no testosterone had been added. After eight days, the half grown in the testosterone environment had developed a thick network of nerve fibres with many interconnections. The specimen grown in the 'female' environment showed only half the number of nerve cells and with few interconnections.

Have these findings any relevance for the human animal? Professor Gerd Dorner of the Institute for Experimental Hormone Research at Humboldt University, East Berlin, believes that the feminized male rat is a valid model to explain male homosexuality. Dorner discovered the rat sex centre before Gorski. He too, by destroying part of the brain of a newborn male rat, could make the male behave as a female, or 'homosexually', as he puts it. Dorner's current line of research is to prove that humans do have a sex centre and that homosexuals have a female one. One research tool he uses is to titrate the male homosexual's ('female') brain with a cocktail of oestrogen which mimics what happens hormonally in a woman who has ovulated, that is, released an egg from her ovary. Dorner claims that many male homosexuals' brains respond to the 'phantom' ovulation by increasing the circulating levels of LH or luteinizing hormone, exactly as occurs in the female at this time of the menstrual cycle, thereby – Dorner would argue – demonstrating that the male homosexual has a female brain. Heterosexual males do not respond in this manner under similar hormonal provocation.

Dorner has extended this line of approach to sampling the levels of testosterone in the amniotic fluid of the mother's womb during the critical fourth month of pregnancy. If levels are low and the child is male at birth, Dorner will follow up the subsequent sexual behaviour of the child. If his hypothesis is correct, a significant number of those males should become homosexual, thereby proving that low levels of testosterone in the womb lead to homosexuality. He believes that 'in the future, there may be the possibility of preventing homosexuality, at least in part. If we find abnormalities in sex hormone levels, I think we should ask the mother if we should correct – only correct – these abnormalities of sex hormone levels. This is a question for society as a whole, not only for me.'

Not all research workers agree with Dorner. Anke Ehrhardt, one of Money's associates, has said : 'Dorner has made the jump from rat behaviour to human homosexuality in a way which I find unacceptable. We went through a particular development where somebody found higher levels of testosterone in heterosexual males compared with controls. It took about 15 years for other investigators to refute that finding – to finally find out that it just wasn't holding true, that it probably had something to do with the sample selection. So the finding which Dorner claims, just has to be established by other investigators.'

Sadly, not everyone ends up as an acceptable anatomical or psychological male or female. Mrs Daphne Went, an attractive maternal 'woman' in her fifties, is happily married with two adopted children and an intelligent, devoted husband. Inside her abdomen are two normal testes. She is one of about 500 'women' in the UK who harbour this arrangement of gonad. Genetically she is XY. In the normal way, when in utero, the testes secreted their first hormone and so her female parts were absorbed. In due course, her testes produced normal amounts of testosterone and dihydrotestosterone, but the target organs in her body were insensitive to it, including her 'female' external genitalia. Accordingly, apart from the womb that had melted away a few months after her conception, everything else developed as in a female. At puberty she failed to develop pubic hair and menstruation never occurred since she had no womb. She was in the darkest of limbos until, at twenty-three, she saw a gynaecologist who examined her and then told her frankly : 'There's nothing I can do for you – nothing anybody can do for you. There's no treatment. You just haven't got a womb, and you have a very short vagina, and I would think that if you intend getting married, you must explain these things to your husband, since there will be no children and intercourse will be strictly limited.'

When she finally met her husband he said he had no objection at all to adopting children, and so, after they got married, they adopted two. They are now in their mid-twenties.

Mr Blackwell is also somewhat exceptional. He is a true hermaphrodite, one of only 303 such people on record. A handsome young Bantu, he was born with a small vagina as well as a penis, presumed to be a boy and reared as such. At fourteen he developed breasts and on investigation was found to have a normal active ovary on one side of his body and a normal active testis on the other. He made up his mind to have his body made up as male, and so his womb and other female parts were removed.

Mrs Went and Mr Blackwell are interesting in the context of Professor Dorner's work. Mr Blackwell, a true hermaphrodite, has a 'female' brain; he ovulated once a month and went through a complete menstrual cycle like a normal female before his hysterectomy. Yet, in spite of his 'female' brain, he does not display the female sexual behaviour Dorner's theory would predict. He is, in fact, somewhat of a womanizer.

Mrs Went's sexual orientation also refutes Dorner's theory. Though her testes are normal and though her brain was masculinized in utero and afterwards in the usual way, her sexual behaviour is and has always been female, though when given the 'phantom womb' test, she responded like a normal male. The behaviour of the Caribbean children, however, supports Dorner's view, though it does not prove it.

Perhaps in the final analysis, individual members of the species are of no more intrinsic importance to the evolution of genes than the shell of the hermit crab is to the crab; perhaps the gene, not man, is Nature's true buccaneer after all.

REFERENCES

G. Dorner, quoted by Edward Goldwyn in 'The Fight To Be Male', *The Listener*, Vol. 101, 1979, p. 79.

Anke Ehrhardt, ibid.

14
Male and Female Homosexuality

In the last chapter we established that the reproductive anatomy in mammals is dimorphic or 'dual-purposed'. On common-sense grounds, therefore, it seems foreordained, if a species is to reproduce itself, that sexual behaviour must also be dimorphic. It must exist in two different behavioural manifestations each distinct enough to permit conception to take place. The male and female must each be able to carry out their complement of behaviour appropriately. The origin of this dimorphism, or duality, of sexual behaviour needs to be considered. Recent evidence from animal sexology suggests that sexually dimorphic behaviour is not uniquely male or uniquely female. It seems rather to be bisexual, although predominantly male or predominantly female in its manifestation. Each sex may, and does on occasion, display mating behaviour, or elements of mating or sexual behaviour, that belong primarily to the other sex.

When one looks at human beings, a similar picture emerges. Ford and Beach studied seventy-seven primitive societies and reported that in forty-eight, homosexual behaviour between males was considered normal or socially acceptable. In a few of these societies it was so common at a certain age as to make anyone who did not indulge feel an odd-man-out. They have furthermore reported that homosexual behaviour is reasonably common in most mammalian species, although exclusive homosexuality in the presence of the opposite sex was considered unusual. From all the evidence available it seems reasonable to assume that homosexual practice is so universal as to be regarded as a normal in a majority of mammalian species, including man.

Alfred Kinsey in his classic study, *Sexual Behaviour in the Human Male* (1948), reported that 37 per cent of American men had experienced orgasm during homosexual contact at some point in their lives; 10 per cent had been exclusively homosexual for at least three years and 4 per cent exclusively homosexual throughout their lives. On the basis of his findings, Kinsey proposed a continuum of homosexuality/heterosexuality, which can be applied to both men and women. There are seven types, numbered from zero to six:

(0) Exclusively heterosexual with no homosexual tendencies
(1) Predominantly heterosexual and only incidentally homosexual
(2) Predominantly heterosexual but more than incidentally homosexual
(3) Equally homosexual and heterosexual
(4) Predominantly homosexual but more than incidentally heterosexual
(5) Predominantly homosexual but incidentally heterosexual
(6) Exclusively homosexual

The brilliant studies of Ford and Beach have shown that where gender identity is concerned, the higher the position in evolutionary development, the more important is learning and experience as opposed to 'instinct'. As Dr P. D. Scott pointed out, if the culture requires the male and the female to eliminate all evidence of bisexuality, to be monogamous and entirely heterosexual, then that pattern of behaviour has to be learned. In this situation, the capacity to learn well and truly and indelibly is of more importance than the content of the desired sexual behaviour; peculiarities and preferences become perversions only when they are not susceptible to needful adaptation – to what convention or culture or religion require.

According to Ford and Beach, in those societies where adult homosexual activities are said to be very rare, strong and specific social pressure is deployed against such behaviour. The opposite also holds true. At various periods in certain civilizations homosexual love affairs were socially approved. As everyone knows, this was true amongst the early Greeks. Writers like Plato considered homosexual love a lofty passion. In his *Symposium* he suggests that the army should be made up of pairs of male lovers, 'abstaining from dishonourable deeds and rivalling one another in honour, such that when fighting side by side, although few in number, they would overcome the whole world. . . . What man would desert his loved one or fail him in the hour of danger? The very coward himself would become the bravest hero at such a time. Love would give him inspiration.'

The Greeks, however, did not encourage indiscriminate infatuations and Socrates' penchant for young boys brought him little credit. Indeed, the cult of effeminacy in young men and buying or selling of sexual favours evoked strong disapproval. Some of the laws concerning homosexual abuses date from Solon's enactments of the sixth century BC. Children were protected from seduction; for a sexual outrage against a minor, a man could be sentenced to death.

As with its analogous male counterpart, the central feature of lesbianism is a preferential erotic attraction to another female which usually, but not always, involves some mode of physical expression of that attraction. This may take the form of mutual kissing and petting, mutual breast and genital contact, or mutual manual, oral-lingual or digital stimulation of the genitalia. As in the male population of homosexuals, lesbianism may be either a transient sexual adaptation or a fixed, life-long phenomenon. Like male homosexuality, it may be associated with a well-adjusted personality, with psychiatric disorder entirely unrelated to sex, or be encountered clinically as depression or another mental disorder that is directly related to the homosexual's conscious or latent sexual misgivings. Kinsey's continuum of course applies to all post-pubertal women, and reminds us again that for males and females, homosexuality is a matter of degree rather than a simple black-and-white phenomenon. Few lesbians therefore fit into the stereotype of the 'butch' or the 'femme', and only a minority play the active or passive role in a relationship exclusively.

Kinsey's survey of female sexuality, published in 1953, reported that 13 per cent of American women experienced homosexual orgasm at some stage of their lives. About 4 per cent of the single women in the survey remained more or less exclusively homosexual from the ages of twenty to thirty-five, and about 2 to 3 per cent had been exclusively homosexual throughout their entire lives. For the UK, Kenyon gives an estimate of 2.2 per cent for exclusive homosexuality in the adult female population.

Generally speaking, overt homosexuality is much rarer in the female, and this seems to apply not only to sub-human mammals but also to the so-called 'primitive' people studied by Ford and Beach and other research groups. Lesbians also seem to be less promiscuous, more emotionally stable and to have longer-lasting relationships than male homosexuals. There seems to be no true prostitution among lesbians and, apart from their sexual orientation, lesbians retain most of the basic female characteristics.

The attitude of the medical profession towards homosexuality has, throughout history, been somewhat schizophrenic. It has echoed the prevailing social and religious posture of the time, rather than emerging as a purely scientific appraisal. The ancient medical writers seem to have concerned themselves chiefly with the man who took the passive role in sodomy. The active partner was usually considered normal, someone getting sexual pleasure in an alternative way, a debauchee perhaps, but not a sufferer from disease, whereas the passive partner, who showed effeminate characteristics and mannerisms, might sometimes be excused his perversion on the basis of a disease process. The predisposition to his passive homosexual role was regarded as hereditary, or alternatively as acquired by force of habit.

Parmenides considered the underlying condition to be a purely mental one, while Aristotle held that it was an inherited disease of the rectum, in which, due to an anatomic aberration, the anus had become the main erotic zone. The opinions of the medical profession remain obscure or silent during the Middle Ages when the legal definition of homosexual sodomy was '*pecatum illud horrible inter christianos non nominandum*' – a sin so horrific that it should not be spoken of by Christians. Until quite late in the nineteenth century attitudes hardly changed. Benjamin Rush, Professor of Medicine at Philadelphia University, bracketed homosexuality with masturbation as a 'kind of insanity'. In 1830 this pillar of the establishment thundered from his chair : 'If one indulges in undue or promiscuous intercourse with the female sex or in onanism [masturbation], it produces seminal weakness . . . feminisation . . . and death' – that is, death by homosexuality, a fate worse than (common-or-garden) death itself.

Sir Alexander Morison (1799-1866), consulting physician to Bethlem Hospital, referred to homosexuality – when diagnosed in some of his patients – as 'monomania with unnatural propensity'. He added revealingly, 'Being of so detestable a character, it is a consolation to know that it is sometimes the consequence of insanity.' His consolation, as Dr J. H. J. Bancroft of Oxford University points out, may have derived from the knowledge that homosexual acts were sometimes committed by people otherwise held in high repute : their insanity gave them a moral let-off.

That homosexuality could be acquired or learned, rather than being inborn, was held by a few physicians at the end of the nineteenth century. Schenck-Notzing, writing in 1895, inclined to this view, whereas Havelock Ellis, a noted liberal sexologist, seems to have got everything from masturbation to homosexuality all muddled up. Writing in 1901 he said, 'In the constitutionally disposed, masturbation may lead not only to neurasthenia [torpitude] but to premature ejaculation, impotence and aversion to coitus – the latter helping to furnish a soil on which the inverted impulse [homosexuality] may develop.' Ellis, whose wife was a lesbian, later seems to have rejected the acquired component in favour of an 'inborn' or 'constitutionally disposed' causality.

Freud considered homosexuality as arising from the innate potential bisexuality of the male and female child. He considered that it became manifest due to damage to personality development as a result of anxiety-provoking experiences during the child's Oedipal phase. He was pessimistic about treatment.

In the 1940s, Rado, challenging Freud's concept of bisexuality, saw homosexuality more as an ongoing defence to cope with the threat of heterosexuality rather than as resulting from early traumatic Oedipal anxieties. This change of emphasis seems to have resulted in less therapeutic pessimism amongst contemporary psychoanalysts, some of whom, perhaps because they adopted a more directive role in therapy, reported encouraging success rates. We are here referring to homosexuals genuinely seeking treatment. Bancroft, a behaviour therapist and physician, delimits the brief of the therapist quite succinctly. Having pointed out that for many men and women homosexuality is often the most successful and acceptable role they can expect in life, he then goes on to state frankly that it would be morally wrong to expect them to change their way of life radically simply as a gesture towards social conventions, family pressure or the sometimes dour (heterosexual) 'morality' of the physician from whom they seek advice.

A genetic or inherited explanation for male and female homosexuality continues to hold some sway, but is becoming more of historical interest than an ongoing area of viable enquiry. In the nineteenth century Ulrichs postulated a congenital aetiology, essentially suggesting that the homosexual has the body of one sex but the mind and soul of the other. In the 1930s Mantegazza spoke of 'an error of nature', and in the 1950s Hirschfeld proposed a 'third sex', an intermediary stage between man and woman. Lang's theory, which suggested that homosexuals had the genes of the opposite sex, was demolished when nuclear sexing and more reliable chromosomal investigations became possible in the 1960s. Although lesbians have not been investigated in great detail, it has been conclusively demonstrated that there is no chromosomal abnormality in male homosexuals.

When one looks at twin studies, the concordance rates for lesbianism in MZ (identical) twins is unimpressive. However, one study of male MZ twins by Heston and Shields, reported in 1968, is of special interest. Among the fourteen siblings of a remarkable working-class London family were three pairs of male MZ twins; in two of these pairs both twins were homosexual, the third pair being both heterosexual. Both homosexual pairs spent much of their time apart in early life, at times living in different homes. The pair of heterosexual twins were the result of the mother's second pregnancy and were born twelve and fifteen years respectively before the two homosexual pairs. The father, a hard-drinking wife-basher, was thoroughly hated by all the family, while the mother was much loved by all the siblings. In the same report Heston and Shields reviewed the twin records of the Maudsley Hospital for twelve (male) pairs in which one or both were homosexual. They concluded that MZ pairs *per se* are not prone to homosexuality; that there was a tendency for concordance to be incomplete in their previously studied series of MZ twins (two pairs homosexual out of a total of five pairs) but to be nonetheless higher than in the corresponding DZ pairs (one pair homosexual out of a total of seven pairs). They stressed the importance of both environmental as well as genetic factors in the aetiology of homosexuality.

Most experienced research workers like Slater, Shields, Kenyon, Bancroft, Cowie and others would probably agree that the genetic component, if it does exist, and if it makes a contribution towards explaining male and female homosexuality, may well have been somewhat overstressed by earlier writers. The most probable way in which it might exert its influence would be in terms of personality predisposition and the resulting personality structure, shaped and moulded by environmental experiences, both prenatal and postnatal. Generally speaking, as we are all born with a greater or lesser predisposition towards average or above average intelligence, neuroticism, psychotic breakdown, hyperthyroidism, duodenal ulcer, cancer of the stomach, tuberculosis, etc., so also are males and females born with differing degrees of genetic predisposition to homosexual behaviour. Where homosexuality is concerned, environmental factors and learning (and non-learning) experiences are, with very rare exceptions, of crucial importance.

Anthropological studies of so-called primitive societies and sociological reports from developed societies are again of relevance. The findings of Ford and Beach seem to reflect the lower incidence of lesbianism generally reported in our own societies, compared with that of male homosexuality. Whereas in forty-nine (64 per cent) of seventy-seven societies investigated homosexual activities were considered normal and socially acceptable for certain members of the community, in only seventeen of these forty-nine societies was specific information obtained on female homosexuality. Even allowing for the fact that most of those interviewed by Ford and Beach were male, lesbianism still would seem to be less frequent than male homosexuality.

Only among the Mohave Indians, of all those preliterate groups recently studied, are there reports of exclusively lesbian patterns of behaviour that have been openly sanctioned. Lesbianism was known in ancient Greece and almost certainly practised in ancient Rome, though little seems to have been written about it. In ancient China it was quite common, viewed with tolerance and often encouraged in the women's quarters of the household, according to the historian Kiefer.

Among the socially approved forms of homosexual behaviour for the male in preliterate societies is that whereby he assumes the feminine role and may be regarded by other members of the community as a shaman, a religious 'entrepreneur' possessing supernatural power. This is found among the Chukchee of Siberia, where the shaman wears women's clothes, displays feminine mannerisms and may end up as the 'wife' of another man who copulates with him per anum, the shaman always playing the (receptive) female role. The 'husband' usually has a real wife whom he uses for heterosexual coitus. Not to be left out, the shaman may in turn have a female mistress, and thereby be the father of children. He enjoys a complicated position of prestige and power in the community.

Male children may be reared from infancy to play the female role among the Koniag of Northern Canada, who live quite close to the borders of Russia. These boys learn wifely duties and when old enough each becomes the 'wife' of one of the more prestigious members of the society. He is accorded much respect and credited with magical powers. Some of the West African Lango men dress as women, simulate menstruation and become the 'wives' of other males. They are welcomed by the feminine co-wives. Their impotence, which is assumed, is considered to be due to some supernatural agency. Their social standing, however, is not very high.

All adult men and boys among the Siwans of North-east Africa engage in anal intercourse, but in contrast to those examples cited above, these men adopt the feminine role only in strictly sexual situations. Males are considered odd if they do not practise active homosexuality. The Siwan fathers lend their sons to each other and talk about their homosexual love affairs as openly as their heterosexual romances. Both married and single men are expected to have homosexual and heterosexual love affairs.

What of homosexual paedophilia 'proper' in these societies? Paederasty or sodomy between unmarried men and uninitiated boys of ten or twelve years old, is found among many of the Australian aborigines. Indeed it is regarded as a recognized custom. Among the Aranda of Central Australia these prepubertal boys often live as the 'wives' of adult men for several years until the older man marries, by which time the 'wife' may cease to have been regarded as a mere boy and accorded the status of a young man. This youth originally had to belong to the proper marriage class from which the older man might later take a real wife. Unmarried men among the Keraki of the east coast of New Guinea universally practise sodomy. Each young boy, in the course of puberty, is initiated into anal intercourse by the older men. After the first year of playing the passive partner the boy then spends the rest of his bachelor days sodomizing the newly initiated. These customs are believed to be necessary for the physical development of these boys. A lime-eating ceremony is celebrated regularly to keep the youths from becoming pregnant. All rituals are fully sanctioned by the older men, but are supposed to be kept secret from the women. To explain this sort of behaviour in terms of endocrine imbalance or genetic aberration would clearly amount to pure physiological farcicality.

With reference to lesbian practice among these preliterate societies and in our own, female homosexuality seems to have received less attention than homosexual practices among males. As a consequence our knowledge is more limited. Lesbian techniques among the Australian Aranda include mutual tickling of the clitoris with the finger. Later, one woman will lie on top of the other and the two women will rub their 'chelia' together. There are variations elsewhere. The Chukchee women of Siberia may employ a penis skilfully fashioned from the calf muscle of the reindeer. Its method of use remains a closely-guarded secret. In South-west Africa Mbundu and Nama women use an artificial penis during sessions of mutual masturbation. Among the wives of important men of the Azande of Central Africa, a carefully fashioned wooden phallus, or occasionally a banana, manioc or indeed a sweet potato may be tied round the waist of one of the women, who then simulates male copulation with her partner.

When we consider the homosexual-heterosexual continuum along which the human animal has to migrate in the hope of finding a satisfactory niche, whether at the homosexual end or the heterosexual end, that journey has entailed a compromise between the prevailing ethnic-sociocultural environment and the human's innate capacity for bisexual behaviour. In other words, exclusive preference for one's own or the opposite sex is a learned or acquired trait and involves, in either case, the repression of a certain amount of homosexual or heterosexual feeling which, from all the evidence available, seems to be deep-rooted in, and natural to, the human animal of both sexes. If Kinsey's survey is at all representative then 18 per cent of men are ambisexual (or bisexual) between the ages of sixteen and fifty-five, as are 4 to 11 per cent of women between the ages of twenty and thirty-five.

Although one cannot extrapolate from the behaviour of lower, subhuman animals to man (or indeed from man to lower animals), their behaviour may provide 'models' or 'examples' which are valuable, enabling us to study and analyse human behaviour more open-mindedly, more perceptively and more critically.

Konrad Lorenz has analysed the male and female mating patterns of ravens, jackdaws and geese where sexual dimorphism, as to gross body shape and colour, is limited to difference only in degree. Under these conditions the female behaves in a female way only when the male is more 'impressive' in size or strength, intensity of colouring, or readiness for threat display or fight; the same is true, vice versa, for the male. In other words, the sex roles in pair formation and copulation depend heavily on dominance and submission; the bigger, more impressive, stronger animal will adopt the male role, the smaller, less impressive, weaker animal the female role, whatever its physiological sex. The behaviour of the male laughing dove makes the point clearer: if the cage of a male dove happens to be near that of a bigger male of the same species, the first male ceases to display in a male fashion and begins to respond in a female fashion. These phenomena also seem to be important in mammals even in a 'non-sexual' context. Primates tend to adopt a masculine role when they are high on the social dominance-submission scale and a female role when low, irrespective of their actual sex or gender-role identity. Thus if a dominant male monkey approaches a less dominant male aggressively, the less dominant animal may posture in the manner of the female monkey when she is sexually receptive. An analogous and comparable set-up might arise in the human situation if a punitive, detached father had produced in his son a fear of older men.

Sexual behaviour has two main components: the choice of sexual object or partner, and the technique of approaching, relating to or involving that partner. Relating behaviour will reflect the gender identity of the individual, that is, his or her prevailing degree of masculinity or femininity irrespective of actual anatomical sex. Thus the human male who seeks the passive role in sexual or other relationships, whether in terms of social dominance-submission or in terms of anal eroticism, is more likely to seek a male partner. There are several other factors which may also impinge to make a homosexual 'object-choice' more likely and in many of these factors the sexual loading or motive may be minimal or somewhat obscure. The relative importance of these factors is a matter for speculation and debate. They can be grouped into negative or 'push-away-from-heterosexuality' factors, and positive or 'pull-towards-homosexuality' factors. They apply and have exerted their influence on every man and on every woman whatever their prevailing gender identity.

'Push' factors might involve anxiety about playing the heterosexual role. This could arise during childhood and early teens spent in a prudish family environment that inhibited the boy or girl from making heterosexual contacts. Formative years spent in a family in which the frank discussion of sex, and in particular heterosexual topics, were considered dirty, sinful or taboo could also be disruptive, as could those homes where discussion was so furtive and limited that fear of the sexual unknown was engendered in the younger members.

Incestuous feelings and anxieties about the mother or father could also act as a 'push' factor. These incestuous Oedipal-Electra tensions might be unconsciously provoked in the male or female offspring by a mother or father who, at the same time, frowned on or actively condemned the child's healthier sexual interests. In this sort of situation fear of maternal or paternal reprisals for conscious or unconscious sexual hankerings might give rise to tension and 'castration anxiety'. Guilt about incestuous feelings towards siblings could also arise.

The lack of confidence of the young adult in his or her sexual competence or physical attraction, and the fear of failure or rejection in heterosexual relations, might also act as 'push' factors. These in turn might be related to worry about the apparent smallness of the boy's penis, or in the girl about smallness of the breasts or other real or imaginary deficiencies. Finally and more generally, lack of confidence in one's masculinity or femininity might result in an impaired gender identity. This in turn could be related to one's physical constitution – for example, gynaecomastia or breast-enlargement at puberty in the male or the growth of hair on the breasts in the female, both completely normal phenomena.

'Pull-towards-homosexuality' factors include sexual tension or 'appetite', need or 'drive' calling out, loudly, or more yearningly, for sexual stimulation, contact and fulfilment, as a means of achieving tension-reduction. Choice of the love or sexual 'object' or person is inevitably involved here, whether this be narcissistic-onanistic (masturbation), homosexual-lesbian, zoophiliac-fetishistic or indeterminate-epicene.

Whether there is in the human ape a perceptual gestalt, an inherent responsivity to certain heterosexual stimuli, remains the subject of debate. Many writers maintain that humans and subhuman mammals are ill-directed in the type of stimuli that turn them on sexually, until conditioning, or experiential events, either rewarding or nocuous, enable them to discriminate. It remains something of a mystery why sexual drive should not be adequately allayed by orgasmic masturbation, why another sexual object needs to be involved.

Perhaps the human lot is so insecure and solitary that man basically needs to communicate not only verbally with another person, but sexually too, in order to have the reassurance of physical 'feedback' or sensual recognition from that other being or outside entity – a human herd of two mutually nudging each other towards their separate affirmations of being individualized and alive.

Another 'pull' factor which Bancroft, the late P. D. Scott and others have drawn attention to, is the security deriving from an emotionally close one-to-one relationship. This does not necessarily end in a homosexual liaison, but it could do so if an impaired relationship with the father or mother resulted in an inordinate need in the son or daughter for an emotionally warm and rewarding relationship with an older male or an older female. Other 'pull' factors for a person with low self-esteem include the reward of being liked or sincerely loved in a sexual relationship, be it homosexual or heterosexual.

The American psychoanalyst Bieber has suggested that one method of dealing with a threatening figure is to involve it in a sexual relationship – the 'eroticization' of a threatening object. Thus, as we have seen, a female primate may deal with a hostile female or male by adopting a sexually inviting female posture; alternatively a male primate, lower in the peck order or social hierarchy, may appease an aggressive male superior by proferring himself in the passive female sexual manner.

We could extend the above 'model'. The American, G. V. Ramsey, noted that boys between ten and twelve often reported erections in exciting or frightening non-sexual situations. Similar incidents were much less common in an older group of boys. It is possible that between the ages of ten and twelve non-specific, non-sexual arousability occurs most often. Such a physiological response to a frightening and non-sexually exciting person might lead, at this sexually ill-directed but impressionable age, to an eroticization of this person (e.g. a strict, punitive teacher). The ensuing confusion is self-evident. Here too is a possible 'model' for the genesis of masochism (or indeed sadism, where the punisher is concerned), when sexual arousal is provoked and associated with receiving and possibly with giving physical punishment. An alternative model for masochism could obtain in those situations where the physical punishment of young people is postponed for a certain length of time. On the part of the child, there would be a strong desire and longing for the punishment, so as to get it over with, and, after the punishment has been administered, the 'painful' pleasure of having done so. I have come across a few relevant cases where children were, for the most part, physically and emotionally ignored by their parents, but nonetheless materially well provided for. These children enjoyed being physically punished because it meant that the parent 'still loved them' and did not totally ignore their existence.

It is also possible that in analogous circumstances non-specific or spontaneous sexual arousal might coincide with and get conditioned onto an inanimate object, which might then take on the status of the fetishistic.

In the psychodynamic or Freudian concept of sexual development, male and female alike run the gamut, or indeed the gauntlet, of the following life adventures : an innate biological predisposition towards bisexuality 'shaped' towards becoming male or female by intrauterine maturation, and influenced after birth by infantile mothering experiences; the development of a male or female gender identity; infantile sexuality and the component drives or instincts towards sexual pleasure derived from the erotogenic zones (mouth, anal area, genitalia); the triangular Oedipal love/hate affair (i.e., mother-father-daughter; mother-father-son); the latency period; drive resurgence and physical maturity at puberty and early adolescence; and finally, if all went well, maturity itself which brings a capacity to both sexes for emotional and physical intimacy and parenthood. Difficulties and disruptions can arise at any of these stages, including the intrauterine period.

During the Oedipal phase, as we have seen, children of both sexes are said to be attracted sexually and emotionally to both parents. The emphasis is on the boy's attraction to the mother – associated with envy, jealousy and fear of the father's reprisals – and on the girl's attraction to the father – accompanied by envy, jealousy and fear of the mother's anger and revenge. For the child, whether male or female, the result is jealousy and anxiety – castration anxiety and penis envy. If the Oedipal phase is handled successfully by the parents, the child emerges more or less intact, having abandoned his or her incestuous wishes in favour of more realistic co-operative sharing. However, the Oedipal fantasies and wishes remain dormant and may later reassert themselves in the child's future choice of sexual partner.

Where female homosexuality is concerned, many different permutations and combinations of parental relationships have been postulated in its aetiology. One recurring theme pivots around the girl's difficulty with her father which may involve hatred, rejection and fear. Bene gave the Bene-Anthony family relations test to thirty-seven lesbians and eighty married controls. Lesbians were more often hostile towards and afraid to their fathers and considered them weak and incompetent when compared with the control (non-lesbian) group. Kenyon compared 123 lesbians and controls with the following results: 21 per cent of the lesbians had poor relationships with their mothers compared with 0.8 per cent of controls; with their fathers the ratio was 30 per cent compared with 8 per cent; fewer lesbians thought their parents happily married (46 per cent compared with 84 per cent) and more had parents who had been separated or divorced (23 per cent compared with 5 per cent). Fifteen per cent of the mothers of lesbians had a positive psychiatric history compared with 4 per cent of control mothers. Seduction by an older lesbian only occured in 8 per cent of Kenyon's group. Twenty-eight per cent of lesbians but only 10 per cent of controls thought their parents would have preferred a boy; 19 per cent of lesbians felt they had not been brought up as girls.

What about traumatic 'potting-shed' experiences of little girls with adult men? In Kenyon's study, 41 per cent of lesbians and 25 per cent of controls had been disgusted or frightened as young children by the sexual behaviour of a man.

In an interesting study in the USA, Kaye, Berl and co-workers found a good deal of evidence for a basic and fundamental heterosexual drive in their lesbian group but concluded that this drive had been blocked by anxiety and inhibition in developing heterosexual drives. Sometimes this fear and inhibition were aided and abetted by the parents. In the UK, Kenyon found, rather similarly, that 46 per cent of lesbians in his group had at some times in their lives actually wanted to get married, 58 per cent admitted sexual intercourse with a man, and 20 per cent had been pregnant. A common finding in the backgrounds of homosexuals is a prudish, puritanical upbringing as regards sexual matters. In Kenyon's group only 22 per cent of lesbians, compared with 40 per cent of controls, considered that their family's attitude towards sex was normal, healthy and accepting. We parents have a lot to expiate and reparate.

15
Sexual Deviations and Frank Perversions

In no area of his behaviour is man's capacity for bizarre, daft or downright crazy behaviour better illustrated than among the sexual deviations and, most especially, the frank perversions.

The dividing line between what is regarded as normal and abnormal or perverted is a vague one, which shifts in different places and times. Freud, very much aware of the acceptable elements of regression and infantile behaviour intrinsic even in normal (vaginal-penile) intercourse and orgasm – for example, sucking of the breasts, fellatio, anal and genital fondling, and cunnilingus – as well as the normal elements of sadism in the male and masochism in the female, stated that 'If a perversion, instead of appearing merely alongside the normal sexual aim and object . . . takes place in all circumstances – if, in short, a perversion has the characteristics of exclusiveness and fixation – then we shall usually be justified in regarding it as a pathological symptom.'

Deviation or perversion, in general terms, can profitably be considered in the context of interpersonal relationships. The pervert substitutes a part against the whole and by so doing avoids a relationship with a person as a whole person. The totality of the whole person, his needs, qualities and aspirations, are ignored for the sake of a mere part of him such as youthfulness, largeness or smallness of penis or breasts, colour of hair, absence of pubic hair, and so on. This attitude, this selfish, attenuated posture towards another person, this sacrifice of wholeness or totality to a part, is often associated with adults who have marked obsessive-compulsive personalities. The perverted adult is often ruthless, determined, single-minded, egocentric and 'anal', compulsively driven by his obsessional need to satisfy his particular sexual craving. All perversions – and in this chapter we shall be looking at paedophilia, exhibitionism or indecent exposure, zoophilia or bestiality, transvestism, transsexualism, fetishism, kleptomania, saliromania, coprophagia, sadism and masochism – seem to derive from and to express those preoccupations, anxieties and fear which characterize the various stages of psychosexual and pyschological development which prevail in infancy and childhood and which have already been discussed in both Freudian and Eriksonian terms.

We have already noted that in certain 'primitive' societies paedophilia – the desire of an adult to engage in sexual activity with children of either sex – is regarded as normal and healthy. In communities in the South-west Pacific studied by Davenport, adults of both sexes fondled young children sexually as naturally as an adult in our society would stroke a child's face, nor did some parents hesitate to masturbate their children in order to pacify them. In our own lewd, law-wracked, taboo-tainted, puritanical society, these spontaneous, ethnically-acceptable, essentially innocent gestures and manoeuvres would be regarded as perversions.

Any normal adult of either sex, parent or non-parent, if they are sensitive and honest, will readily admit to deriving sensual pleasure from nursing, caring for and innocently handling young children, or being themselves innocently petted by an attractive child of either sex. Normal mothers who breast-feed their babies may become sexually aroused and pleasurably excited if the child sucks the nipple in a certain way. I have observed children of two or three years spontaneously and passionately exploring their parents' genitalia until tactfully and gently diverted.

As the analyst Rosemary Gordon points out (and Freud would certainly agree with her), pathology is merely the unfavourable outcome of the vicissitudes of basic drives and endowments. It should not surprise us, therefore, that recent reports from biologists, physiologists, ethologists and psychoanalysts suggest that the perverted variety of paedophilia rests upon perfectly normal drives, instincts and endowments. Most of us, thank the gods, are paedophiles in the original meaning of the term : we like or love children, especially our own. Indeed, adults who dislike children are probably abnormal.

The normal and healthy origins of abnormal paedophilia are pretty self-evident. The adult's love for the young has protective and therefore survival value for the young. It is also an essential ingredient in that instinct which binds parents to their children and evokes mutual trust and tenderness. Konrad Lorenz has this to say of the parental instinct: 'It is a distinct and indubitable sensuous pleasure to fondle a nice plump appetising human baby. Furthermore I can assert that my pleasurable sensations in fondling a sweet human child are of the same quality as those I experience in fondling a chow-puppy or a baby-lion.' (I don't think we're justified in calling Lorenz either a paedophile or a zoophile because he enjoys these pleasures.)

What triggers off the 'parenting' instinct? It is probably something as simple as the shape of the child: a short face in relation to a high forehead, round, protruding cheeks, and maladjusted limb movements that remind us of its helplessness if attacked or abandoned. This instinct prompts the adult to feed the young, to protect them against danger and predators and to encourage them, through play, to become strong and confident and to develop the skills they will need as adults.

It has been suggested that in the case of the human animal, this love of child and youth takes on another important dimension because of the adult's need to preserve his own inner child – those childlike qualities derived and retained from his early life, which include playfulness, the ability to continue 'growing' and learning, curiosity, innocence and freshness of perception and outlook, and a continual aspiring responsiveness and willingness to open himself to experiences of wonder and awe at the magical world about him. In other words, only while child and youth persist as functional, representational entities in the psyche, can a person be said to do more than just exist. Only when the child inside him has been successfully protected is a person truly alive.

When does this quite natural paedophilic drive become pathological? Much depends on the prevailing social and cultural mores, and on where the line is drawn between childhood and adulthood. The evidence suggests that most perverts, and in particular paedophiles, harbour, indeed treasure, an obsessional, eternal, unconscious hankering for an idealized childhood and youth, which they conceive of as an idyllic state of purity and innocence. Their obsessionality with this makes them generally resistant to change or reorientation. Many psychiatrists consider this fear of change to be closely interlinked with unconscious dependence, self-doubt and anxiety, lest new experiences prove overwhelming and so – as they did in the pervert's own infancy and childhood – revive and re-enact all the old painful experiences of shame, anger, helplessness, anxiety and inadequacy. Accordingly many paedophiles remain prisoners, locked forever in a pathetic state of infantile sexuality, for which they themselves are not to blame, and which – though now a true perversion, because they are adult – may nevertheless provide them not only with an acceptable outlet for sexual desires, but in the manner least likely to unleash in them those unconscious, unmetabolized, infantile anxieties and fears that still lurk and brew in the archives of their sad, parent-mutilated childhoods.

A few examples from the London-based psychoanalyst Rubinstein will, I hope, make this discussion clearer. During the analysis of a man in his early forties it emerged that his paedophilia was related to his unconscious Oedipal desires and love-hate for his mother (who had put him in an orphanage at the age of one), complicated by his deep resentment of her desertion, and of various mother-substitutes who had ill-treated or neglected him throughout his childhood. For him the attraction of young boys consisted in their representing or symbolizing himself as a child, when he felt most in need of love, and, notwithstanding this, how at the same time he could behave towards them like a 'bad mother' by beating them in a cruel and selfish way. (He had himself been severely beaten during toilet-training.) He made some progress during therapy but retained the ambivalent wish to try to find his mother – partly in order to make peace with her, partly to tell her at last what he really thought of her.

Another middle-aged male patient illustrates the paedophile's 'cross-identification' as well as the obsessive-compulsive determination to satisfy his perversion. He had served several long prison sentences for his escapades but admitted that the attraction to boys was so strong that it was 'worth going to prison for'. He was the unwanted child of an unwanted pregnancy in a mother who neglected him from birth. He married in his twenties and managed to get his wife pregnant. When she had a miscarriage and told him that she was glad not to be having his child, 'the bottom fell out of life'. Subsequently, whenever he saw a mother making an indulgent fuss of her son, 'it literally hurt me and I felt the desire to do it instead of her'. During analysis it became clear that loving and making love to young boys was a re-enactment of the way he once wished, and still unconsciously wished, to be loved by his own mother.

The form of paedophilic behaviour exhibited by the latter individual is much more typical than the aggressive behaviour of the first man. Sexual advances made to children generally take the form of verbal approaches through the use of exciting or vulgar sexual phrases or words; genital exhibition; persuading the child to manipulate the genitals of the adult or to allow its own genitals to be caressed. Buggery or sexual intercourse rarely if ever takes place. The urge or impulse to seduce children occurs much more frequently in men than in women and can take either a heterosexual, homosexual or bisexual form.

It was the German poet and philosopher Goethe who said, 'Nature in her abnormalities reveals her secrets.' At no time in his life does the crazy ape seem to me more pathetic than when he 'flashes' or exhibits his sexual organs, usually to strangers, with the object of achieving that sexual excitement and satisfaction which other more normal and conventional sexual manoeuvres fail to provide.

Indecent exposure was first specified as an offence in the UK in the 1824 Vagrancy Act, whereby 'every person wilfully, openly, lewdly and obscenely exposing his person with intent to insult any female', could be convicted as a rogue and vagabond and become liable to a prison sentence or fine. Havelock Ellis (who himself had a penchant for regaling himself by drinking his own urine) has referred in his writing to a case of exhibitionism, which went on record in 1476, when a London priest had to appear before an ecclesiastical court charged with showing his privates to the ladies of his own parish. Probably one of the first cases ever recorded is to be found in the Bible (Genesis 9 : 21-25) when the drunken Noah was found 'uncovered within his tent', to the horror of Ham, his youngest son. He had been drinking his own homemade wine. His daughters Shem and Japheth fretfully and ingeniously managed to cover his nakedness.

The French, with their usual flair for the obvious, describe three types of exhibitionism : *supérieur*, *postérieur* and *antérieur*. The first refers to breast exposure by women; the second to something almost as rare, buttock exposure in the male, one of the most famous Gallic practioners being the young Rousseau; the third type is genital exposure in the male. Most exhibitionists are in fact men, usually young men, many of whom seem to have an irresistible, often repetitive, impulse to show their sexual organs to strangers.

In 1877 Lasègue, the humane old master and founding-father of French exhibitionology, shrewdly observed that those who suffered from the condition he called *'l'exhibitionnisme'*, were nearly always men, often of previous good character, who described experiencing sudden powerful urges to display their genitals, often with little attempt to avoid arrest or capture, sometimes at the same place and time of day and in front of the same victim. Apart from the genital display, there were no erotic or other obscene gestures, nor any attempt to enter into any kind of relationship with the victim. Lasègue's exposers found their behaviour quite inexplicable. In Garnier's classic paper of 1900 he too noted that exhibitionism had both obsessional and impulsive features. The early writers on the subject also distinguished between primary or true exhibitionism and secondary forms in which the acts of exposure were symptomatic of major mental illness, such as psychosis, dementia or brain tumours.

Fashions change. Categories nowadays, in order of increasing seriousness, and which probably have some value in predicting future violence, are : simple exposure without masturbation; exposure with masturbation; exposure with masturbation and with some form of communication, such as speaking, shouting obscenities or whistling at the victim; and exposure where the victim is handled in some way and rape may (rarely) be attempted.

Among exposers the personality traits which are especially common are emotional immaturity, passivity and obsessionality. Some are also sociopathic. They seem to fall into two main groups : in the first we have an inhibited young man of near normal personality and good character, who struggles hard against his impulse to expose, but finds it irresistible. His behaviour makes him feel anxious, guilty and humiliated. He exposes with a flaccid penis, doesn't masturbate and derives little pleasure from the act. The second group of exposers are more sociopathic and therefore less inhibited, expose in a state of great excitement and with an erect penis, masturbating if possible at the time of exposure. They enjoy the act and experience little guilt. There may be a marked element of sadism in their behaviour, so some of them are dangerous; they may also suffer from other psychiatric illnesses as well, including additional sexual disorders, and many have relatives who also suffer from psychiatric disease. Some exhibitionists have features from both these groups.

In most surveys, 45 to 70 per cent of exhibitionists are under twenty. No social class or level of intelligence is immune. They usually look younger than their age would indicate and most have a rather boyish manner. If married, their wives invariably look much older than their husbands. In their general behaviour they often show a profound egocentricity, their mood is unduly sensitive to even minor upsets, their pride easily hurt. They tend to be easily discouraged from their goals in life and are reluctant to accept either authority or responsibility. Their passivity and inability to assert themselves socially seem to be linked with difficulties in expressing anger and aggression constructively, so that angry feelings often lead on to self-defeating behaviour – being caught in the act – that sometimes seems designed to punish the person who has offended and upset them. The sociopathic type are more impulse-ridden and therefore more likely to appear in court.

What reaction does the exhibitionist expect from his victim and why does he exhibit? As with most things in psychiatry one can only speculate. It is best to think of the sad cabaret act itself as a piece of acting-out or 'substitute' behaviour, which in some perverse way may alleviate mounting tensions, anxieties and frustrations. Alternatively, it may in some cases represent a desire for punishment. A proportion of exhibitionists expose from vehicles whose number plates may readily be noted. Others expose so blatantly and openly that police arrest soon follows. Only about 10 to 20 per cent expose in circumstances which make police arrest unlikely. Deliberate risk-taking is often associated with recent traumatic experiences in the exhibitionist's life. For example, they often describe exposure activity as increasing in amount and recklessness in ratio to mounting tension and distress arising from current psychosocial difficulties. At other times the increase in activity is frequently associated with a severe depressive mood swing with no obvious cause. In these kinds of situations the exhibitionist often describes relief at being caught by the police; capture seems to mean not only punishment for himself and, by extension, someone close to him, but also escape from increasingly unbearable emotional pain in a life-situation that has become intolerable.

Girls at about the age of puberty, and occasionally children, seem to be selected most often as the witness or victim, possibly because they are more likely to be shocked or impressed than older women. The reactions least desired are indifference or mockery. What does the act itself signify? The usual theme or leitmotiv would seem to be one of dominance or mastery; the exhibitionist, generally frightened of and unassertive with women, now suddenly performs a personality about-turn and aggressively confronts and challenges a female with his penis, briefly arrests her total attention and evokes in her some powerful emotion of fear, shame, disgust or shock, or indeed sexual curiosity and arousal. If the response coincides with the exposer's 'ideal', and this is almost invariably precisely and fetishistically defined in his mind, then for a fleeting moment he enjoys and experiences intense involvement in a scene where he himself is in total and absolute control. If the response does not coincide exactly with what he desires, he may continue to seek out other likely witnesses until successful. He may then immediately masturbate to orgasm or hurry off and masturbate later to his memory of the scene. It is usually at this point that excitement ends and guilt, remorse, sadness and fear take over.

Many exhibitionologists, including Havelock Ellis and Freud, have commented on the aggressive aspect of exposing, which Ellis referred to as 'psychic defloration'. Paradoxically, despite the nature of the act, it is seldom intended as an invitation to intercourse, and sexual advances from the witness are rarely welcomed. Occasionally, however, exposure does lead to intercourse. The impulse to exhibit manifests itself after puberty and may last throughout life. Many of these men discover after they have married or have found females who are willing to have intercourse with them, that it is the exhibitionism which provides their real gratification and that coitus is only a poor second best. Many are deeply unhappy, not only because they realize the risks to which their impulses expose them, but also because they have insight into their impoverished, lonely method of sexual gratification.

Exhibiting the genitalia is frequent and normal in both sexes in childhood and later usually undergoes repression. In some male children repression may be exaggerated, leading to severe inhibitions both social and sexual, or repression may be incomplete. These alternatives (severe repression or incomplete repression) may occur where there has been either intense prohibition of, or alternatively overstimulation of interest in, the boy's genital functions by an indulgent, seductive mother who is often at the same time overtly prudish towards her son. Unrepressed exhibitionistic urges may possibly serve later on in life to hold deeper sexual wishes towards the mother in unconscious control. Some exhibitionists seem to be fixated at Freud's oral stage of psychosexual development. One of Rosen's patients described himself pathetically as a 'mouth in trousers'. Rosen suggests that the hostility of the oral phase, which may manifest itself in biting and 'devouring' in childhood, is projected onto the outside world by the exhibitionist and a similar retaliation is expected (and indeed is often provided by onlookers other than the victim, or by police arrest). Christoffel postulated colpophobia – fear of the female genitals – as being the really basic fear in this perversion : the exhibitionist is afraid that the vagina might bite off and devour the penis.

The family backgrounds of exhibitionists resemble in many respects those of male homosexuals, and vividly and movingly illustrate some of the Freudian, Eriksonian and other interpretations and explanations we have discussed in earlier chapters. The mother is typically dominant and overprotective of the future exhibitionist who develops a close, warm, but ambivalent relationship with her. She may, as already mentioned, behave towards the son in a seductive but at the same time prudish manner, exhibiting her own naked body to the child while disapproving of his healthy interest in his own genitalia, for instance, or alternatively showing undue interest in the boy's penis. The future exhibitionist's father plays a rather less damaging role. He is usually passive and ineffectual, and less often harsh and punitive towards his son. Nevertheless, few exhibitionists speak well of their fathers and most show a marked preference for the mother. A sort of ongoing, ambivalent, 'jealousy-love-anxiety-resentment' romance seems to embroil mother and son.

Many reports agree that the development of exhibitionism is associated, as we would expect, with the seductive type of skewed relationship with the mother, leading on to severe castration anxiety that arises from the child's incestuous yearnings. This anxiety is increased if the father is frightening or remote to the child, and if the family attitude towards sex is puritanical and repressive, especially at the time when the son reaches puberty. The psychoanalytic view suggests, therefore, that the act of exposure enables the exhibitionist to act out and express his revolt against his 'love-hated' mother, thus finding an outlet for his frustrated incestual yearnings. In addition, in its own bizarre way, it allows him to assert his individuality and masculinity to a female who, at the time of exposure, symbolizes his mother.

Few exhibitionists are motivated to seek professional help and be cured. When they are motivated, behaviour therapy offers the most practical form of treatment.

Bestiosexuality is most germane to our attempts to observe and interpret the seemingly crazy behaviour of man and woman. It cuts across the whole gamut of sexual/conceptive deployment, from onanistic and mythological copulations, Christian incarnation, reincarnation and metempsychosis, to more down-at-soul, sub-Arcadian, intra-species, non-procreative pleasurings and barnyard gymnastics. St Thomas Aquinas regarded man as basically a polygamous animal; there are times when he is also polysexual.

As is usual, the Greeks may have thought of, or at least improved on, the joys of zoophilia first. Zeus, the All-High, god of the sky, fell in love with Leda, the wife of Tyndareus. He changed himself into a swan of dazzling whiteness and made love to her, having surprised her bathing in a pool. In his poem celebrating the event, Yeats asked :

> 'Did she put on his knowledge with his power
> Before the indifferent beak could let her drop?'

The short answer is yes. As a consequence she bore him two children, Pollux and Helen, so she must have learned something too.

Pasiphae, the wife of King Minos, torn by monstrous and bestial passion, fell in love with a bull and had intercourse with it. She later gave birth to the Minotaur, which was, as she must have expected, half ox, half man.

The Romans, as usual trying literally to ape the Greeks, staged carefully rehearsed exhibitions of mass public bestiality, employing bulls, giraffes, boars, large dogs and apes which had been painstakingly trained by ringmasters using the technique of operant conditioning (the carefully timed administration of reward or punishment).

Generally, however, bestiality has been condemned throughout history. The Hittite code, the Bible and the Talmud all – under certain carefully defined circumstances – imposed the death penalty on the offender. The laws prohibiting and punishing sexual intercourse between human and subhuman animals illustrate the idiosyncrasies of the law-givers themselves as much as the grotesque gymnastics of the protagonists. The Hittite code ruled that, 'If a man lie with a cow the punishment is death'; 'If a man lies with a hog or dog, he shall die'; 'If a bull rear upon a man, the bull shall die, but the man shall not die'; however, 'If a man lies with a horse or mule, there is no penalty, but he shall not come near the king, and he shall not become a priest.'

The medieval courts continued to punish with death anyone found having intercourse with an animal. The animal was sometimes executed too, its degree of complicity being determined by strict legal procedures. The vengefulness and righteousness of the law (for man, woman and beast) only slowly abated: in his book *The Criminal Prosecution and Capital Punishment of Animals*, E. P. Evans refers to the case of M. Jacques Ferron, who was hanged in 1750 at Vanvres for having intercourse with a she-ass. The ass was only acquitted after the court had received a testimonial signed by witnesses vouching for the animal's previous good behaviour. Signatories included the prior of the local convent. It was decided that the beast had not yielded to Ferron's advances of her own free will.

Other animals were not so lucky. Legal records in New Haven document that in June 1662 one of its male citizens was condemned to death for multiple bestialities. He was executed only after he had been forced to witness the execution of the pigs, sheep and cattle of which he had had carnal knowledge.

Zoophilia continues to be practised in both developed and developing societies. In his book, *The Sexual Relations of Mankind*, Mantegazza remarked that 'The Chinese are famous for their love affairs with geese'; at the moment of ejaculation the man would pull the head off the unfortunate bird so as to enjoy the pleasurable last spasms of the bird's anal sphincter muscles. Kinsey, Pomeroy and Martin estimated that 8 per cent of males in the USA indulged in sexual contact with animals. The incidence was much lower in males who had been reared in urban areas, but as high as 50 per cent for boys with an agricultural background, 17 per cent of whom reached orgasm during this type of contact. This suggests that availability of animals and perhaps prohibition or scarcity of consenting human females (or males) may be factors relating to causation. It is relevant to refer here to the sexual behaviour of male members of the Masai tribe in Kenya who are, for the most part, nomadic cattle herders. Not only is male homosexuality permitted, but 'it is customary', according to Ford and Beach, 'for older boys to have sex relations with she-asses'. Ford and Beach refer to several other tribes where bestiality is permitted. The Copper Eskimos of the Arctic coast of North America bugger animals alive or dead; the Hopi Indians of Arizona are another example. Sometimes, as among the Fez of Morocco, bestiality may be associated with the practice of magical rites intended to augment the male's sexual prowess.

Kinsey and his co-workers recorded that dogs masturbated by humans at regular intervals may transfer their sexual interest to the person who stimulates them and fail to respond sexually to bitches on heat. There are many cases in the literature in which the animal itself sometimes took the initiative. Yerkes describes a female gorilla called Congo who responded sexually to male and female dogs (but preferentially to the male). She also responded to men and would sometimes grasp a man's head, put it in contact with her vagina and masturbate with it.

This brings to mind a speculation made in his recent book, *Ever Since Darwin*, by Dr S. J. Gould of Harvard University. Encouraged by the genetic closeness of humans and chimpanzees, he suggests that 'interbreeding may well be possible', although he himself has little inclination to partake personally. Would any of us, I wonder, be accepted? Are we good enough for them? A more likely candidate than Gould to discover the answer to this fascinating question might be the Oxford zoologist Richard Dawkins. He considers that 'a chimp-human hybridisation would provide exactly the come-uppance that human dignity needs.'

Freud pointed out – as Kinsey later confirmed – that bestiosexuality is not uncommon amongst farmers and those who have regular access to animals. However, the Freudian explanation of zoophilia would also hold that in some cases the animal may be used as a maternal substitute to avoid the Oedipal anxiety and castration fear which intercourse with a woman (symbolizing the real mother) might engender. An analogous situation might obtain for the female consorting sexually with a male animal.

Bestiosexual sadism will be mentioned briefly. On 10 September, 1954, the *Daily Telegraph* reported the case of a boy of fifteen, from a good home, who had used a ball-point pen or a tool called a 'fish disgorger' to stab and maim horses in or near the left eye. The boy was 'always pleasant, helpful and friendly', according to his father. Freud might have suggested that the boy was 'always pleasant', etc., because he feared the father's castration wrath should he have behaved otherwise; that he resented his over-controlling father and symbolically killed him, like Oedipus had done, by maiming the horses who here represented the father.

That a proportion of the male population prefer to dress, and even to live, like women, was also known to the ancient Greeks. Hippocrates noted that such behaviour was particularly common among the Skyths. He rather naïvely attributed this to excessive horse-riding, which presumably he suspected might damage the Skyth genital. The French also seem to have been at heart a nation of transvestites. Famous cross-dressers in French history include St Joan of Arc, Chevalier d'Eon de Beaumont, the Duc d'Orleans and the Abbé de Choisy. Chevalier d'Eon de Beaumont is a particularly interesting case. Born in 1728, he became a distinguished diplomat in the service of Louis XV. He lived until 1810, having spent forty-nine years living and behaving as a man and thirty-three as a woman. Anatomically he was a normal male. The taste for transvestism has by no means died out in France. Most cities in France, including the capital, have thriving female-impersonation clubs.

Transvestites wish to wear the clothes of the opposite sex, often for the purpose of sexual gratification. In symptomatic transvestism, the cross-dressing is a symptom of homosexuality or – where the desire of the person is to use or wear some specific article of clothing for sexual gratification – of fetishism. When masochists or homosexuals don cross-sex clothing during sexual escapades, transvestism is playing second fiddle to the main deviation. In simple transvestism the anomaly is confined to the wish to dress and behave as a member of the opposite sex. There is usually no other sexual deviation. Simple transvestites experience a feeling of contentment and self-assurance when cross-dressed, in contrast to the frustration and anxiety they feel when obliged to wear the dress of their own sex. There also seems to be a rare type of male and female transvestite who is totally asexual. These people have no sexual component whatsoever in their lives, but nevertheless derive a sort of 'neuter' pleasure from wearing clothes of the other sex.

Theories attempting to explain transvestism postulate the concept of a phallic woman – a woman under whose clothes a penis can be found – whom the male transvestite tries to mimic and emulate. By so doing he can not only unconsciously deny his castration-Oedipal anxiety complex (associated with the father) but at the same time unconsciously feel that by putting on women's clothes he is actually enhancing his virility. Cross-dressing enables him to identify with the powerful phallic woman, i.e. his concept of his mother during the phallic phase of his development. Alternatively, it may be that the male transvestite is unable to accept the existence of penisless people (e.g. mother). He thus symbolically creates a phallic woman by donning women's clothes. This 'proof' that the penis does indeed exist for the woman permits sexual arousal, reassurance and erection, since he himself (now as phallic woman) does indeed conceal a penis under his clothes.

The concept that transvestism necessarily represents a homosexual orientation has been challenged by Randell in the UK. Half the male transvestites he studied were at the heterosexual end of the Kinsey scale; many had married and had children, although some had been divorced by their wives. Sometimes these divorces were related to their transvestite practices and additional transsexual drives. On the other hand, some transvestites undoubtedly are homosexuals, who dress like females to advertise or express their orientation towards men.

Related to transvestism is transsexualism. Transsexuals want to become, and to function as, members of the opposite sex. Not content with 'assuming' the alternative gender role, they wish to 'live it' totally – physiologically, anatomically and, of course, sexually. Some male and female transsexuals are prepared to undergo major surgery and complex plastic procedures to achieve this ambition. The pioneer was Christine Jorgensen, who popularized the idea that men who felt like women could change their sex. Christine's operation, carried out in Denmark in 1952, rocked the medical world to its conservative foundations, and posed many ethical, legal, surgical and psychiatric questions.

Many male and some female transsexuals are not homosexual; however, most females seeking sex reassignment are. The records show that the majority of people seeking a sex change have been anatomical males. In the USA the ratio is about three men to every woman. This imbalance between the sexes can be explained if we remember our discussion of the anatomical and psychological bipotentiality of the human foetus. Neuroendocrinologically, the basic mammalian state, both anatomically and probably behaviourally, is female. So-called man is really, in one sense, a monstrous self-perverted woman. We have already seen how foetus-produced androgen, the masculinizing hormone, is necessary to produce maleness in the foetus. No sex hormones are required for femaleness. Prenatal androgen, as we have also seen, appears to influence postnatal behaviour in a masculine direction. Thus a developmental system (anatomical maleness and behavioural masculinity) requiring the addition of specific amounts of specific substances at critical times is, on common-sense grounds, more vulnerable to incomplete or 'imperfect' outcomes than a system that does not require such chemical intervention. Non-masculinized or feminine men are therefore more likely to occur than masculine women.

A Freudian or psychodynamic explanation might also be offered. All children identify first with the mother; she is the most significant other person in their world. Thus, as Richard Green puts it, the male must disidentify with a female on the road to his male identity, while the female skips that first hurdle as she journeys towards her femaleness.

The sociological viewpoint is also relevant. Society today allows women more latitude for cross-sexed expression. It is permissible and at times fashionable for women to dress like men, to live together, and to indulge in romantic relationships, without anything like the same degree of ostracization or stigmatization encountered by men who behave in a similar manner. Thus perhaps the pressure to reduce social alienation by trying to bring anatomy into conformity with conventional behaviour is greater for males.

Finally, from the practical point of view, the surgical construction of a cosmetically acceptable and functional vagina is a great deal more simple to achieve than the fashioning of a penis for the female.

Most special centres for sex reassignment in the USA advise their patients to dress all day and every day in the preferred sex role, to get a job in that role, to move to a new neighbourhood where they can live out their new life and see how it really is. They also test their patients' motivation for having a sex-change operation. The patients are told that they don't need genital surgery in order to get a better understanding of what their new life could be like. This trial period should last for one to two years. Concurrent with 'passing' in the desired role, contra-sex hormones are given. The man undergoes (reversible) chemical castration with oestrogens, and is also advised to undergo the costly, painful and prolonged process of facial hair expilation, while the female is given androgens to lower her voice, promote the growth of a beard, and cause her periods to cease. When taken regularly for a year or more, androgens also cause the clitoris to grow by up to two inches.

If they negotiate the trial period successfully, and still wish to change their sex, patients then undergo surgery. This, as we have said, is easier for the male wishing to become a female than it is for the female wishing to become a man. In 1963 Dewhurst reported on the case of a female transsexual (who was also a transvestite) who had a female-to-male sex change at the age of twenty-two. A brief outline of the case will show some of the difficulties involved.

The patient was anatomically as well as chromosomally a normal XX female. While still a schoolgirl, aged about twelve, she began to feel much more masculine than feminine and soon afterwards began to wear boys' clothes whenever she could. This upset her family, especially the father, who on several occasions burned the male clothes. She would then save up her money and buy more.

After leaving school at the age of fifteen, her belief in her masculinity became even more pronounced and she wore male clothing on all occasions. At seventeen she fell deeply in love with another girl, proposed marriage and was accepted, but only on the understanding that a medical examination would prove that she was a man. She was seen by Professor Dewhurst, who found her to be a completely normal anatomical female. She was later admitted to hospital and examined under anaesthesia. The existence of a normal uterus was proved and her cells were found to be chromatin positive, that is female. Her hormonal levels were normal and her chromosomes XX. Nevertheless, the patient had no intention of returning to the female role and asked to have her breasts removed and an artificial phallus constructed. This was not advised. It was arranged for her to see a psychiatrist with the view to getting her to accept her true gender role, but she saw him only once and then defaulted. Later she consulted another gynaecologist who also refused her request for surgery.

Three years later, after a high-level conference at yet another hospital, at which gynaecologists, psychiatrists and a plastic surgeon were present, it was agreed to re-register her in the male sex and for plastic surgical measures to be undertaken to make her as mannish as possible. At a hospital many miles from her home she underwent a hysterectomy; her ovaries, fallopian tubes and breasts were removed. She was then given large doses of testosterone which masculinized her facial appearance considerably. After her recovery from the hysterectomy and the other operations, a tube of skin, and the subcutaneous tissue beneath it, was raised from the front of her abdomen and a piece of rib cartilage incorporated within it. Then, after a series of grafts, involving ingenious craftiness and high-powered plastic surgery, she ended up with a 'penis' through which she could urinate and which hung in a posture of semi-permanent erection from her re-arranged 'ex-vagina'. During this time she was officially re-registered as a man. Sometime later 'he' married his fiancée.

Sadly, however, within a year this patient was back in hospital with retention of urine, and he has since required regular surgical dilations of the urethra.

When asked, having spent one and a half years out of three in hospital, 'Was it worth it?', he replied, 'Oh yes, well worth it.' He added later that he felt a far more self-reliant and confident person after the operation than he ever had done as a female. He furthermore insisted that sexual intercourse was satisfactory; it was not possible to confirm this with his wife.

Although the operation on the male transsexual is somewhat simpler, it is not without its dangers. In 1968 Symmers reported in the *British Medical Journal* on two cases of cancer of the breast in male transsexuals 'after surgical and hormonal interference with the primary and secondary sex characteristics'. Both had died of the disease, which may have been caused by the type and amount of oestrogen given and the length of time over which it was administered.

The first of these two cases, who had died at the age of thirty, had as a child regularly heard both his parents say that they had wanted a daughter. He was their only child. At boarding school he was exploited sexually by a group of older boys with whom he had a preference for playing the passive role. At university he had sexual intercourse with a number of females, but it left him with the feeling of having done something sordid and wrong: 'I felt myself an unwilling lesbian associating physically with what I acknowledged to be one of my own sex, when what I wanted was a man.' He felt himself to be, without any doubt whatever, a 'psychological' woman. At the age of twenty-four he had the first of a series of operations. These included castration, partial removal of the penis and transplantation of the glands of the penis. A 'vagina' was formed from a length of bowel, and bilateral mammoplasty, which in this case entailed inserting silicone into the breasts, was undertaken. Oestrogens were administered by mouth and by injection. When satisfied with the results he bought an expensive wardrobe and returned to his parents' home.

They decided to introduce him to their friends as a niece from overseas. He went to the family doctor, who did not recognize him, and obtained a prescription for contraceptive pills which he then took regularly. On several occasions afterwards he passed himself off in fashionable resorts as an expensive prostitute, and also enjoyed playing the street-walker successfully. When aged thirty, he noticed a lump in one breast which proved to be a cancer. He died seven months after having his breast removed. At post mortem, cancer secondaries were found in his spine and lungs. Sex chromatin tests proved that he was a male.

The other transsexual male also died in his early thirties. None of the surgical operations in either case were carried out in the UK.

The most exciting recent work in the field of transsexualism has been done by Richard Green and by Robert Stoller, John Money and their associates in the USA. It concerns pre-adolescent boys who have been identified as individuals at high risk for developing adult transsexualism. A fairly typical case is a boy aged nine who had been in treatment since the age of five. His mother reported that his first feminine behaviour occurred when he was less than two years old : he regularly put on her high-heeled shoes. By three he was enticing his older sister to dress him in her clothes and to put make-up on his face. The mother said, 'From the very beginning he preferred being a girl and acted like a girl because he felt he was very pretty.' He insisted that she buy him feminine dolls and she willingly complied because she did not want to 'see him develop a tantrum'. His maternal grand mother, a strong personality, helped him to obtain jewellery and admired his interest in 'artistic things'. By five he was dressing exclusively in feminine clothes, using cosmetics and openly insisting that when he grew up he would be a woman. Up till this time neither parent thwarted his femininity. Then all three began therapy.

As in the retrospective reports of adult males who want sex-change surgery, the very feminine young boys investigated by Green and coworkers strongly preferred dressing in girls' clothes; they liked girls' games and toys, female activities and the companionship of girls and steadfastly avoided activities typical of normal young boys. It is relevant to mention here that Green and Money are of the opinion that gender identity becomes established between the ages of eighteen months and three years. Typically these young boys were very close to their mothers, and the majority of fathers tended to be negative, passive and dominated by their wives. The mothers' relationships with their sons was excessively close. One could speculate here and suggest that the boys' fathers were so negative, so dominated by their wives and so psychologically absentee, that the idyllic Oedipal romance between mother and son was never threatened by castration anxiety, because the father was too weak and because, in his own eyes, the little boy was really a little girl.

All three, father, mother and son, had to be taken into treatment. This basically consisted of directing the boy towards a close relationship with a male therapist; stopping parental encouragement of feminine behaviour; interrupting the excessively close relationship between mother and son; enhancing the role of father and son and generally promoting the father's role within the family. The success achieved by this approach, based as it is on carefully and actively supervised unlearning and relearning of gender-role behaviour for the boy (i.e. behaviour therapy) and similar supervision, amendment and reassignment of the role played by the parents towards their son and consequently towards each other, was impressive. The results indicate the capacity for gender-role preference in the pre-adolescent male to undergo considerable modification towards masculinity. Green justifies this type of therapeutic intervention on the grounds that, in Western culture, males with an extremely feminine identity suffer considerable social hardships at all ages.

Finally, as a fascinating side-light on the question of transsexualism, and as further evidence for those readers who may still have doubts about the anatomical bisexuality and psychic bipotentiality of the 'Great Ape', I will briefly describe and discuss a true human hermaphrodite examined and operated on in London in 1950. He was a fourteen-year-old Hindu, the youngest of four children, the elder ones being normal girls. The mother was a healthy normal woman who continued to enjoy good health after the birth of the hermaphrodite. She later gave birth to a normal son. For convenience I shall continue to refer to the patient as 'he'. He had two large normal female breasts, a small penis about two inches long, a normal testicle in the scrotum on the right side and normal pubic hair. It was decided to establish his true sex by opening his abdomen. At operation a normal womb, left ovary and left fallopian tube were discovered and removed. The pathologist's report noted, 'The general architecture of the ovary appeared normal . . . with more than the average number of late ripening follicles [eggs or ova].' The left fallopian tube was also normal. With regard to the testis, a tiny portion of which was removed for microscopic examination, the report stated, 'All phases of the germ-cell lineage up to spermatids and [mature and normal] spermatozoa were seen.' There were an above-average number of sperms found in the tubules of the testis. There was no vagina. (Many similar cases of true hermaphroditism have been described in the scientific journals.)

This patient might, technically at least, have conceived of himself, since he possessed a normal womb and produced normal ova and sperms. These sperms might have leaked from his testis, migrated fortuitously into the womb and up the fallopian tube where fertilization with a ripened follicle (or ovum) from his healthy ovary could have taken place. He would not only have cloned himself – literally reproduced himself – but would have done so without the loss of either of his two virginities – parthenogenesis. He might even have produced twins, or quadruplets, each possessing the same two sexes. Since he had no vagina, delivery would have required caesarean section.

He had been reared as a boy, and therefore, as we should expect by now, he was entirely masculine in his outlook. He enjoyed playing boys' games and foresaw himself as the father of a family. He was sexually inexperienced at the time of his operation. There was no physical reason why at a later date he should not 'father' many healthy children even if he hadn't had his hysterectomy.

For the sake of completeness we will briefly mention a few more of the rather bizarre sexual perversions man is subject or subjected to. It is worth reminding ourselves that 'perversion' here refers to an individual's habitual sexual behaviour rather than to some occasional manifestation. This habitual behaviour is such as to interfere seriously with the biological function of reproduction. A perversion is therefore persistent, repetitive and excludes a loving sexual relationship with a person of the opposite sex.

Fetishism, even when it takes strange forms, is in essence no more than a caricature of certain important features of normal sexual love. The fetish (Portuguese *feitico*: amulet) is an inanimate object worshipped by savages for its magical powers, or regarded by them as inhabited by a spirit; in other words, it is endowed with special powers. Hence a fetish in the pathological sense is any object which the fetishist endows with sexual significance and in the absence of which he is incapable of sexual excitement. It may be an inanimate object, for instance clothes, ladies' fans, boots, or a non-sexual part of a person, a foot or hair. It has been suggested that at a critical phase of development some powerful erotic stimulus may condition a person's sexual preference onto a certain object, present at that time, for ever after. Sexual histories taken from fetishists offer some support for this theory; the story of the shoe-fetishist who, as a little boy, got an erection while being tickled on the belly by his adored nursemaid's shoe-clad foot, is part of psychiatric folklore. Most fetishists are men and most men are to some extent fetishistic and most women know it and pander to it even in their everyday public attire.

Sexologically, kleptomania refers to an obsessive inclination to steal and thereby achieve sexual pleasure. Kleptomaniacs are usually women. Pyromania refers to those cases in which firesetting is required for sexual arousal and excitement.

Most children go through a period during which they are very preoccupied with examining, playing with and tasting their urine and faeces as part of their exploration of themselves, each other and their environment. Some young children 'parcel' their faeces and hide the parcels away, possibly because they think their faeces are part of their own body and therefore valuable. Later on 'naughty' words are the object of their special interest. We've all used naughty words – 'shit', 'piss', 'fart' – as kids, and still do as adults, especially when we verbally regress when angry – 'Go and fuck yourself.' Many normal adults seem preoccupied with their bowel actions and with regular purging of themselves with pills or other concoctions and potions. Some adults, however, never evolve away from early childish preoccupations with urine, faeces and dirt, which maintain their sexual connotations with the penis, vagina and the anal-erotic. If this interest in dirt 'in general' predominates, it is referred to as saliromania (French *salir* : to dirty).

The anonymous saliromaniac Victorian author of *My Secret Life* describes repeatedly in great detail how he gratified his perversion by hiding himself in public lavatories, or by paying prostitutes to pee while he sat back and watched. Some go far beyond the bounds of polite Victorian watchfulness and themselves wish to urinate and defecate on others, literally putting the 'shit on you', or 'piss on you', of impolite conversation into practice; others prefer to be on the receiving end or ends. Similarly, some find it sexually pleasurable to ingest the excreta of others. A young male patient of mine described with sincere relish the joys of drinking his girlfriend's urine and eating her faeces. Such behaviour is called coprophagia (Greek *kopros* : manure; *phago* : to eat). These perversions are closely related to sado-masochism and to exhibitionism and voyeurism. Their regressive features should be by now quite obvious.

Some people derive sexual pleasure in using vulgar expressions, attacking passers-by with obscene remarks, making obscene telephone calls to strangers, or writing crude letters anonymously to others. These cases are referred to as coprolalia (Greek *lalein* : to talk).

Sadism long antedated that talented French writer, the Marquis de Sade, who has lent the perversion his distinguished name and who himself probably only suffered from what D. H. Lawrence would have called 'sadism in the head'. It is unlikely that he was a practitioner, whereas the Hungarian aristocrat, Countess Erzsbet Bathory, was; she derived sexual pleasure from inflicting pain and humiliation on others. In 1611, when aged fifty, she was walled up alive in her own castle for having killed several hundred young girls in various gruesome ways, in order to pleasure herself sexually. At her trial the judge was especially concerned that she had murdered noblewomen rather than confining herself to the sadistic slaughter of mere servant-girls. The blood of her unfortunate victims was sometimes collected and warmed for the countess's bath.

Count Leopold von Sacher-Masoch gave his name to the perversion masochism, in which the pervert derives sexual pleasure from being humiliated and physically beaten. Sadism and masochism are pathological exaggerations of the normal aggressive and submissive components of sexuality.

There is a 'sade-masoch', to a greater or lesser degree, in every man, woman and child. It is only when self-respect or consideration for others are violated that these normal urges become perversions.

REFERENCES

Richard Dawkins, review of *Ever Since Darwin, Nature,* Vol. 276, 1978, p. 121.

Sigmund Freud, *Collected Papers,* Hogarth Press, London, 1924.

S. J. Gould, *Ever Since Darwin,* André Deutsch, London, 1978.

Richard Green, *Sexual Identity Conflict in Children and Adults,* Duckworth, London, 1974.

Raymond Greene, D. Matthews *et al.*, 'A Case Study of True Hermaphroditism', *British Journal of Surgery*, Vol. 40, 1952-3, p. 263.

Konrad Lorenz, quoted by Rosemary Gordon in 'Paedophilia: Normal and Abnormal', in W. Kraemer (ed.), *The Forbidden Love*, Sheldon Press, London, 1976, p. 37.

P. Mantegazza, *The Sexual Relations of Mankind,* Brandon, North Hollywood, California, 1966.

W. St C. Symmers, 'Carcinoma of the Breast in Trans-sexual Individuals after Surgical and Hormonal Interference with the Primary and Secondary Sex Characteristics', *British Medical Journal*, Vol. 2, 1968, p. 83.

16

The Ape in Extremis

In case the reader remains unconvinced of the endemic madness inherent in the human ape's bio-methodology, in this final chapter I shall discuss examples of neurotic/hysterical and crazy/deluded behaviour which can occur under certain extremes of internal or external environmental stress. These disorders are so implosive for the individual that his repertoire of normal responses and personality resources is overtaxed and he literally 'freaks out' and loses all touch with reality. We shall also touch briefly on the phenomenon of mass hysteria, when large groups of people are infected with the same madness.

Koro is an acute anxiety reaction in which the patient develops a desperate sense of fear and becomes convinced that his penis is shrinking. He believes that it may disappear into his abdomen, in which case he will die. The patient's family or friends don't laugh; they rush him to the nearest doctor for they too believe the sick man to be in mortal danger. The patient meanwhile isn't taking any chances; he grasps and holds his organ very tightly in his hand, or he may loop a stout noose of string round it. Some victims of *Koro* clamp their penis in a wooden box.

The *Koro* syndrome is found almost exclusively among inhabitants of the Malay archipelago and among the South Chinese. The latter refer to the phenomenon, the patient and the imagined plight of the penis, as *Suk-yeong.*

Female cases of *Koro* or *Suk-yeong* have also been reported, the patient complaining of shrinkage of her labia majora and breasts.

Koro is extremely rare. Yap, who made a comprehensive survey of all cases reported in the world literature, was able to collect only nineteen cases over a period of fifteen years. I have personally seen only one case in the UK in the last ten years. The patient was referred to me from a VD clinic. He was native English, of low intelligence, and his delusion about his shrinking penis was part of a broader schizophrenic delusional system.

What causes this odd syndrome? Ignorance and ethnically elaborated old wives' tales about the dangers of masturbation, sexual over-indulgence or nocturnal emissions may act on the anxious, predisposed individual's fears and apprehensions regarding sexual competence or fertility. Yap considers sudden exposure of the penis to cold water or cold air, which would naturally make it shrink, coupled with stories about others who were said to have died of *Koro*, to be the precipitating factors in an attack. In women, shrinkage following exposure of the smooth muscle in the labia to cold air or water, could perhaps trigger off a panic attack. The resulting rise in circulating adrenaline would cause a generalized contraction of the skin, including the skin and smooth muscle of the breasts and nipples.

Yap's series of patients were treated by their physicians with tranquillizing drugs and psychotherapy. A few cases required electric shock therapy; others received the now obsolete insulin coma treatment. Long-term prognosis depends on the type of personality that existed before the attack. In Yap's survey, about a third recovered completely, half ceased to have attacks but remained anxiety-prone, and one patient made no progress.

Another bizarre syndrome, *Latah*, is also mostly confined to Malaysians. Occurring in two varieties, it may unleash a quite spectacular display of behavioural dressage. In one variety, a sudden stimulus causes the person to stop all normal activity and triggers off a sequence of inappropriate body movements and even more bizarre verbal behaviour, over which the person has no voluntary control. The other type of *Latah* is a mimetic or echo reaction. Here the sudden stimulus seems to compel the victims to imitate any action or words to which they are exposed, so that they show sustained and complete echopraxia (repeating the same movements over and over) and echolalia (repeating the same words or phrases). Automatic obedience often occurs. Although the victims of the *Latah* reaction cannot control their odd behaviour, they are nonetheless aware of their predicament and may, for example, protest against being asked to undress in public even while they are actually doing so. The unfortunate person is sometimes the butt of practical jokers and is totally at their mercy. The *Latah* reaction may also be triggered off by sudden embarrassment or tickling. The affected person may then amuse or embarrass the onlookers by uttering obscenities or asking indiscreet questions. The jokes and fun may end unhappily for the victim and her family, as the disease occasionally becomes chronic, leading on to permanent automatic obedience and echo behaviour and forcing the unfortunate individual into hiding and eventually causing profound personality deterioration.

Latah occurs chiefly in women and affects all the Malaysian races, especially the Javanese. In the nineteenth century it seems to have been confined mainly to the male; it was then quite common and found in all classes of society. H. B. M. Murphy, who has studied the epidemiology of *Latah* over the last half century, notes that since the 1930s the condition has become more rare and is almost completely confined to women of middle age, the majority of whom were employed as domestic servants. After the Second World War, cases of *Latah* were difficult to find in Indonesia. Conditions similar to, and at times identical with, *Latah* have been reported in people from other cultures, including Africans, Siberian aboriginals, Laplanders and North Americans (who became known as 'the jumping Frenchmen of Maine').

Latah is obviously set off by an intense fright-reaction, during which self control, consciousness or, more specifically, ego synthesis, are totally obliterated and ego boundaries are thus severely disrupted. During this sort of 'instant brainwash' or instant hypnosis, when perceptual and motor integration are wiped out or inhibited, the victim is unable to react selectively and purposefully to his environment; he remains in a state of passive, hypnotic-like suggestibility and is unable to resist responding to whatever maximal stimulus he is bombarded with from outside.

Intelligent people are affected by *Latah* reactions more often than those who are mentally defective. Between attacks there is usually no personality disturbance, but it may prove difficult to get a patient out of the *Latah* state and back to normality, especially if she is of neurotic or hysterical personality. Murphy has compared the *Latah* reaction, often associated, as we have seen, with outbursts of agitated behaviour and obscenity in otherwise highly respectable servants, to the obscenities and blasphemies uttered by religious men undergoing general anaesthesia for an operation. He has also pointed to the Malayans' belief in demonic possession, and to one of their children's games in which a trance-like state is produced, the players behaving as if they are real-life animals. The reaction seems to be basically a periodic psychogenic, possibly even an auto-hypnogenic, disorder. The most effective treatment is a combination of tranquillizers and supportive psychotherapy. Sometimes electric shock therapy is required.

Clérambault's syndrome, variously referred to as *psychose passionelle* or erotomania, is a disorder in which a female has the delusional conviction that a man – who hardly knows her – is passionately in love with her. Alternatively, this syndrome may refer to patients uttering explosive and absurd rubbish, who hear their thoughts echoed aloud and are convinced that they are possessed or being influenced by an outside or dissociated force. In reality, however, Clérambault's syndrome is a diagnostic figment, which exists only in the disordered minds of some Brazilian, Italian, French and North American psychiatrists. These gentlemen were in fact dealing with patients suffering from paranoid schizophrenia. Dr G. Clérambault himself, however, is not a delusion : I have established beyond doubt that he did exist in the 1920s and wrote papers with special reference to his own clinical observations and diagnostic ultra-aberrations.

Another syndrome that doesn't really exist in its own right, independent of the psychiatrist writing about it, is *dèlire de négation*, or Cotard's syndrome, in which patients complain of having lost not only their possessions and status but also their strength, heart, blood and intestines. Trees, houses and other people no longer exist for them; time itself stops and so, as a result, the patient has become unhappily immortal. A German psychiatrist, Dr H. Dietrich, recently described a case in which the deluded patient, a psychiatrist by profession, became so fed up with his impoverished immortality that he called it a day and committed suicide. Dietrich's patient was probably suffering from nihilistic delusions (not uncommon nowadays in elderly depressives) or senile dementia (erosion and loss of cells from the cortex of the brain).

These syndromes put me in mind of James Clarence Mangan, the brilliant, cowed, self-effacing, father-battered, early-nineteenth-century Irish poet, who translated poems into English, the originals of which never existed.

Human animals sometimes find each other emotionally infective and addictive, and each other's behaviour, at certain times, quite contagious. *Folie à deux* or *folie communiquée* was first described by Lasegne and Falret in 1877. ('Double insanity' and 'psychosis of association' have been proposed as the equivalent English terms.) The illness is characterized by psychotic symptoms, including delusions, shared by two people living together in a close and intimate situation. *Folie à trois*, *folie à quatre* and *folie à cinq* have been observed. In 1964 Goduco-Agular and Wintrob reported a case of *folie à famille* affecting seven members of a family in the Philippines. The eldest daughter infected her brother, parents and three sisters with a madness that reached its climax in a state of frenzied religious sadism, during which an aunt was savagely beaten to death. Waltzer went five better in a paper entitled 'A psychotic family : folie à douze'.

Lehmann has described an interesting case of *folie à deux* involving a poorly educated mother who was deeply attached to her well-educated, paranoid schizophrenic daughter and had adopted her daughter's delusions. When they were separated, being placed in different wards in the same hospital, the mother lost her delusions but became so lonely and depressed that it was feared she might die. She was therefore transferred to the same ward as her daughter. Within a week she had gained six pounds in weight, was happy and active, but had re-adopted her daughter's delusions. After both had been discharged, they continued to live in the same room, worked together in the same laundry and continued to share the same paranoid delusions which by then had taken on an even more grandiose nature.

Folie à deux can occur in the aged. In one fascinating case the dominant and submissive partners reversed roles after the submissive partner had become ill, but there was no change in their shared persecutory delusions.

In the *folie* phenomenon, whether it is *à deux* or *à douze*, we are seeing what is essentially an induced madness : one person infects one or more other people with whom he or she comes into close, sustained contact. This seems to provide a simple model, or example, of what can happen at more catastrophic levels when a truly mad or grossly self-inflated ape, like Hitler, infects a whole nation with his egomaniacal delusions. Hitler dragooned into mass action an intelligent but obsessive-compulsive race by presenting himself as a righteous, totally self-convinced 'Fatherland figure', thereby evoking in a vulnerable population that unquestioning allegiance and obeisance that may lead ultimately, as it did in this case, to racial, national and international disaster. Hitler and the Germans are not the only example. Napoleon ruthlessly implemented and for a time lived out his megalomaniacal dreams in this way; so too, in the more provincial setting of the Uganda of the late 1970s, did Idi Amin. The induced madness, culminating in the mass suicides and poisonings (even of infants) in Jonestown, Guyana, carried out by an American religious sect in November 1978 in response to their lunatic leader, also comes to mind here.

Witch-hunting and witch trials were among the more dangerous and prevalent infective group-disorders of the Middle Ages. Many of the thousands of victims were probably innocent schizophrenics, hysterics or normal people, suspected by a frenzied mob of being possessed by some demonic force that had turned them into a witch, a wolf (lycanthropy) or some other animal. Some of the unfortunate victims may themselves have believed they were so possessed and proceeded to twitch, howl, bark or growl in a manner appropriate to their imposed or newly espoused role. Less dangerous collective disorders include the dancing mania, first observed and recorded in Germany in 1374. Dancing mania swept through many parts of Europe for more than a century. Localized sudden epidemics of hysterical laughing also occurred in the Middle Ages.

Epidemics of hysteria still occur. Sirous published a review in 1973 of twenty epidemics of mass hysteria reported during the previous sixty years. Witch-hunting still takes place in parts of Kenya, Uganda and other undeveloped and not so underdeveloped countries.

Another type of collective mental disorder, characterized by the sudden release of irrational, loutish and unusually aggressive behaviour, may be observed in the lynchings that still take place on occasion in the USA and elsewhere, and in the Orangemen's deranged drumming and pathetic capering during the annual 'festivities' in Ulster on the twelfth of July.

The crazed Orangemen celebrating 'King Billy's' victory at the Battle of the Boyne, the American lynching gangs, the mobs looting an earthquake-ravaged city – all seem to be influenced by a mass eruption of strong emotion and herd-instinct behaviour, in which each participant augments the wild behaviour of another, culminating in a transitory loss of rational and moral control, so that violence, to some extent foreign to the participants' usual personalities, is given full vent.

In almost all cultures, to a greater or lesser extent, belief in demoniacal possession is still prevalent and potent, and has been identified as the cause of strange or crazy behaviour. *Piblokto* (sometimes referred to as 'Arctic hysteria') affects the inhabitants of the Artic regions. It is characterized by periods, lasting about two hours, during which the victim, usually a woman, begins to grunt like a seal or call like a penguin, or to imitate the cry of some other animal or bird. Then, even though the temperature is well below zero, she will throw herself about in the snow, pulling off her clothes. After the attack she becomes completely normal again. During these attacks the victims are not touched by anyone because the Eskimos think that evil spirits may be involved.

A more dramatic type of psychosis is *Wihtigo*, confined to the Cree, Ojibway and Salteaux Indians of North America. A Wihtigo is a giant monster that eats human flesh. During times of famine a man may become deluded that he has changed into a Wihtigo and may even express a craving for human meat. This disorder is probably hysterical – that is, dissociative in nature – and may therefore be unconsciously mediated and contrived in an ethnic environment where myths, including that of demoniacal possession, are intermingled with existing disease concepts and the ever-present struggle for survival.

Belief in, or at least awareness of, demonology is still universal, as indeed is religious belief, which has been inculcated or conditioned into many of us in learning situations, or indoctrinations, from a very early age. Throughout the world and in even the most 'advanced' societies, there are those who ascribe certain illnesses and mental disorders to possession by evil spirits. In 1969 Obeyesekere described the Sanni demons, still believed to possess patients in Ceylon. More recently Wintrop reported that 10 per cent of psychotic male patients in a Liberian psychiatric centre had delusions relating to possession by 'mammy water'. I have myself invited a white Anglican clergyman, who practised exorcism, to speak to members of the psychiatric department of the Middlesex Hospital Medical School in London. He seemed to me to be a kind, level-headed, psychosis-proof citizen, but he believed firmly in possession and practised what he preached.

The anthropologist W. B. Cannon carefully investigated the phenomenon of voodoo death – a person's belief that he is the victim of an evil spell or of black magic. Cannon convinced himself that such deaths have indeed occurred in South America, Africa, Australia, New Zealand, Haiti and in the Pacific Islands. Some of these deaths may have been due to the victim's refusal to eat or drink, or the consequence of adrenaline or cortisol exhaustion, these two hormones being secreted in times of anxiety, fear and stress. Another anthropologist, Lester, also accepts the authenticity of voodoo deaths and explains them in his 1972 report in terms of Engel's 'giving up-given up' complex, a psychological crisis in which a person is very susceptible to the development of serious physical disease, and so die.

This takes us back to the complex relationship between psyche and soma. As suggested earlier, it is best to conceive of this relationship in terms of a two-way arrow system, wherein each system – the mind and the body – acts and reacts on the other. An excellent example of the seeming dominion at certain times of psyche over soma is pseudopregnancy or pseudocyesis. Typically this occurs in a childless married woman with a strong desire to have a child. She develops and demonstrates many of the signs of true pregnancy, including amenorroea (cessation of periods), abdominal enlargement (due, in this case, to retained wind in the bowels), fullness and tingling of the breasts, morning sickness, urinary frequency and a darkening pigmentation of the skin or freckles. For a non-pregnant woman to develop some of these signs postulates an amazing neurohormonal sleight of hand. It involves inhibiting the secretion of follicle-stimulating hormone from the pituitary gland (which ripens the egg in the ovary); maintaining high levels of progesterone to prevent the lining of the womb from breaking down into menstrual bleeding; and altering hormonal secretion from the adrenal glands and melanocyte-stimulating hormones from the pituitary gland, so that skin pigmentation deepens and freckles darken and become more noticeable. Unlike the leopard, the human female can literally change her spots.

The sad day finally comes when the pseudopregnant woman must be told the truth, given a general anaesthetic, and have the air released from her bowels. It is sometimes advisable that her husband or a close friend should be present so that later he can convince the woman that her baby was not stolen by the doctor.

Many other phenomena – including perhaps the most intriguing, grotesque and abnormal phenomenon of all, human genius – illustrate what a bizarre, valiant, crazy grotesquerie is man. Only two further examples will be given : the curious phenomenon of autoscopic experience and – returning us full-circle to the start of our journey – the 'siamese twins' born of the surgeon's knife after he has split a single brain in two and thereby created a human with – and between – two minds.

Autoscopy has a long history. It has recently come back into vogue since it has become possible to resuscitate patients who have been physically 'dead', or very close to it. A number of writers have taken to button-holing these patients after recovery in order to try to get information about the next life, Hamlet's 'undiscovered country'. (If there is such a thing, let us hope, in the words carved on W. C. Fields's tombstone, that it is 'better than Philadelphia'.)

Autoscopic phenomena are essentially autonomous hallucinatory experiences in which a part or all of a person's body is observed by him from outside, as though seen in a looking-glass. It is often colourless and may even be transparent, but it is observed clearly. It usually appears suddenly without warning and imitates the 'owner's' movements. Classically, these phantoms, or dislocated body images, last only a few seconds and appear at dusk : they may be accompanied by auditory and other types of hallucinations. The person usually maintains a detached insight into the unreality of the experience and may react with sadness or perplexity. When these phenomena are experienced by schizophrenics, their reaction is generally one of emotional indifference.

As usual, the Greeks were probably the first to note the phenomenon. Aristotle commented with relish on a man who could not go out without seeing his double coming towards him. The German poet, statesman and philosopher, Johann Wolfgang von Goethe, had a vivid autoscopic experience while out on horseback as a young man. He saw approaching another horseman who turned out to be his double and who disappeared after a few seconds. Many famous writers seem to have had these experiences, including Guy de Maupassant (who was most probably in a state of alcohol-induced delirium tremens at the time) and Edgar Allan Poe (who was probably similarly afflicted). William Wordsworth seems to have had the knack of whipping his mind up into states of pseudo-autoscopic deliria whenever he caught glimpses of the world through the 'vision splendid' of his childhood.

Resuscitated patients not infrequently give accounts of how they saw their own bodies very clearly, and the medical team rushing about trying to revive them. Some patients claim to have heard the conversation of the doctors and nurses, despite the fact that they were unconscious. Others tell of passing into a sort of transcendental phase in which they experienced a review of their past life, encountered friends who were long dead, and evaluated their own achievements and omissions. Many of these experiences might be explained in terms of the effects of drugs, including the anaesthetic used by the medical team, or of an inadequate supply of oxygen to the brain. Alternatively, they might be simply remembered dream experiences that took place while the patient was unconscious.

What causes the autoscopic phenomenon in the natural, non-resuscitative setting? No one really knows. Some have suggested an irritation of the temporal lobe (where memory traces of past experiences are stored); others hold that the hallucination represents the projection of especially elaborated memory traces. (Presumably the nerve cells associated with these memory traces fire off spontaneously.) In a few individuals the experience may be symptomatic of schizophrenia or depression. Indeed Lukianowicz and others who have studied these experiences suggest that some normal subjects with well-developed imaginations – for example, a visualizer with a narcissistic personality – may occasionally see their doubles under conditions of emotional elation or stress. Ostow considers autoscopy as a manifestation of the wish for death and rebirth – but surely that is why we go to bed at night and hope to wake up feeling braver? A more prosaic explanation is that the phenomenon may be simply the aura which sometimes precedes a migraine attack.

We have referred in an earlier chapter to humans with split brains. Let us look briefly at what happens to their personalities when their brains are split in two.

The two halves or hemispheres of the brain are connected by a bridge of tissue called the corpus callosum, which keeps one half informed of what is happening in the other half. When the corpus callosum is divided surgically in sub-humans, the two halves show a functional separation from one another, so that each side can perform many tasks on its own, and can also perceive, remember and learn independently. For example, each hand of the split-brain monkey can be trained to discriminate between different wooden shapes, but the animal is incapable of transferring what it has learned from one hand to the other. Because it lacks a viable corpus callosum, it literally cannot let its right hand know what its left hand has learned to do.

In the mid-1970s in Los Angeles Bogan and Vogel performed full split-brain surgery on a small number of patients in order to relieve severe intractable epilepsy. In 1977 Wilson operated on a new series on the East Coast of the USA. After recovering from their operations, these patients presented a picture of two separate people inhabiting the same body. The brain has been divided and so too has the mind. Although the speech area, as we have seen, is located in either the left or right side of the brain, the mechanisms of perception – seeing, hearing, feeling, etc. – are duplicated within the two cerebral hemispheres. Split-brain patients therefore have no difficulty in analysing the information coming from the outside environment to either hemisphere, but like the monkey they are unable to relate the information received by one hemisphere to that received by the other. Indeed, each hemisphere seems to comprise a separate realm of experience almost unknown to the other.

All messages or information received or transmitted via the nerve cells, cross to the opposite side of the brain. The split-brain patient with the speech area located in the left hemisphere can therefore see and report everything that falls in the right field of his vision; it crosses over and stimulates the left (major) hemisphere. But he is unable to speak about things that fall in the left field, because they cross to the right (minor) hemisphere, where there is no speech area, and because communication between the hemispheres has been stopped by the operation. While the left-hemisphere 'personality' can eloquently describe his feelings and experiences in speech and writing, the right-hemisphere 'personality' cannot.

Using special tests, it is possible to get to know both 'people'. Although the right hemisphere cannot communicate very effectively, it does have its own specializations, particularly for gestalt (whole-figure) perception and also in mediating spatial recognition and function. Each side of the brain can possess particular knowledge and construct and organize its own individual inner realm of experience. For example, patients are able to spell out answers to questions using cardboard letters manipulated by the left hand (and the right hemisphere). The examiner poses the written question, 'Who are you?', projecting the words only to the right (minor) hemisphere. The left hand then spells out the patient's name : 'JOHN'. In one case in the USA the right hemisphere's favourite person was Henry Winkler. Its favoured career was different from that of the left.

The left and right hands were also capable of mediating and expressing the distinct and conflicting wills of the two 'personalities'. One patient, for instance, tied his dressing-gown with one hand while simultaneously untying it with the other. When mowing the lawn he sometimes experienced conflict between the two hemispheres, one side wanting one hand to push the mower in one direction, the other side in a different direction. Another patient had to sit on his left hand when reading a book, otherwise it would turn over to pages which the major left hemisphere was not reading at that time, and the right hand would continuously have to correct what the left hand had done. A female patient was very aware that her left hand had a mind of its own : on several occasions – as, for example, when she had overslept – it slapped her.

Mother Nature's nods can sometimes be quite homeric. As a student at St Thomas's Hospital Medical School in London, I examined a dead cyclopean child, 'complete' with only one eye. I have also had the opportunity to observe a two-headed child in the United States; one head was wide awake, the other seemingly fast asleep. Very few of these unfortunate children live to adulthood. One who did was Zhang Ziping, a deaf mute who lives in a mountain village 170 miles north-east of Kunming in China. Zhang had a parasitic head growing from the right-hand side of his true head; it had a sparse covering of hair, eyes that did not open, eyebrows, eyelashes, nostrils, a beard, protruding teeth, a tongue and an underdeveloped brain that did not function. When Zhang ate, this head imitated the eating movements of the host head.

Zhang was one of thirteen children, of whom ten had died. His mother originally wanted to abandon him, but allowed him to live because he was the only son in the family. He was clever and a good worker, but rarely went out. Until he reached the age of thirty-five, his parents refused to allow him to have his second head removed, for fear that he would die. Eventually, however, in 1980, surgeons removed the head in an eight-hour operation. On recovery, Zhang indicated that he wished to go home and get married.

So here in this strange epoch, at this moment in time, we stand on the dizzy high horse of our ever-vaunting hind legs and very possibly on the brink of the second Neutron Azoic; so many half-eked, ambivalent, ill-defined entities trammeled up in one skull 'in ratio' to the one multi-individual behind that transparent face-mask; brain abundled into that hollow bone and growing out through its sockets like a fistful of forgotten corn through foramina in old rock; heckled, betimes driven mad by ancestral voices calling from the Mesozoic, from the Oligocene, voices echoing from the first glaciation to Mount Olympus – Hydra-headed centaurs, skulls chock-full of

yeasting teratoma
rostral ghosts
zooid metastases
snoring yahoos :

Homunculoid archetypes
mislaid imagos
introjections
of living ancestry
and other emetic bric-à-brac
hankered
innocently bought in
harboured
suckled
augmented
fermented
traitorous beasts culled from the market-place
of infantile despairs
from lonelinesses forlorn / long-winded / endless as the
  Nile / beginningless
as a Yangtzekiang flowing backwards –

Peace, unquiet ape, most consummate, consequential ape, most self-surpassing, most heroic of primates.

Select Bibliography

Adrian, E. D., *The Physical Background of Perception*, Clarendon Press, Oxford, 1947.

Alvarez, A., *The Savage God: A Study of Suicide*, Weidenfeld & Nicolson, London, 1971.

Barchas, J. D. *et al.*, *Psychopharmacology*, Oxford University Press, New York, 1977.

Bloch, S. *et al.*, *News Bulletin on Psychiatric Abuse in the Soviet Union*, No. 2, London, October 1979.

Bowlby, J., *Attachment and Loss*, Hogarth Press, London, 1969.

Bradshaw, J. S., *Doctors on Trial*, Wildwood House, London, 1978.

Bridges, P. K. and Bartlett, J. R., 'Psychosurgery: Yesterday and Today', *British Journal of Psychiatry*, Vol. 131, 1977, pp. 249-60.

Brooksbank, B. W. L. and MacSweeney, D. A., 'The Fate of Androsta-4 16-dien-3-One and the Origin of 3a-hydroxy-5a-androst-16-ene in Man', *Journal of Endocrinology*, Vol. 2, 1972, p. 239.

Brown, J. A. C., *Freud and the Post-Freudians*, Penguin Books, Harmondsworth, 1964.

Browne, G. W. and Harris, T., *The Social Origins of Depression*, Tavistock, London, 1978.

Chorover, S. L., 'The Pacification of the Brain: From Phrenology to Psychosurgery', in T. P. Morley (ed.), *Current Controversies in Neurosurgery*, W. B. Saunders, Philadelphia, 1976.

Coppen, A., 'The Marke-Nyman Temperament Scale' (an English translation), *British Journal of Medical Psychology*, Vol. 39, 1966.

Coppen, A. and Walk, A. (eds), *Recent Developments in Affective Disorders*, Headley Brothers, Ashford, Kent, 1968.

Crow, T. J., Johnstone, E. and Owen, F., 'Recent Advances in Research on Schizophrenia', in K. Granville-Grossman (ed.), *Recent Advances in Clinical Psychiatry*, Churchill Livingstone, Edinburgh, 1979.

Dewhurst, C. J. and Gordon, R. R., *The Intersexual Disorders*, Baillière Tindall & Cassell, London, 1969.

Dimond, S. J., *Introducing Neuropsychology*, Charles C. Thomas, Springfield, Illinois, 1978.

Dixon, N. A., *On the Psychology of Military Incompetence*, Jonathan Cape, London, 1976.

Eccles, J. C., *Facing Reality: Philosophical Adventures of a Brain Scientist*, Springer, New York, 1970.

——, 'The Physiology of Imagination', *Scientific American*, Vol. 119, 1958, pp. 135-46.

——, *The Understanding of the Brain*, McGraw-Hill, New York, 1977.

Erikson, E. H., *Childhood and Society*, Imago Publishing Co., London, 1951.

Eysenck, H. J. and Eysenck, S. B. G., *Psychoticism as a Dimension of Personality*, Hodder & Stoughton, London, 1977.

Eysenck, H. J. and Wilson, G. D., *The Experimental Study of Freudian Theories*, Methuen, London, 1973.

Ford, C. S. and Beach, F. A., *Patterns of Sexual Behaviour*, Harper & Row, New York, 1951.

Ganong, W. F., *Review of Medical Physiology*, Lang, Los Altos, California, 1979.

Gay, P., *Freud, Jews and Other Germans*, Oxford University Press, New York, 1978.

Gazzaniga, M. S., 'Consistency and Diversity in Brain Organization', *Annals of the New York Academy of Sciences*, Vol. 299, 1977, pp. 415-23.

Goldwyn, E., 'The Fight to Be Male', *The Listener*, Vol. 101, 1979, p. 709.

Gould, S. J., *Ever Since Darwin*, André Deutsch, London, 1978.

Green, R., *Sexual Identity Conflict in Children and Adults*, Duckworth, London, 1974.

Green, R. *et al.*, 'Treatment of Boyhood "Transsexualism" ', *Archives of General Psychiatry*, Vol. 26, 1972, p. 132.

Greene, R., Matthews, D. *et al.*, 'A Case of True Hermaphroditism', *British Journal of Surgery*, Vol. 40, 1952-3, p. 263.

Hardin, G., *The Limits of Altruism*, Indiana University Press, London, 1978.

Hare, E. H. and Moran, P. A. P., 'Age in Psychiatric Patients:

Evidence for the Constitutional Hypothesis', *British Journal of Psychiatry*, Vol. 134, 1979, p. 169.

Hecker, J. F. C., *Epidemics of the Middle Ages*, Sydenham Society, London, 1844.

Hill, Sir D., 'The Qualities of a Good Psychiatrist', *British Journal of Psychiatry*, Vol. 133, 1978, p. 97.

Hunter, W. R. *et al.*, 'The Sex of Teratoma in (Human) Males and Females', *The Lancet*, 25 September, 1954.

Jones, K., 'Society Looks at the Psychiatrist', *British Journal of Psychiatry*, Vol. 132, 1978, p. 321.

Jung, C., *Memories, Dreams, Reflections*, Collins and Routledge & Kegan Paul, London, 1963.

Kelly, D., 'Psychosurgery Today', in K. L. Granville-Grossman (ed.), *Recent Advances in Psychiatry*, Vol. 2, Churchill Livingstone, Edinburgh, 1976.

Kinsey, A. *et al.*, *Sexual Behaviour in the Human Male*, W. B. Saunders, Philadelphia, 1948.

Kinsey, A. *et al.*, *Sexual Behaviour in the Human Female*, W. B. Saunders, Philadelphia, 1953.

Köhler, W., *The Mentality of Apes*, Penguin Books, Harmondsworth, 1957.

Kraemer, W. (ed.), *The Forbidden Love: The Normal and Abnormal Love of Children*, Sheldon Press, London, 1976.

Kraepelin, E., *Manic Depressive Insanity and Paranoia*, 8th ed., Churchill Livingstone, Edinburgh, 1921.

Lancet, The, 'Split Brains' (editorial), 3 March, 1979.

Leakey, R. and Lewin, R., *People of the Lake; Man: His Origins, Nature and Future*, Collins, London, 1979.

Loraine, J. A. (ed.), *Understanding Homosexuality: Its Biological and Psychological Bases*, Medical and Technical Publishing Co., Lancaster, 1974.

Lovelock, J. E., *Gaia: A New Look at Life on Earth*, Oxford University Press, Oxford, 1979.

Lukianowicz, N., 'Autoscopic Phenomena', *Archives of Neurological Psychiatry*, Vol. 80, 1958, p. 199.

MacLean, P. D., 'The Triune Brain, Emotion and Scientific Bias', in F. O. Schmitt (ed.), *Neurosciences*, Rockefeller University Press, New York, 1970.

MacSweeney, D. A., 'Tryptophan versus ECT in the Treatment of Unipolar Depression', *The Lancet*, Vol. 2, 1975, pp. 510-11.

——, *So Why Do You Kill Me?*, Eoten Press, London, 1980.

MacSweeney, D. A., Timms, P. and Johnson, A. J., 'Thyro-endocrine Pathology, Obstetric Morbidity and Scizophrenia : Survey of a Hundred Families with a Schizophrenic Proband', *Psychological Medicine*, Vol. 8, 1978, p. 151.

Miller, H., 'Psychiatry – Medicine or Magic?', in T. Silverstone and B. Barraclough (eds), *Contemporary Psychiatry*, Headley Brothers, Ashford, Kent, 1975.

Money, J., 'Clinical Aspects of Prenatal Steroidal Action on Sexually Dimorphic Behaviour', in C. Sawyer and R. A. Gorski (eds), *Steroid Hormones and Brain Function*, University of California Press, Berkeley, 1972.

Morley, T. P. (ed.), *Current Controversies in Neurosurgery*, W. B. Saunders, Philadelphia, 1976.

Murphy, E. A., 'The Epistemology of Normality', *Psychological Medicine*, Vol. 9, 1979, p. 409.

Murphy, H. B. M., 'History and Evolution of Syndromes : The Striking Case of Latah and Amok', in M. Hammer, K. Salzinger and S. Sutton (eds), *Psychopathology: Contributions from the Social, Behavioural and Biological Sciences*, John Wiley, New York, 1973.

Obeyesekere, G., 'Ritual Drama of the Sanni Demons : Collective Representation of Disease in Ceylon', *Comparative Studies in Social History*, Vol. II, 1969, p. 174.

Richter, D. (ed.), *The Challenge of Violence*, Ardua Press, Tadworth, Surrey, 1972.

Rosenthal, D. and Kety, S. S. (eds), *The Transmission of Schizophrenia*, Pergamon Press, Oxford, 1968.

Russell, A. T. *et al.*, 'Emotional Problems of Residents in Psychiatry', *American Journal of Psychiatry*, Vol. 132, 1975, p. 263.

Rycroft, C., *A Critical Dictionary of Psychoanalysis*, Penguin Books, Harmondsworth, 1972.

Sachir, M. T. and Robins, E., *Male and Female Homosexuality*, Williams & Wilkins, Baltimore, 1973.

Sherrington, C. S., *The Integrative Action of the Nervous System*, Cambridge University Press, Cambridge, 1947.

Sirois, F., 'Les épidemies d'hystérie : Revue de la litérature : Réflexions sur le probléme de la contagion psychopathologique', *Union Medicale Canadienne*, Vol. 102, 1973, p. 1906.

Slater, E. and Cowie, V., *The Genetics of Mental Disorder*, Oxford University Press, Oxford, 1971.

Smith, M., *Evolution of Sex*, Cambridge University Press, Cambridge, 1978.

Szasz, T., *The Myth of Mental Illness*, Secker & Warburg, London, 1972.

Usdin, E. *et al.*, *Endorphins in Mental Health*, Macmillan Press, London, 1979.

Valenstein, E. S., *Brain Control*, John Wiley, New York, 1973.

Vispo, P., 'On Human Maturity', *Perspectives in Biology and Medicine*, Vol IX, 1966, pp. 586-640.

Westerman, G., 'The Trees and the Wood', *British Journal of Hospital Medicine*, Vol. 21, 1979, p. 101.

Wilson, C., *The Strength to Dream*, Abacus, London, 1976.

Wilson, J. E., *On Human Nature*, Harvard University Press, Cambridge, Mass., 1978.

Yap, P. M., 'Koro : A Culture-Bound Depersonalisation Syndrome', *British Journal of Psychiatry*, Vol. 3, 1965, p. 43.

Young, J. Z., *Programmes of the Brain*, Oxford University Press, Oxford, 1978.

Zangwill, O. Z., *An Introduction to Modern Psychology*, Methuen, London, 1965.

Index